EVERY ONE A WITNESS

THE NORMAN AGE

Preface by Lord Wolfenden

ALSO BY A.F. SCOTT

EVERY ONE A WITNESS: THE PLANTAGENET AGE
EVERY ONE A WITNESS: THE TUDOR AGE
EVERY ONE A WITNESS: THE STUART AGE
WITCH, SPIRIT, DEVIL
(White Lion Publishers, London)

MEANING AND STYLE
POETRY AND APPRECIATION
MODERN ESSAYS (three series)
TOPIC AND OPINIONS (three series)
THE SPOKEN WORD (two series)
SPEAKING OF THE FAMOUS
VITAL THEMES TODAY
THE CRAFT OF PROSE
CURRENT LITERARY TERMS
(A Dictionary of their Origin and Use)
ANGLO-BENGALI SCHOOL FINAL ENGLISH
COMPOSITION AND TRANSLATION
(with Professor Dharanimohan Mukherjee)
NEW HORIZONS, in ten books (with N.K. Aggarwala)
(Macmillan)

ENGLISH COMPOSITION (Books I-IV)
POEMS FOR PLEASURE (Books I-III)
THOUGHT AND EXPRESSION
PLAIN ENGLISH (Books I-V)
THE POET'S CRAFT
(Cambridge University Press)

ILLUSTRATED ENGLISH (Books I-VIII)
(Max Parrish)

NEW READING, in sixteen books
(The Reader's Digest Association)

ODHAM'S YOUNG PEOPLE'S ENCYCLOPAEDIA
(four books, section on English Literature)

CLOSE READINGS
(Heinemann)

TABARIN TALES (Books I-VI)
(Geoffrey Chapman)

WHO'S WHO IN CHAUCER
(Elm Tree Books, Hamish Hamilton)

EVERY ONE A WITNESS
The Norman Age

COMMENTARIES OF AN ERA

A. F. SCOTT

WHITE LION PUBLISHERS
London New York Sydney Toronto

First published in the United Kingdom by
White Lion Publishers, 1976

ISBN 7274 0101 7

Made and printed in Great Britain
for White Lion Publishers Limited,
138 Park Lane, London W1Y 3DD
by Hendington Limited,
Deadbrook Lane, Aldershot, Hampshire

CONTENTS

List of Illustrations	
Acknowledgements	
Preface	
Royalty	1
Towns and Buildings	18
Family	44
Social Life	46
Food and Drink	63
Dress	59
Education	70
The Arts	74
Sports and Pastimes	85
Health	95
Work and Wages	99
Religion	131
Travel	196
Law and Crime	198
Famous People	225
Historic Events	259
Warfare	291
England and the Sea	320
Select Bibliography	323
Biographies	325
Index	331

LIST OF ILLUSTRATIONS

The author and publisher acknowledge with thanks permission to reproduce the illustrations listed below.

1. William I 2
2. William II 7
   The Trustees of the British Museum
3. Henry I 9
   The Trustees of the British Museum
4. The Nightmares of Henry I 11
   The Master and Fellows of Corpus Christi College, Oxford
5. The Wedding Feast of Matilda 14
   The Master and Fellows of Corpus Christi College, Cambridge
6. Stephen 15
   The Trustees of the British Museum
7. The Royal Builders 16
   The Trustees of the British Museum
8. Domesday Book 19
   Public Record Office, London
9. Westcott Barton, Marwood, North Devon 20
   F.L. Attenborough
10. Framework of a cruck building 23
11. Barn at Godmersham, Kent 26
   Quentin Lloyd
12. Twelfth century builders 29
   Herrad von Landsberg: Hortus Deliciarum
13. The Great Hall, Castle Hedingham, Essex 32
   Royal Commission on Historical Monuments (England) Crown copyright
14. Wasdale in Cumberland 35
   Aerofilms Ltd
15. Cadbury, in Devon 38
   Aerofilms Ltd
16. Celtic hamlet and open fields near Cape Cornwall 41
   Aerofilms Ltd
17. Braunton Great Field, Devonshire 44
   Dr. J.K. St.Joseph
18. Jew's House, Lincoln 45
   A.F. Kersting

19. Bathing a child 50
Trustees of the British Museum
20. Norman midwife 55
Bodleian Library, Oxford
21. Curtained bed, twelfth century 58
The Master and Fellows of Trinity College, Cambridge
22. Eleventh century dress 59
Trustees of the British Museum
23. A Cistercian monk 60
Dugdale: Monasticon Anglicanum
24. Women's Costume 60
Herrad von Landsberg: Hortus Deliciarum
25. Short tunics 61
Trustees of the British Museum
26. Embroidered super tunic 62
Trustees of the British Museum
27. After-dinner drinking 65
Trustees of the British Museum
28. Boiling meat and slaughtering animals 68
Trustees of the British Museum
29. Students from England crossing to France 71
The Master and Fellows of Trinity College, Cambridge
30. Twelfth century writing lesson 72
The Master and Fellows of Trinity College, Cambridge
31. The Crucifixion, Winchester Psalter 75
Trustees of the British Museum
32. Domesday Book 76
Controller of H.M. Stationery Office
Crown copyright
33. Psalter of St. Alban 77
34. Claverley Church, Shropshire 77
Tristam: English Medieval Wall Painting, the Twelfth Century
35. The adoration of the Magi 79
Victoria and Albert Museum
36. Seal of Merton Priory 80
Controller of H.M. Stationery Office
Crown copyright

37. Gloucester candlestick 81
Victoria and Albert Museum
38. John of Salisbury's *Entheticus* 82
Trustees of the British Museum
39. The Marriage of Christ and the Church 83
The Provost and Fellows of Kings College, Cambridge
40. Clerestory window, Canterbury Cathedral 84
Crown copyright
41. Chess 86
Trustees of the British Museum
42. Hawking 87
Trustees of the British Museum
43. Hunting 88
Trustees of the British Museum
44. Wrestling 89
Trustees of the British Museum
45. Puppet show 90
Herrad von Landsberg: Hortus Deliciarum
46. Playing bells 91
Trustees of the British Museum
47. Mummers 92
Bodleian Library, Oxford
48. Twelfth century chessmen 93
Trustees of the British Museum
49. Balancing 94
Bodleian Library, Oxford
50. Sugeyethistell 96
Bodleian Library, Oxford
51. Twelfth century cripple 97
Trustees of the British Museum
52. Twelfth century trepanning 98
The Master and Fellows of Trinity College, Cambridge
53. Saxon Calendar 102
Trustees of the British Museum
54. The first smith 106
National Buildings Record
55. The plough, eleventh century 111
Bodleian Library, Oxford
56. Husbandry 114

57. Master mason discussing building plans 118
Trustees of the British Museum
58. A smith at work 122
The Master and Fellows of Trinity College, Cambridge
59. Dyeing cloth 129
Trustees of the British Museum
60. Pilgrimage to the shrine of St. Edmund 133
Trustees of the British Museum
61. Western doorway, Llandaff Cathedral, Glamorgan 135
The Master and Fellows of Trinity College, Cambridge
62. Winchester Cathedral 137
Martin Hurlimann
63. Tewkesbury Abbey, Gloucestershire 139
Edwin Smith
64. The Choir of Canterbury Cathedral 141
National Monuments Record. Crown copyright
65. Norman gatehouse of the abbey of Bury St. Edmunds 142
Courtauld Institute of Art
66. Crypt of Worcester Cathedral 144
Dean of Worcester
67. Fountains Abbey 147
Aerofilms Ltd
68. Chapter House, Wenlock Abbey 149
National Buildings Record
69. Winchester Cathedral 151
Courtauld Institute of Art
70. South porch, Malmesbury Abbey, Wiltshire 153
Edwin Smith
71. South doorway, Kilpeck Church, Herefordshire 155
Royal Commission on Historical Monuments (England) Crown copyright
72. Rievaulx Abbey 159
Cambridge University Press
73. The choir of Rievaulx Abbey 161
British Travel and Holidays Association
74. The nave, Durham Cathedral 164
B.C. Clayton
75. St. Michael's Mount 167
Cambridge University Press

76. Dunfermline Abbey, in Fife 169
Cambridge University Press
77. The Abbey of St. Mary in Furness 172
Cambridge University Press
78. Calder Abbey, near Egremont 175
Cambridge University Press
79. Forde Abbey, in Dorset 176
Cambridge University Press
80. Twynham Priory, soon called Christchurch, in Hampshire 178
Cambridge University Press
81. Bolton Abbey, Yorkshire 180
Cambridge University Press
82. Lacock Abbey, near Chippenham, Wiltshire 184
Cambridge University Press
83. Whitby Abbey, Yorkshire 186
J. Dixon-Scott
84. Corn brought to the mill 188
Bodleian Library, Oxford
85. Shepherds at Bethlehem 191
Bodleian Library, Oxford
86. Christ and two disciples 193
The Master and Fellows of Pembroke College, Cambridge
87. St. George and the Dragon 194
National Monuments Record
88. Norman execution 207
The Master and Fellows of Trinity College, Cambridge
89. Twelfth century executioner 220
St. Alban's Psalter (Hildesheim)
90. Hugo, the illuminator 227
Bodleian Library, Oxford
91. Geoffrey Plantagenet, Count of Anjou 231
92. Henry of Blois 234
Trustees of the British Museum
93. Eadwine, monk and scribe 238
The Master and Fellows of Trinity College, Cambridge
94. Seal of Gilbert de Clare 242
Trustees of the British Museum
95. Dunstan copying the Rule of St. Benedict 246
96. Seal of William FitzEmpress 249
After Stenton: Early Northamptonshire Charters

97. William Longespee, Earl of Salisbury 252
98 –The Bayeux Tapestry
103 *Variously: Phaidon Press Ltd and The Folio Society*
104. Tintagel 276
Aerofilms Ltd
105. The Tower of London 279
106. Warwick Castle 280
107. Berkhamstead Castle 283
Dr. J.K. St.Joseph. Crown copyright reserved
108. Carlisle Castle, Cumberland 285
Department of the Environment. Crown copyright reserved
109. Pembroke Castle 287
110. Rochester Castle 289
Department of the Environment. Crown copyright
111. Chepstow Castle, Monmouth 290
Department of the Environment
112. Sword dance 295
Trustees of the British Museum
113. A quintain 300
Bodleian Library, Oxford
114. Sling used in hunting and warfare 305
Trustees of the British Museum
115. A joust 310
Trustees of the British Museum
116. Twelfth century cavalrymen 316
Herrad von Landsberg: Hortus Deliciarum

ACKNOWLEDGEMENTS

The author and publishers are grateful to the authorities named for permission to use copyright material. Furthermore, the publishers have tried to trace the owners of all copyright material, and apologise for any omissions. Should these be made known to us proper acknowledgements will be made in future editions.

To Esmé Woodland

PREFACE

by Lord Wolfenden

"England itself, in foolish quarters of England, still howls and execrates lamentably over its William Conqueror, and rigorous line of Normans and Plantagenets; but without them, if you will consider well, what had it ever been?"

This rhetorical question about England comes from the rather patronising Scottish pen of Thomas Carlyle. I suppose 1066 is still the one date in history which every schoolboy can be relied upon to know. And by many it is still regarded as marking an abrupt and total break with the country's past, a date of catastrophe when the simple and blameless local inhabitants were overwhelmed by brutal and licentious soldiery from across the English Channel.

In real life things were not quite like that. Arthur Scott's latest book gives us a vivid picure of what England became and was during The Norman Age, of how the Normans adopted and adapted many existing English customs, and of how the complications of dynastic relationships worked themselves out in changes which have ever since affected the history of England and of the wider world. As his practice is throughout this series, Arthur Scott goes straight back to contemporary sources. There is nothing here that is second-hand, nothing that is based on the historian's *post eventum* hindsight. We meet the chroniclers of the day, writing in their own language as eye-witnesses of events that were taking place around them – such men as Ailred of Rievaulx, Eadmer, John of Salisbury, Richard of Hexham.

The surviving written records are, naturally enough, sparse. So side by side with the documents we have set before us the evidence of architecture, sculpture, art, dress, weapons, coins and all the practical realities of daily living, in a splendid multi-dimensional re-creation of what life was really like in The Norman Age. This is the stuff of which history is made; and we are once again in Arthur Scott's debt for this further example of his industry, discernment and taste.

Wolfenden

Royalty

HAROLD, KING OF THE ENGLISH, *c.* **1022-1066**

On taking the helm of the kingdom Harold immediately began to abolish unjust laws and to make good ones; to patronize churches and monasteries; to pay particular reverence to bishops, abbots, monks and clerks; and to show himself pious, humble and affable to all good men. But he treated malefactors with great severity, and gave general orders to his earls, ealdormen, sheriffs and thegns to imprison all thieves, robbers and disturbers of the kingdom. He laboured in his own person by sea and by land for the protection of his realm.

Florence of Worcester, *English Historical Documents,* Vol.II

And Earl Harold was now [1066] consecrated king and he met little quiet in it as long as he ruled the realm.

Anglo-Saxon Chronicle, English Historical Documents, Vol.II

WILLIAM THE CONQUEROR, 1066-1087

This king excelled in wisdom all the princes of his generation, and among them all he was outstanding in the largeness of his soul. He never allowed himself to be deterred from prosecuting any enterprise because of the labour it entailed, and he was ever undaunted by danger. So skilled was he in his appraisal of the true significance of any event, that he was able to cope with adversity, and to take full advantage in prosperous times of the false promises of fortune. He was great in body and strong, tall in stature but not ungainly. He was also temperate in eating and drinking. Especially was he moderate in drinking, for he abhorred drunkenness in all men and disdained it more particularly in himself and at his court. He was so sparing in his use of wine and other drink, that after his meal he rarely drank more then thrice. In speech he was fluent, and persuasive, being skilled at all times in making clear his will. If

1. William I from the Bayeux Tapestry. His title of Bastard was exchanged for that of Conqueror. The son of duke Robert and Arlette, the tanner's daughter, William was a self-made man, an outstanding soldier and a capable king. He had an iron will and achieved sound administration and a remarkable record of the country in the Domesday Book, 1085.

'A master of politics, war and the management of men, a convinced ecclesiastical reformer, and a king whose constructive powers had not been equalled since Charlemagne.' R. Allen Brown

his voice was harsh, what he said was always suited to the occasion. He followed the Christian discipline in which he had been brought up from childhood, and whenever his health permitted he regularly, and with great piety, attended Christian worship each morning and evening and at the celebration of mass. And so, at last, it seemed to everyone that he could be given no more honourable grave than in the church which out of love he had built at Caen to the honour of God and of St Stephen, the first martyr. This indeed, he had previously arranged. Therefore in that church he was buried and a monument of gilded silver was erected over his tomb by his son, William, who succeeded him as king of England.

A Monk of Caen, *English Historical Documents,* Vol.II

This King William of whom we speak was a very wise man, and very powerful and more worshipped and stronger than any predecessor of his had been. He was gentle to the good men who loved God, and stern beyond all measure to those people who resisted his will. In the same place where God permitted him to conquer England, he set up a famous monastery and appointed monks for it [Battle Abbey], and endowed it well. In his days the famous church [Christ Church] at Canterbury was built, and also many another over all England. Also, this country was very full of monks and they lived their life under the rule of St Benedict, and Christianity was such in his day that each man who wished followed out whatever concerned his order. Also, he was very dignified; three times every year he wore his crown, as often as he was in England. At Easter he wore it at Winchester, at Whitsuntide at Westminster, and at Christmas at Gloucester and then there were with him all the powerful men over all England, archbishops and bishops, abbots and earls, thegns and knights. Also, he was a very stern and violent man, so that no one dared do anything contrary to his will. He had earls in his fetters, who acted against his will. He expelled bishops from their sees, and abbots from their abbacies, and put thegns in prison, and finally he did not spare his own brother, who was called Odo; he was a very powerful bishop in Normandy (his cathedral church was at Bayeux) and was the foremost man next the king, and had an earldom in England. And when the king was in Normandy, then he was master in this country; and he [the king] put him in prison. Amongst other things the good security he made in this country is not to be forgotten – so that any honest man could travel over his kingdom without injury with his bosom full of gold; and no one dared strike another, however much wrong he had done him. And if any man had intercourse with a woman against her will, he was forthwith castrated.

He ruled over England, and by his cunning it was so investigated that there was not one hide of land in England that he did not know who owned it, and what it was worth, and then set it down in his record. Wales was in his power, and he built castles there, and he entirely controlled that race. In the same way, he also subdued Scotland to himself, because of his great strength. The land of Normandy was his by natural inheritance, and he ruled over the country called Maine, and if he could have lived two years more he would have conquered Ireland by his prudence and without any weapons. Certainly in his time people had much oppression and very many injuries.

Anglo-Saxon Chronicle, English Historical Documents, Vol.II

WILLIAM THE CONQUEROR'S OBITUARY ENDS WITH THIS SHARP VERSE, 1087

He had castles built
And poor men hard oppressed.
The king was so very stark
And deprived his underlings of many a mark
Of gold and more hundreds of pounds of silver,
That he took by weight and with great injustice
From his people with little need for such a deed.
Into avarice did he fall
And loved greediness above all,
He made great protection for the game
And imposed laws for the same.
That who so slew hart or hind
Should be made blind.

He preserved the harts and boars
And loved the stags as much
As if he were their father.
Moreover, for the hare did he decree that they should go free.
Powerful men complained of it and poor man lamented it
But so fierce was he that he cared not for the rancour of them all
But they had to follow out the king's will entirely
If they wished to live or hold their land,
Property or estate, or his favour great,
Alas! woe, that any man so proud should go,
And exalt himself and reckon himself above all men,
May Almighty God show mercy to his soul
And grant unto him forgiveness for his sins.

Anglo-Saxon Chronicle, English Historical Documents, Vol.II

WILLIAM II, 1087-1100

Should anyone be desirous, however, to know the make of his person, he is to understand that he was well built; his complexion florid, his hair yellow; of open countenance; different-coloured eyes, varying with certain glittering specks; of astonishing strength, though not very tall, and his belly rather projecting; of no eloquence, but remarkable for a hesitation of speech, especially when angry.

William of Malmesbury, edited by J.A. Giles

He was very strong and fierce to his country and his men and to all his neighbours, and very terrible. And because of the counsels of wicked men, which were always harassing this nation with military service and excessive taxes, so that in his days all justice was in abeyance, and all injustice arose both in ecclesiastical and secular matters. He kept down God's church, and all the bishoprics and abbacies whose incumbents died in his days he sold for money or kept in his own hands and let out for rent, because he intended to be the heir of everyone, cleric or lay, and so on the day he died he had in his own hands the archbishopric of Canterbury, and the bishopric of Winchester and that of Salisbury, and eleven abbacies all let out for rent. And though I prolong it further – all that was hateful to God and just men was all customary in this country in his time, and therefore he was hateful to nearly all his people, and odious to God, just as his end showed, because he departed in the midst of his injustice without repentance and any reparation.

Anglo-Saxon Chronicle, English Historical Documents, Vol.II

Greatness of soul was pre-eminent in the king, which, in process of time, he obscured by excessive severity; vices, indeed, in place of virtues, so insensibly crept into his bosom, that he could not distinguish them. The world doubted, for a long time, which way he would incline; what tendency his disposition would take. At first, as long as Archbishop Lanfranc survived, he abstained from every crime; so that it might be hoped he would be the very mirror of kings. After Lanfranc's death, for a time, he showed himself so variable that the balance hung even between vices and virtues. At last, however, in his latter years, the desire after good grew cold, and the crop of evil increased to ripeness: his liberality became prodigality; his magnanimity pride; his austerity cruelty. I may be allowed, with permission of the royal majesty, not to conceal the truth; for he feared God but little, man not at all. If anyone shall say this is undiscerning he will not be wrong; because wise men should observe this rule, 'God ought to be feared at all times; man according to circumstances!' He was, when abroad, and in public assemblies, of supercilious look, darting his threatening eye on the bystander; and with assumed severity and ferocious voice, assailing such as conversed with him. From fear of poverty, and of the treachery of others . . . he was too much given to greed and to cruelty. At home and at table, with his intimate companions, he gave loose to levity and to mirth. He was a most facetious railer at anything he had himself done amiss, in order that he might avoid blame, and make it a matter of jest.

William of Malmesbury, translated by J.A. Giles

WILLIAM II, or RUFUS, 1087-1100

He was a man of meane stature, thicke and square bodied, his belly swelling somewhat round; his face was red, his haire deepely yealow, by reason whereof he was called *Rufus;* his forehead foure square like a window, his eyes spotted and not one like the other; his speech unpleasant and not easily uttered, especially when he was mooved with anger. He was of great abilitie in body, as well for naturall strength, as for hardiness to endure all ordinary extremities both of travaile and of want. In Armes he was both expert and adventurous; full of inward braverie and fiercenesse; never dismayed, alwayes forward, and for the most part fortunate; in counsaile sudden, in performance a man; not doubting to under-

2. William II or Rufus was vainglorious, complex and eccentric; a ruffian only pious when lying on his sick bed. Away from his hunting companions, he was killed by an arrow in the New Forest; his body, picked up by Purkess, a charcoal-burner of Minestead, was carried in a cart to Winchester.

take any thing which invincible valour durst promise to atchieve. Hee had bene bred with the sword; alwayes in action; alwayes on the favourable hand of Fortune: so as, albeit he was but yong, yet he was in experience well grounded; for invention subtill, in counsaile quicke, in execution resolute; wise to foresee a danger, and expedite to avoid it. In a word, the generall reputation of his valour and celeritie made him esteemed one of the best Chiefetaines in his time.

His behaviour was variable and inconstant; earnest in evry present passion, and for the most part accompanying the disposition of his mind, with outward demonstrations. Of nature he was rough, haughtie, obstinate, invincible, which was much enlarged both by his soveraigntie and youth: so singular in his owne conceit, that he did interprete it to his dishonour, that the world should deeme, that he did not governe by his owne judgement. In publicke he composed his countenance to a stately terrour; his face sowerly swelling, his eyes truculent, his voyce violent and fierce, scarce thinking himselfe Majesticall in the glasse of his understanding, but when he flashed feare from his presence. And yet in private he was so affable and pleasant, that he approched neere the degree of levitie: much given to scoffing, and passing over many of his evill actions with a jeast. In all the other carriages of his life, he maintained no stable and constant course; but declared himself for every present, as well in vertue as in vice, strong, violent, extreeme.

In the beginning of his reigne he was esteemed a most accomplished Prince; and seemed not so much of power to bridle himselfe from vice, as naturally disposed to abhorre it. Afterwards, either with variation of times, or yeelding to the pleasures which prosperity useth to ingender even in moderate minds, or perhaps his nature beginning to disclose that which hee had cunningly concealed before; corruptions crept up, and he waved uncertainely betweene vertue and vice. Lastly, being imboldned by evill teachers, and by continuance both of prosperitie and rule, he is said to have made his height a priviledge of looseness, and to have abandoned himselfe to all licentious demeanour; wherein he seemed little to regard God, and nothing man.

Sir John Hayward, from *Lives of the III Normans, Kings of England*, following the early chronicles.

COURT LIFE IN THE REIGN OF WILLIAM II, A.D.1098

The sacred honours of the church, as the pastors died, were exposed to sale: for whenever the death of any bishop or abbot was announced, directly one of the king's clerks was admitted, who made an inventory of everything, and carried all future rents into the royal exchequer. In the meantime, some person was sought out fit to supply the place of the deceased; not from proof of morals, but of money; and at last, if I may so say, the empty honour was conferred, and even that purchased, at a great price.

These things appeared the more disgraceful, because, in his father's time, after the decease of a bishop or abbot, all rents were reserved entire, to be given up to the succeeding pastor; and persons truly meritorious, on account of their religion were elected.

But in the lapse of a very few years, everything was changed. There was no man rich except the money-changer; no clerk, unless he was a lawyer; no priest, unless he was a farmer. Men of the meanest condition or guilty of whatever crime, were listened to, if they could suggest anything likely to be advantageous to the king; the halter was loosened from the robber's neck, if he could promise any emolument to the Sovereign. All military discipline being relaxed, the courtiers preyed upon the property of the country people, and consumed their substances, taking the very meat from the mouths of these wretched creatures. Then was there flowing hair and extravagant dress; and then was invented the fashion of shoes with curved points; then the model for young men was to rival women in delicacy of person and to mince their gait.

William of Malmesbury, *Chronicle*, IV, i, translated by J.A. Giles

HENRY I, 1100-1135

Henry, the youngest son of William the Great, was born in England the third year after his father's arrival; a child, even at that time, fondly cherished by the joint good wishes of all, as being the only one of William's sons born in royalty, and to whom the kingdom seemed to pertain. The early years of instruction he passed in liberal arts, and so thoroughly imbibed the sweets of learning, that no warlike commotions, no pressure of business, could ever erase them from his noble mind: although he neither read much openly, nor displayed his attainments except sparingly. His learning, however, to speak the truth, though obtained by snatches, assisted him much in the science of governing; according to that saying of Plato, 'Happy would be the commonwealth, if philosophers governed, or kings would be philosophers.' Not slenderly tinctured by philosophy, then, by degrees, in process of time, he learned how to restrain the people with lenity; nor did he ever suffer his soldiers to engage but where he saw a pressing emergency. In this manner, by learning, he trained his early years to the hope of the kingdom.

[Henry] was active in providing what conduced to the strength of his dominions, and firm in defending it. He refrained from war so long as he could do so with honour, but when he resorted to

3. Henry I, the youngest son of William I, a well-educated, hard and efficient man, did much to improve relations in England by making no distinction between Saxon and Norman. He married an English princess, Matilda, daughter of Malcolm, King of Scotland, and grand-daughter of Edward the Exile. The order and progress he brought suffered under his successor, Stephen.

arms he was a most severe requiter of injuries, dispelling danger by his energy and courage. He was constant alike in his enmities, and in his general benevolence, giving too much rein in his anger in the one case and displaying his royal magnanimity in the other. For he reduced his enemies even to ruin, and he exalted his friends and dependents, so that all men envied them. Does not philosophy propound this to be the first and greatest concern of a good king, 'to spare the suppliant and wear down the proud'? Inflexible in the administration of justice, he ruled the people with moderation, and with a seemly dignity restrained the great. He ruthlessly sought after robbers and counterfeiters, and signally punished them when caught. Nor was he negligent in matters of less importance. When he heard that traders refused broken money, though of good silver, he commanded that the whole of it should be broken or cut in pieces. The measure of his own arm was used to correct the false ell of traders, and he made that arm the standard for all England. He made it a rule for the followers of his court that no matter on which of his estates he might be, they should observe his orders as to what they should take without payment from the country folk, and how much and at what price they should purchase; and he punished those who transgressed this rule by heavy fines or even loss of life. At the beginning of his reign, that he might awe transgressors, he usually decreed punishment by mutilation, but later he resorted more to fines. Thus in consequence of the rectitude of his conduct, as is natural to man, he came to be feared by the magnates and beloved by the common people. If at any time the better sort, regardless of their plighted oath, wandered from the path of fidelity, he immediately recalled them to the straight road by the wisdom of his unceasing exertions; the refractory he brought back to reason by the wounds he inflicted on their bodies. I cannot easily describe the watch he kept on such persons and he allowed nothing to go unpunished which had been to the detriment of his dignity. Normandy was the chief source of his wars, and there in the main he resided, yet he also took special care of England so that none dared rebel by reason of his prudence and courage. Rebellions among his nobles never caused him to be treacherously attacked by his attendants, save only once when a certain chamberlain of plebian birth, but distinguished as the keeper of the king's treasure, was detected in such an attempt, and, after confession, suffered a bitter penalty. With this exception the king remained secure throughout his life: fear restrained the minds of all and admiration controlled their conversation.

He was of middle stature, neither unduly short nor tall: his hair was black and set back on his forehead; his eyes were mildly bright; his chest brawny; his body well fleshed. He was facetious in proper season, and even when preoccupied with business he was pleasant in company. He was not personally pugnacious, for he seemed to recall the saying of Scipio Africanus: 'My mother bore me to be a commander not a soldier.' Therefore he preferred to gain his ends by diplomacy rather than by the sword, and in this he was inferior in wisdom to no king of modern times, and indeed might without exaggeration be said to have in this matter

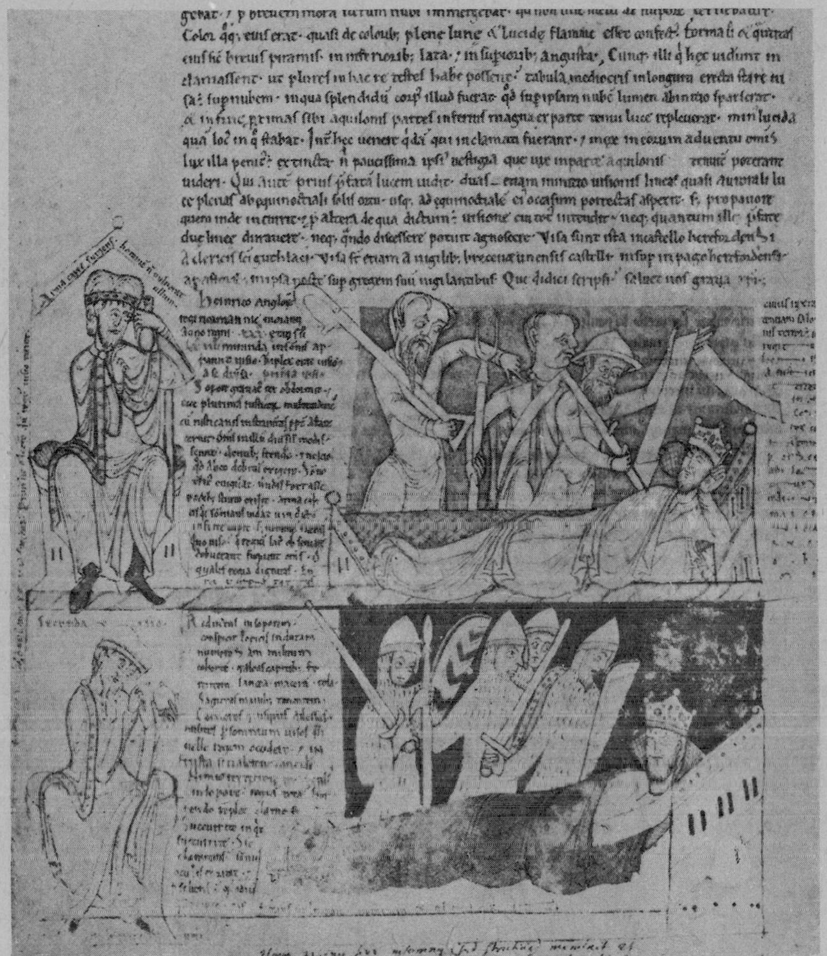

4. . The nightmares of Henry I, 1130-1140.
The king is threatened by bishops. From *John of Worcester's Chronicle*, written *c*.1130-1140.

surpassed all his predecessors. If he could, he made his conquests without violence, and if that was unavoidable, with as little bloodshed as possible . . . he was the master of his passions rather than their slave. He was plain in his diet, seeking to satisfy his hunger than to sate himself with a multitude of delicacies. He drank simply to allay his thirst, and he deplored the least lapse into drunkenness both in himself and others. His sleep was heavy and marked by much snoring. His eloquence was rather natural than premeditated, and deliberate rather than fluent.

William of Malmesbury, *English Historical Documents,* Vol.II

On the death of the great King Henry the verdict of the people was freely expressed concerning him, as is usually the case after the death of a notable personage. Some said that he was eminently distinguished for three splendid qualities; great wisdom, for he was most deep in counsel, keen foresight and outstanding eloquence; success in war, for besides other fine achievements he had overcome the king of France, and riches, for he was more wealthy than any of his predecessors. Others, however, taking a different view, attributed to him three vices; gross avarice through which, though himself wealthy like all his ancestors, he devoured the poor by tolls and exactions, entangling them in the toils of his informers; cruelty in that he put out the eyes of his kinsman, the count of Mortain, during his captivity, about which nothing could be known until death revealed the king's secrets, and other examples of greed were also cited which I forbear to mention; and also incontinence, for like Solomon he was perpetually enslaved by the rule of women. Such diverse opinions were freely expressed by the common people. But in the terrible times which followed later through the insensate treachery of the Normans, whatsoever King Henry had done, whether in the manner of a tyrant or of a true king, appeared most excellent in comparison with their evil deeds.

Henry of Huntingdon, *Historie Anglorum*,
English Historical Documents, Vol. II

ST MARGARET, MOTHER OF MATILDA, WIFE OF HENRY I

To the honourable and excellent Matilda, Queen of the English, Forasmuch as you have requested, you have also commanded me, to present to you in writing the story of the life of your mother .... You are wont to say that in this matter my testimony is especially trustworthy, since you have understood that by reason of her frequent and familiar intercourse with me I am acquainted with the most part of her secrets....

She made the King himself most attentive to works of justice, mercy, almsgiving, and other virtues. From her also he learned to keep the vigils of the night in prayer. . . . Also the books which she used either in her devotions or for reading, he, though unable to read, used often to handle and examine, and when he heard from her that one of them was dearer to her than the others, this he also regarded with kindlier affection, and would kiss and often fondle it. Sometimes also he would send for the goldsmith, and instruct him to adorn the volume with gold and precious stones, and when finished he would carry it to the Queen as proof of his devotion. The Queen, on the other hand, herself the noblest gem of a royal race, made the splendour of her husband's royal magnificence much more splendid, and contributed much glory and honour to all the nobility of the kingdom and their retainers. For she brought it to pass that merchants who came by land and sea from divers lands, brought with them for sale many and precious kinds of merchandise which in Scotland were before unknown, among which, at the instigation of the Queen, the people bought garments of various colours, and different kinds of personal ornaments; so that from that time they went about clothed in new costumes of different fashions, from the elegance of which they might have been supposed to be a new race. She also appointed a higher class of servant for the King, that when he walked or rode abroad numerous bodies of them might accompany him in state; and this was carried out with such discipline that wherever they came none of them was permitted to take anything from anyone by force; nor did any of them dare to oppress or injure the country people or the poor in any way. Moreover, she increased the splendour of the royal palace, so that not only was it brightened by the different coloured uniforms worn in it, but the whole house was made resplendent with gold and silver; for the vessels in which the King and nobles of the kingdom were served with food and drink, were either of gold or silver, or were gold or silver plated. And this the Queen did not because the honour of the world delighted her, but because she felt compelled to do what the royal dignity required of her. For when she walked in state clad in splendid apparel, as became a Queen, like another Esther, she in her heart trod all these trappings beneath her feet, and bore in mind that under the gems and gold there was nothing but dust and ashes.

Turgot, *Life of St Margaret* in *Ancient Lives of Scottish Saints*,
translated by W.M. Metcalfe

MATILDA (1080-1118), queen of Henry I

Now it is true that this Matilda was brought up from early childhood in a convent of nuns and grew up there to womanhood, and many believed that she had been dedicated by her parents to God's service as she had been seen walking abroad wearing the veil like the nuns with whom she was living. This circumstance, when, long after she had discarded the veil, the king fell in love with her, set the tongues of many wagging and held back the two from embracing one another as they desired. Accordingly, as all were looking for a sign from Anselm on this question, the girl herself went to him and humbly besought his advice and help in the matter . . .

'But that I did wear the veil', she said, 'I do not deny. For when I was quite a young girl and went in fear of the rod of my Aunt Christina, whom you knew quite well, she to preserve me from the lust of the Normans which was rampant at that time ready to assault any woman's honour, used to put a little black hood on my head and, when I threw it off, she would often make me smart with a good slapping and most horrible scolding, as well as treating me as being in disgrace. That hood I did indeed wear in her presence, chafing at it and fearful; but, as soon as I was able to escape out of her sight, I tore it off and threw it on the ground and trampled on it and in that way, although foolishly, I used to

5. The wedding feast of Matilda, daughter of Henry I, and the Emperor Henry V, 1114

vent my rage and the hatred of it which boiled up in me. In that way, and only in that way, I was veiled, as my conscience bears witness.'

Eadmer, monk of Canterbury, *Historia Novorum in Anglia*, translated by Geoffrey Bosanquet

STEPHEN, 1135-1154

Stephen, therefore, in order that he might be elevated to the throne equally against right both human and divine – transgressing the one by not being the legitimate heir, and the other by his perfidy – promised everything which the prelates and nobles demanded: but his want of faith rendered all these of no avail; for by the judgements of God that good, for the attainment of which those wise and powerful men had resolved on the commission of such an atrocious crime, was not permitted to take effect.

William of Newburgh, translated by J. Stevenson

6. Stephen, the son of Adela, William I's daughter, had much of his mother's intelligence and also considerable charm. He usurped the throne that belonged to Matilda, daughter of Henry I; this was a cause of much unsettlement. His reign of nineteen years was one of continuous strife and anarchy.

Stephen (by the grace of God), king of the English, to the justices, sheriffs, barons and to all his servants and liegemen, both French and English, greeting. Know that I have granted, and by this present charter confirmed, to all my barons and vassals of England all the liberties and good laws which Henry, king of the English, my uncle, granted and conceded to them. I also grant them all the good laws and good customs which they enjoyed in the time of King Edward. Wherefore I will and firmly command that both they and their heirs shall have and hold all these good laws and liberties from me and from my heirs freely, fully and in peace.

7. The Royal Builders, by Matthew Paris, *c.* 1250
(top) William I, Battle Abbey; William II, Westminster Hall;
Henry I, Reading Abbey; Stephen, Faversham Abbey

And I forbid anyone to molest or hinder them, or to cause them loss or damage in respect of these things under pain of forfeiture to me.

Coronation Charter of Stephen, *English Historical Documents*, Vol.II

He was a man of activity, but imprudent: strenuous in war; of great mind in attempting works of difficulty; mild and compassionate to his enemies and affable to all. Kind, as far as promise went; but sure to disappoint in its truth and execution. Whence he soon afterwards neglected the advice of his brother, befriended by whose assistance, as I have said, he had supplanted his adversaries and obtained the kingdom.

William of Malmesbury, translated by J.A. Giles

Towns – Buildings

THE BUILDING OF WESTMINSTER ABBEY

Outside the walls of London, upon the River Thames, stood a monastery dedicated to St Peter, but insignificant in buildings and numbers, for under the abbot only a small community of monks served Christ. Moreover, the endowments from the faithful were slender, and provided no more than their daily bread. The king [Edward the Confessor] , therefore, being devoted to God, gave his attention to that place, for it both lay hard by the famous and rich town and also was a delightful spot, surrounded with fertile lands and green fields and near the main channel of the river, which bore abundant merchandise of wares of every kind for sale from the whole world to the town on its banks. And, especially because of his love of the Prince of the Apostles, whom he worshipped with uncommon and special love, he decided to have his burial place there. Accordingly he ordered that out of the tithes of all his revenues should be started the building of a noble edifice, worthy of the Prince of the Apostles . . . And so the building, nobly begun at the king's command, was successfully made ready; and there was no weighing of the costs, past or future, so long as it proved worthy of, and acceptable to, God and St Peter. The princely house of the altar, noble with its most lofty vaulting, is surrounded by dressed stone evenly jointed. Also the passage round that temple is enclosed on both sides by a double arching of stone with the joints of the structure strongly consolidated on this side and that. Furthermore, the crossing of the church, which is to hold in its midst the choir of God's choristers, and to uphold with like support from either side the high apex of the central tower, rises simply at first with a low and sturdy vault, swells with many a stair spiralling up in artistic profusion, but then with a plain wall climbs to the wooden roof which is carefully covered with lead.

8. Domesday Book. These two volumes, on top of an iron-bound chest, contain a record of the ownership, area, and value of the lands of England, and of the numbers of tenants, livestock and so on, made by order of William the Conqueror in 1086. The name 'Domesday' originated 'as a final and conclusive authority on all matters connected with land-tenure'. The book is open at a page giving details of Westminster.

Above and below are built out chapels methodically arranged, which are to be consecrated through their altars to the memory of apostles, martyrs, confessors and virgins. Moreover, the whole complex of this enormous building was started so far to the East of the old church that that brethren dwelling there should not have to cease from Christ's service and also that a sufficiently spacious vestibule might be placed between them.

The Life of King Edward the Confessor, edited by F. Barlow

STORM IN LONDON, 1091

At this time also, winds, blowing from all quarters in a way marvellous to relate, began on 17 October to blow so violently that they shattered more than 600 houses in London; churches were reduced to heaps, as also houses, stone walls like those of timber . . . . The fury of the wind lifted up the roof of the Church of St Mary, which is called at Bow, and crushed two men there.

Rafters and beams were carried through the air, and of these rafters four of 26 feet in length, when they fell in the public street, were driven with such force into the ground that they scarcely stood out four feet, and as they could in no way be pulled out, orders were given to cut them off level with the ground.

Thanks to O.U.P. for quotations from L.F. Salzman, *Building in England down to 1540.*

9. Westcott Barton, Marwood, North Devon: a Domesday demesne farm.

MONASTERIES AND CHURCHES REBUILT

[Soon after the Conquest] the City of Canterbury was set on fire by the carelessness of some persons, and the rising flames caught the mother church thereof . . . and the whole was consumed. . . . [Lanfranc] pulled down to the ground all that he found of the burnt monastery, whether of buildings or the wasted remains of buildings and having dug out their foundations from under the earth, he built in their stead others which greatly excelled them in beauty and in size.

This year [1093] in the presence of almost all the bishops and abbots of England, on 8 April, with great joy and honour, the monks came from the old monastery at Winchester to the new. On the feast of St Swithin a procession was formed from the new monastery to the old and they brought the shrine of St Swithin and placed it in the new church. Next day, by order of Bishop Walkelin, men began to break up the old monastery; and it was all broken up in that year except one chapel and the high altar.

Thanks to O.U.P. for quotations from L.F. Salzman, *Building in England down to 1540.*

BUILDING REGULATIONS IN LONDON IN THE TWELFTH CENTURY

When two neighbours shall have agreed to build between themselves a wall of stone, each shall give a foot and a half of land, and so they shall construct, at their joint cost, a stone wall three feet thick and sixteen feet in height. And, if they agree, they shall make a gutter between them, to carry off the water from their houses, as they may deem most convenient. But if they should not agree, either of them may make a gutter to carry the water dripping from his own house on to his own land, except he can convey it into the high street. . . .

And if any one shall build his own stone wall, upon his own land, of the height of sixteen feet, his neighbour ought to make a gutter under the eaves of the house which is placed on that wall, and receive in it the water falling from that house, and lead it on to his own land, unless he can lead it into the high street.

Also, no one of two parties having a common wall built between them, can, or ought, to pull down any portion of his part of the said wall, or lessen its thickness, or make arches in it, without the assent and will of the other.

And if any one shall have windows looking towards the land of a neighbour, and although he and his predecessors have long been possessed of the view of the aforesaid windows, nevertheless, his neighbour may lawfully obstruct the view of those windows, by building opposite to them on his own ground, as he shall consider most expedient; except he who hath the windows can show any writing whereby his neighbour may not obstruct the view of those windows. . . .

A decree made by the counsel of the citizens, for the setting into order of the city and to provide, by God's help, against fire.

First, they advise that all ale-houses be forbidden, except those which shall be licensed by the common council of the city at

Guildhall, excepting those belonging to persons willing to build of stone, that the city may be secure. And that no baker bake, or ale-wife brew, by night, either with reeds or straw or stubble, but with wood only.

They advise also that all the cook-shops on the Thames be whitewashed and plastered within and without, and that all inner chambers and hostelries be wholly removed, so that there remain only the house [hall] and bed-room.

Whosoever wishes to build, let him take care, as he loveth himself and his goods, that he roof not with reeds, nor rush, nor with any manner of litter, but with tile only, or shingle, or boards, or, if it may be, with lead, within the city and Portsoken. Also all houses which till now are covered with reed or rush, which can be plastered, let them be plastered within eight days, and let those which shall not be so plastered within the term be demolished by the aldermen and lawful men of the venue.

All wooden houses which are nearest to the stone houses in Cheap, whereby the stone houses in Cheap may be in peril, shall be securely amended by view of the mayor and sheriffs, and good men of the city, or, without any exception, to whomsoever they may belong, pulled down.

The watches, and they who watch by night for the custody of the city shall go out by day and return by day, or they by whom they may have been sent forth shall be fined forty shillings by the city. And let old houses in which brewing or baking is done be whitewashed and plastered within and without, that they may be safe against fire. . . .

They say also that it is only proper that before every house should be a tub full of water, either of wood or stone.

London Assizes, quoted in Hudson Turner, *History of Domestic Architecture,* Vol.I

ZOO IN A PARK, 1119

Paul, Earl of Orkney, though subject by hereditary right to the King of Norway, was so anxious to obtain the friendship of the king [Henry I], that he was perpetually sending him presents; for he was extremely fond of the wonders of distant countries, begging with great delight, as I have observed, from foreign kings, lions, leopards, lynxes or camels – animals which England does not produce.

He had a park called Woodstock, in which he used to foster his favourites of this kind. He had placed there a creature called a porcupine, sent to him by William of Montpelier, of which animal, Pliny the Elder, in the eighth book of his Natural History, and Isodorus, on Etymologies, relate that there is such a creature in Africa, which the inhabitants call of the urchin kind, covered with bristly hair, which it naturally darts against the dogs when pursuing it. Moreover these are, as I have seen, more than a span long, sharp at each extremity, like the quills of a goose where the feather ceases, but rather thicker, and speckled, as it were, with black and white.

William of Malmesbury *Gesta Regum Anglorum*, translated by J.A. Giles

CASTLES, 1140

There were many castles throughout England, each defending their neighbourhood, but, more properly speaking, laying it waste. The garrisons drove off from the fields, both sheep and cattle, nor did they abstain either from churches or church-yards. Seizing such of the country vavassours [yeomen] as were reputed to be possessed

10. Framework of a cruck building, eleventh century. The cruck was a suitably bent oak branch, split to form two equal halves as shown here. A similar branch at the other end could be joined by a ridge pole. A horizontal beam strengthened the cruck.

of money, they compelled them, by extreme torture, to promise whatever they thought fit. Plundering the houses of the wretched husbandmen, even to their very beds, they cast them into prison; nor did they liberate them, but on their giving every thing they possessed or could by any means scrape together, for their release. Many calmly expired in the midst of torments inflicted to compel them to ransom themselves, bewailing, which was all they could do, their miseries to God. And, indeed, at the instance of the Earl [of Gloucester], the legate, with the bishops, repeatedly excommunicated all violators of churchyards and plunderers of churches, and those who laid violent hands on men in holy or monastic orders, or their servants: but this his attention profited little. It was distressing, therefore, to see England, once the fondest cherisher of peace and the single receptacle of tranquillity, reduced to such a pitch of misery that, not even the bishops, nor monks, could pass in safety from one town to another.

William of Malmesbury *Gesta Regum Anglorum*, translated by J.A. Giles

A SURVEY OF THE MANOR OF ELTON, *c.* 1154-1180

And this is the work and the service of [the holder of] I virgate: From Michaelmas to the beginning of August he works for 2 days in each week and ploughs for a third, except at Christmas and Easter and Pentecost. And from the beginning of August to the Nativity of St Mary he works for 3 days each week. And from the Nativity of St Mary he works every day except Saturday. In winter he ploughs half an acre, and sows it with his own seed; and he harrows and reaps this, and also another half-acre in August. And he performs carrying services at his own expense. And he makes 2 mitts of malt from the lord's corn and the sixth part of 1 'milla'.

He makes payments for rights on the common; and he pays 13 pence as 'heusire'. He pays also 4 pence at Michaelmas, and 1 halfpenny for wool. And he shall go errands: if he goes outside the county he shall be quit of his week's work except for ploughing. And in August he gives 1 carrying service of timber, and 1 work at fencing and he performs 2 carrying services of corn in August. And each 5 virgates give 4 pence for fish, and each 2 virgates give 1 cart of thatch, and they make the thatch. When the winnower comes there, all shall go to the court and thresh the corn from day to day until the 'farm' is made up. And if there is such hard frost in winter that he cannot plough, then he shall work on Fridays instead of ploughing. And when the farmer calls for boon-works in August he shall come to them with his whole household, and he shall then be fed by the farmer.

The Cartulary of Ramsey Abbey, *English Historical Documents*, Vol.II

ROMAN ROADWAYS OF ENGLAND

Faire weyes many of ther ben in Englonde;
But four most of all ther ben I understonde,
That thurgh an old Kyng were made ere this,
As men schal in this boke aftir here telle I wis.
Fram the South into the North takith Ermingestrete.
Fram the East into the West goeth Ikeneld strete.
Fram Southest to Northwest, that is sum del grete.
Fram Dover into Chestre goth Watlyngstrete.
The ferth of thise is most of alle that tilleth fram Toteneys.
Fram the one end of Carnwaile anone to Canteneys.

Fram the Southwest to Northest into Englonde ende
Fosse men callith thilke wey that by mony town doth wende.
Thise foure weyes on this londe Kyng Belin the wise [legendary British ruler]
Made and ordeyned hem with gret Fraunchise;

Robert of Gloucester, metrical chronicle of England, c. 1285, *The Antiquities of Warwickshire*, W. Dugdale

A NORMAN LAND GRANT, 1069

By the bounteous grace of Christ, the King of kings who rules everything with a pious government, William, duke of the Normans, having acquired the kingdom of England, when he was in the royal township which in England is called 'Guenitho', by the counsel and request of his liegeman William, son of Osbern the steward who was the chief of the palace, and in the presence of Abbot Rainer and the two monks, Nicholas and William, gave to Holy Trinity of the Mount in perpetual heredity the land which in England is called 'Hermodesodes' with the church and all its appurtenances, to wit, in fields and meadows and pastures and mills and waters and marshes and woods and with the rest of the neighbourhood of this village. This gift was made by the presentation of a dagger and when the king gave it to the abbot, he pretended to stab the abbot's hand. 'Thus', he jestingly exclaimed, 'ought land to be bestowed'. With this clear sign therefore, and with the testimony of the many nobles who stood by the king's side, was this gift made in the year of the Incarnation of our Lord 1069.

Cartulary of Holy Trinity, Rouen, *English Historical Documents,* Vol.II

THE ISLE OF ELY, *c.* 1070

A French knight, who had been captured by Hereward 'the Wake', describes the Isle to William I.

In our Isle men are not troubling themselves about the siege; the ploughman has not taken his hand from the plough, nor has the hunter cast aside his arrow, nor does the fowler desist from beguiling birds. If you care to hear what I have heard and seen with my own eyes, I will reveal all to you. The Isle is within itself plenteously endowed; it is supplied with various kinds of herbage; and in richness of soil surpasses the rest of England. Most delightful for charming fields and pastures, it is also remarkable

11. Barn at Godmersham, Kent. This is an early form of the timber aisled hall, leaving a clear centre, and spaces between the tall posts for animal stalls and human occupation.

for beasts of chase; and is, in no ordinary way, fertile in flocks and herds. Its woods and vineyards are not worthy of equal praise; but it is begirt by great meres and fens as though by a strong wall. In this Isle there is an abundance of domestic cattle, and a multitude of wild animals; stags, roes, goats, and hares, are found in its groves and by these fens. Moreover, there is a fair sufficiency of otters, weasels, and polecats; which in hard winter are caught by traps, snares, or any other device. But what am I to say of the kinds of fishes and of fowls, both those that fly and those that swim? In the eddies at the sluices of these meres are netted innumerable eels, large water-wolves, with pickerels, perches, roaches, burbots [a fish full of prickles], and lampreys, which we call water-snakes. It is, indeed, said by many that sometimes salmon are taken there, together with the royal fish, the sturgeon. As for the birds that abide there and there-abouts, if you are not tired of listening to me, I will tell you about them, as I have told you about the rest. There you will find geese, teal, coots, didappers [or dabchicks], water-crows, herons, and ducks, more than man can number, especially in winter or at moulting time. I have seen a hundred – nay, even three hundred – taken at once; sometimes by bird-lime, sometimes in nets or snares.

Liber Eliensis, translated by J.W. Clark in Cambridge, 1893

AN ACCOUNT OF THE CITY OF CHESTER

The city of Chester paid geld *T.R.E.* [Tempore regis Edwardi] for 50 hides. There are 3½ hides which are outside the city, that is 1½ hides beyond the bridge, and 2 hides in Newton and Redcliff and in the bishop's borough: these paid geld with the city.

There were in the city *T.R.E.* 431 houses which paid geld, and besides these the bishop had 56 houses which paid geld. This city then paid 10½ marks of silver. Two-thirds went to the king, and one-third to the earl.

These were the laws which were then observed:

If the peace given by the king with his own hand, or by his writ, or by his messenger was broken by anyone, the king received a fine of 100 shillings. But if the same peace of the king given by the earl at his command was broken, the earl had the third penny of the 100 shillings which were given in fine for this offence. If, however, the same peace given by the king's reeve, or by the earl's servant, was broken, a fine of 40 shillings was paid, and the earl had the third penny.

If any freeman, breaking the king's peace which had been given, killed a man in a house, all his land and chattels were forfeit to the king, and he became an outlaw. The earl exacted the same penalty, but only when his own man incurred this forfeiture. Nobody, however, could give back peace to any outlaw except by the will of the king.

A man who shed blood from the morning of Monday to noon on Saturday paid a fine of 10 shillings. But from noon on Saturday until the morning of Monday 20 shillings was the amount of the fine for bloodshed. A like 20 shillings was paid as a a fine by the man who shed blood in the 12 days of Nativity, on Candlemas Day, on the first day of Easter, and the first day of Pentecost, on Ascension Day, on the day of the Assumption or of the Nativity of Holy Mary, and on the day of the Feast of All Saints.

He who killed a man on these holy days paid a fine of 4 pounds; but on other days 40 shillings. So too he who committed 'hamfare' [robbery] or 'forsteal' [violence in the streets] on these feast days and on Sunday paid 4 pounds; on other days 40 shillings.

He who incurred 'hengwite' [failure to raise the hue and cry after a thief] in the city paid 10 shillings; but a reeve of the king or earl incurring this forfeiture paid a fine of 20 shillings.

He who was guilty of robbery or theft, or assaulted a woman in a house, paid a fine of 40 shillings.

If a widow had unlawful intercourse with any man, she paid a fine of 20 shillings; a young girl paid 10 shillings for this offence.

A man who seized the land of another in the city and could not prove it to be his, paid a fine of 40 shillings. He who made the claim paid a like fine if he could not prove the land to be his by right.

He who wished to take up his land or the land of his kinsman gave 10 shillings, and if he could not or would not pay this, the reeve took his land into the king's hand.

He who did not pay his 'gafol' at the term when it was due paid 10 shillings as a fine.

If fire broke out in the city, the man from whose house it came paid a fine of 3 ounces of pennies, and to his next-door neighbour

12. Builders using plumb-line, pick-axe, chisel, and a kind of hoe for mixing lime. Twelfth century.

he gave 2 shillings.

Two-thirds of all these forfeitures were the king's and one-third the earl's.

If ships arrived at the port of the city, or departed therefrom without permission of the king, the king and the earl had 40 shillings from each man who was on the ships.

If a ship came against the king's peace, and despite his prohibition, the king and the earl had the ship, and the men, and all that was in the ship.

But if the ship came in the king's peace, and with his leave, then those on board might sell what they had undisturbed. When it left, however, the king and the earl took 4 pence from each last. If the king's reeve ordered those who had martens' pelts not to sell to anyone until the king had seen them and been given an opportunity of buying, then he neglected to do this paid a fine of 40 shillings.

A man or a woman caught giving false measure in the city paid a fine of 4 shillings. Likewise the maker of bad beer was either set in the cucking-stool, or paid 4 shillings to the reeves. The officers of the king and the earl took this forfeiture in the city in whosoever's land it arose, whether the bishop's or that of any other man. In like manner did they take toll, and anyone who delayed it beyond three nights paid a fine of 40 shillings.

There were in this city *T.R.E.* 7 moneyers who, when the coinage was changed, paid 7 pounds to the king and earl over and above the 'farm'.

There were then 12 'judges' of the city and these were taken from the men of the king and the bishop and the earl. If any of them absented himself from the hundred court on the day of its session without proper excuse, he paid a fine of 10 shillings to the king and the earl.

For the repair of the city wall the reeve was wont to call up one man from each hide in the county. The lord of any man who failed to come paid a fine of 40 shillings to the king and the earl. This forfeiture was not included in the 'farm'.

This city then rendered a 'farm' of 45 pounds and 3 'timbres' of martens' pelts. A third of this was the earl's and two-thirds the king's.

When Earl Hugh received it, it was not worth more than 30 pounds for it was greatly wasted; there were 205 houses less than there had been *T.R.E.* There are now the same number as he found there.

Mundret held the city from the earl for 70 pounds and 1 mark of gold. The same Mundret had at 'farm' for 50 pounds and 1 mark of gold all the earl's pleas in the shire court, and in the hundred court, except Englefield.

The land on which the church of St Peter stands, which Robert of Rhuddlan claimed as thegn-land, never belonged to a manor outside the city, and this was proved by witness of the county. It belongs to the borough and always paid dues to the king and the earl like the lands of the other burgesses.

Domesday Book, Vol.I, fol.262b.
Translation based on *The Domesday Survey of Cheshire*, J. Tait

CLAIMS FROM THE SURVEY OF HUNTINGDONSHIRE IN DOMESDAY BOOK

The jurors of Huntingdon say that the church of St. Mary of the borough and the land which is annexed to it belonged to the church of Thorney, but the abbot gave it in pledge to the burgesses. Moreover, King Edward gave it to Vitalis and Bernard, his priests, and they sold it to Hugh, chamberlain to King Edward. Moreover, Hugh sold it to two priests of Huntingdon, and in respect of this they have the seal of King Edward. Eustace has it now without livery, without writ, and without seisin [possession].

Eustace took away wrongfully the house of Leveve and gave it to Oger of London.

They bear witness that the land of Hunef and Gos was under the hand of King Edward on the day when he was alive and dead and that they held of him and not of the earl. But the jurors say that they heard that King William was said to have given it to Waltheof.

Touching the 5 hides of Broughton the jurors say that it was the land of sokemen *T.R.E.* [Tempore regis Edwardi], but that the same king gave the land and the soke over the men to St. Benedict of Ramsey in return for a service which Abbot Alwin did for him in Saxony, and ever afterwards the saint had it.

The shire bears witness that the land of Bricmer 'Belehorne' was 'reeveland' *T.R.E.* and belonged to the king's 'farm'.

They bear witness that the land of Alwin the priest was to the abbot. . . .

They bear witness that Aluric's land of Yelling and Hemingford belonged to St. Benedict and that it was granted to Aluric for the term of his life on the condition that after his death it ought to return to the church, and 'Bocstede' with it. But this same Aluric was killed in the battle of Hastings, and the abbot took back his lands and held them until Aubrey 'de Vere' deprived him of possession.

Touching 2 hides which Ralph, son of Osmund, holds in Hemingford, they say that one of them belonged to the demesne of the church of Ramsey in King Edward's day, and that Ralph holds it against the abbot's will. Touching the other hide, they say that Godric held it from the abbot, but when the abbot was in Denmark, Osmund, Ralph's father, seized it from Sawin the fowler, to whom the abbot had given it for love of the king.

Touching Summerlede they say that he held his land from Turulf who gave it to him, and afterwards from the sons of Turulf, and they had sake and soke over him.

The jurors say that the land of Wulwine Chit of Weston was a manor by itself, and did not belong to Kimbolton, but that nevertheless he was a man of Earl Harold.

Touching a hide and a half of land which was Aelget's, the jurors say that this Aelget held them from Earl Tosti with sake and soke and afterwards of Waltheof.

Godric the priest likewise held 1 hide of land from Earl Waltheof *T.R.E.*, and Eustace holds it now.

They say that the land of Godwine of Weston in no way belonged to Saxi, Fafiton's predecessor.

The men of the shire bear witness that King Edward gave Swineshead to Earl Siward with sake and soke, and so Earl Harold had it, except that the men paid geld in the hundred, and performed military service with them.

Touching the land of Fursa, the soke was the king's. King Edward had soke over 1 virgate of land of Alwin Deule in Pertenhall.

The jurors say that the hide of land which Wulwine Chit had in Catworth was in the king's soke and that Earl Harold did not have it.

13. The great hall, Castle Hedingham, Essex, showing furniture and mural galleries. Twelfth century

In Little Catworth the same Wulwine had 1 hide over which King Edward always had sake and soke. But Wulwine could give and sell the land to whom he wished. But the men of the countess say that the king gave the land to Earl Waltheof.

The shire bears witness that the third part of half a hide which lies in Easton and pays geld in Bedfordshire belongs to the abbot of Ely's manor of Spaldwick. The abbot of Ely thus held it *T.R.E.*, and for five years after the coming of King William. Eustace seized this land wrongfully from the church, and kept it.

The jurors say that Keystone was and is the 'farm' of King Edward, and although Aluric the sheriff resided in that village, he nevertheless always paid the king's 'farm' therefrom, and his sons after him, until Eustace took the sheriffdom. They have never seen or heard of a seal of King Edward that he put it outside his 'farm'.

Alwold and his brother claim that Eustace took away their land from them, and the men of the shire deny that they have ever seen a seal, or seen anyone who gave Eustace seisin of it.

On the day when King Edward was alive and dead, Gidding was an outlying estate of Alconbury in the king's 'farm'.

The men of the shire bear witness that Buckworth was an outlying estate of Paxton *T.R.E.*

They say that 36 hides of land in Brampton which Richard 'Ingania' claims to belong to the forest were of the king's demesne 'farm', and did not belong to the forest.

They say that Graffham was and is the king's sokeland, and that they have not seen the writ, or anyone who gave legal possession of this to Eustace.

Touching 6 hides in Conington they said they had heard that these formerly belonged to the church of Thorney, and that they were granted to Turchill on condition that after [his] death they ought to return to the church with the other 3 hides in the same village. The jurors said that they had heard this, but they had not seen evidence of it, nor were they present when the arrangement was made.

Touching the land of Tosti of Sawtry, they say that Eric, his brother, bequeathed it to the church of Ramsey after his death and after the death of his brother and sister.

Touching Fletton the jurors say that *T.R.E.* the whole belonged to the church of Peterborough, and so it should.

Touching Leuric's land the jurors say that it was in the king's soke, but Bishop Remigius shows the writ of King Edward by which he gave Leuric with all his land to the bishopric of Lincoln with sake and soke.

GRANT OF LAND TO BE HELD BY MILITARY SERVICE MADE BY ROBERT LOSINGA, BISHOP OF HEREFORD, 1085

This privilege Robert, bishop of the church of Hereford, ordered to be recorded as agreed between him and Roger, son of Walter, concerning certain land which is called 'Hamme', [Holme Lacy] and those things which pertain to it. This land belongs to the church of Holy Mary, the Mother of God, and of St. Ethelbert the martyr; and previously the said bishop held this land as his own demesne and for the sustenance of the church. This land the aforesaid knight, to wit, Roger, asked from the bishop through his friends, and he offered money in respect of it. But the bishop, by the counsel of his vassals, gave him this same land in return for a promise that he would serve the bishop with 2 knights as his father did whenever the need arose. This also was part of the contract: that the men of the bishop belonging to King's Hampton and Hereford, and to the estates pertaining thereto, should be at liberty to take timber from the wood for the use of the bishop as often as it should be needed for fuel or for repairing houses; and the pigs of these manors should feed in the same wood. This refers to the men belonging to the bishop. And this contract further enjoins that if Roger becomes a monk, or dies, neither his mother nor his wife nor his sons nor his brothers nor any of his kinsfolk shall have rights in the aforesaid land, but let the bishop receive whatever in the estate may be to the profit of holy Church, and his men shall receive the same without any contradiction whatsoever. This instrument was executed in the year of the Incarnation of our Lord 1085, it being the eighth Indiction. The following were witnesses to this matter: Earl Roger, [first earl of Shrewsbury] and his son, Hugh, and his other son, Everard, and the countess and the sheriff, Warin; Osbert, son of Richard; Drew, son of Pons; Gerard of Tournay-sur-Dive; William 'Malbedan'; Gilbert, Earl Roger's constable. Of the men of the bishop there were these: Gerald, his brother; Humphrey the archdeacon; Ansfrid the priest; William; Leofwine; Alfweard; Saewulf; Alwine. And there were

14. Wasdale in Cumberland, showing the winding lanes and small irregular fields; what W.G. Hoskins calls 'a handmade landscape of medieval colonization'.

these laymen from among the men of the bishop: Udo; Athalard; Franco; Arnulf; Tetbald; Robert; Gozo; Osbert; Peter; Richard the butler. Of the men of Earl Roger there were these clerks: Ralph; Geoffrey; Odo; Gerold. And there were these laymen of Earl Roger: Walter; Heribert 'de Furcis'; Richard of Stanton; Herman 'de Drewis'; Robert of Boscherville; Richard of Ectot; William of Evreux; Ralph of Le Saussey; Nicholas; Godmund. The aforesaid Roger holds other land devoted to the sustenance of the bishop, to wit, at Onibury, on these conditions. As long as he lives he shall give each year on St. Martin's Day 20 shillings, and after his death, or if he becomes a monk, the land shall be returned without question to the bishop in the same condition as it is now. On this matter the following were witnesses: Ansfrid of Cormeilles; Edric of Wenlock; another Edric, to wit, the steward; and all the aforesaid except Earl Roger and his household.

English Historical Review, Vol.XLIV

PROTECTION OF WOODLAND

To William the monk. Concerning the giving of Thorpe wood to the sick I gave no commands, nor do I give nor shall I give; for I appointed thee guardian, not uprooter of that wood. To the sick I will give not wood, but money, when I come to Norwich, as I did last year. Give them this answer and no other. Meanwhile do thou guard the wood of the Holy Trinity [of Norwich] even as thou wouldst wish thyself to be guarded by the Holy Trinity, and to keep my love.

Letter from Bishop Herbert de Losinga of Norwich
to monastic official between 1094 and 1120,
Epistolae H. Losingae

THE CUSTOMS OF OXFORD AND OXFORDSHIRE

The shire of Oxford pays a 'farm' of three nights. It thus pays 150 pounds. As an increase to this it pays 25 pounds by weight. There comes from the borough 20 pounds by weight. From the mint there are 20 pounds in pennies which are reckoned at 20 to the ounce; 4 shillings are paid for weapons; 100 shillings 'by tale' are paid in respect of the queen's gift; 10 pounds are paid in respect of a hawk; 20 shillings in respect of a sumpter horse; 23 pennies reckoned at 20 to the ounce in respect of hounds; 6 sesters of honey and 15 pennies in respect of customary dues.

From the land of Earl Edwin in Oxfordshire and Warwickshire the king has 100 pounds and 100 shillings.

Anyone breaking the king's peace given under his hand and seal to the extent of committing homicide shall be at the king's mercy in respect of his life and members. That is if he be captured. And if he cannot be captured, he shall be considered as an outlaw, and anyone who kills him shall have all his possessions.

The king shall take the possessions of any stranger who has elected to live in Oxford and who dies in possession of a house in that town, and without any kinsfolk.

The king shall take 100 shillings from anyone who breaks into the court or house of another so that he inflicts death or injury upon him by assault.

The king shall likewise take 100 shillings from any man who having been summoned for military service fails to discharge that service.

The king shall be entitled to the body and the possessions of any man who kills another within his own court or house excepting always the dower of his wife, if he has a wife who has received a dower.

Domesday Book, Vol.I, fol.154

CROSSROADS AT DUNSTABLE, Early Twelfth Century

The Lord Henry [I], King of England, son of William the Conqueror had in demesne [in hand] the vills of Houghton and Kenesworth. The country round Houghton where the two royal thoroughfares of Watling Street and Ickneld intersect, is so wooded in every direction and so full of robbers that a law abiding person can scarcely get through without losing his life, his limb, or his goods. The king wanted to remedy this evil so he ordered the whole district to be cleared and then built a royal palace there which he called Kingsbury. This place covers nine acres. He wanted to establish a settlement there, too, so he had a proclamation made in every part of the kingdom declaring that anybody who migrated thither might have land at 12d. an acre a year. Immigrants and their heirs would have the same freedoms and privileges throughout the kingdom as the city of London or any other English borough had ever had. Thus the area was built up by such people across and along the two highways. A robber who used to operate there was called Dunning and so the town was called Dunningstable.

The king kept the town of Dunstable as a free borough in his own hands for 17½ years and its burgesses were free throughout England throughout his reign as explained; and they never had to go outside the town of Dunningstable to answer the justices in eyre or other royal officials, but such judges and officials always made a diversion and came to Dunstable . . . and he established a market twice a week and a three day fair . . . and gallows. . . . At last the king built a church in honour of St. Peter at the end of the town and built a monastery, and, as he had long intended, established there a prior and canons regular [Augustinians, such as his queen had established at Aldgate, London]. He gave them . . . the borough with the market and the fair.

College of Arms MS. translated from *Monasticon Anglicanum, A History of the Abbies and other Monasteries, Hospitals, Frieries and Cathedral and Collegiate Churches,* W. Dugdale

15. Cadbury in Devon: a landscape of dispersed farms

SURVEYS OF CERTAIN MANORS BELONGING TO THE ABBEY OF PETERBOROUGH, 1125 to 1128

This is the description of the manors of the abbey of Peterborough as Walter the archdeacon received them and possessed them in the hand of the king.

In Kettering are 10 hides for the king's geld. And of these 10 hides 40 villeins hold 40 virgates. And these men plough in the spring from each virgate 4 acres for the work of the lord. And besides this they provide ploughs for the work of the lord four times in the winter, and three times in the spring and once in the summer. And these men have 22 ploughs with which they work. And all these men work for the lord 3 days in each week. And besides this they render each year from each virgate by custom 2 shillings and 3 halfpence. And all the men render 50 hens and 640 eggs. And besides this, Ailric holds 13 acres with 2 acres of meadow, and pays for them 16 pence. And there is a mill with a miller and it pays 20 shillings. And 8 cotters each of whom has 5 acres and they work (for the lord) 1 day each week, and twice a year they make malt. And each one of them gives 1 penny for a he-goat (if he has one) and 1 halfpenny for a nanny-goat. And there is a shepherd and a swine-herd who holds 8 acres. And in the court of the demesne there are 4 ploughs with 32 oxen, and 12 cows with 10 calves, 2 beasts for food, 3 draught horses, 300 sheep, 50 pigs, and 16 shillings' worth of the surplus hay from the meadow. The church of Kettering belongs to the altar of the abbey of Peterborough. And for the love of St. Peter it renders 4 rams and 2 cows or 5 shillings. . . .

In Pilsgate there are 3 hides for the king's geld. And 3 villeins hold 1 hide and 1 virgate. And these have 2 ploughs with which they plough for the lord 8 acres for the winter sowing and 8 acres for the spring sowing; and they work 3 days each week for the lord. And there is 1 bordar and 2 ox-herds holding land by service. And there is 1 shepherd. And there are 44 sokemen. And all these together with the villeins pay 44 shillings a year. And all these sokemen have 8 ploughs and with them they plough for the lord three times a year. And each one of them reaps in August half an acre of the lord's corn, and they give boon-work twice in August. And each one harrows 1 day in spring. And there is a mill which pays 4 shillings. And in the court of the demesne there is 1 plough with 8 oxen, and 1 boar and 2 calves and 1 horse for harrowing and 2 foals. And 180 sheep and 20 pigs. On the Feast of St. Peter [is paid] 6 sheep or 1 cow and 5 ells of cloth.

In Thorpe Achurch are 2 hides and 1 virgate for the king's geld. And there are 12 full villeins and each one of them holds 11 acres and works (for the lord) 3 days each week. And 6 half-villeins who perform the same in proportion to their holdings. And all of these make a customary payment of 10 shillings. And besides this they pay for love of St. Peter 5 'multones', and 10 ells of cloth, and 10 baskets and 200 loaves. And all these men plough 16½ acres for the lord's work. And there are 6 bordars who pay 7 shillings. And all these pay each year 22 skepfuls of oats in return for dead wood and 22 loaves and 64 hens and 160 eggs. And one sokeman is there who performs service with a horse. And William, son of Anserad, holds a fourth part of 3 yardlands by knight-service. And William, son of Odard the cook, holds a fourth part of 3 yardlands by service in the abbot's kitchen. And the men of this William perform work for the court, that is to say, they provide their ploughs for the lord twice a year. And on the land of this William there are 4 full villeins who reap half an acre in August. And Godric holds a fourth part of 3 yardlands, and for that he and his horse do the abbot's service, providing their own food. And this Godric has 3 villeins and each one of them reaps half an acre for the abbot in August, and with their ploughs they perform two boon-works. In the court of the demesne there are 2 ploughs with 16 oxen, and 3 cows and 8 beasts for food and 1 draught horse and 8 pigs.

In Collingham there are 4 carucates and 1 bovate less a fifth part of 1 bovate for the king's geld. And there are 20 villeins who hold 1½ carucates. Each one of these works for the lord throughout the year 1 day in each week. And in August he performs 3 boon-works. And all these men bring 60 cartloads of wood to the lord's court, and they also dig and provide 20 cartloads of turves, or 20 cartloads of thatch. And they must harrow throughout the winter. And each year they pay 4 pounds of rent. And there are 50 sokemen who hold 2½ carucated of land. And each one of these must work by custom each year for 6 days at the deer hedge. And in August each shall work 3 days. And all these have 14 ploughs and with them they shall work for the lord four times in

16. Celtic hamlet and open fields near Cape Cornwall in the far west of the Penrith peninsula. The buildings and boundaries of the fields are made of granite, known as moorstone.

Lent. And they plough 48 acres, and harrow, and reap in August. And the aforesaid sokemen pay 12 pounds each year. And in the court of the demesne are 2 ploughs with 16 oxen, and 4 cows and calves and 1 beast for food and 160 sheep and 12 pigs. . . .

Taken from the 'Black Book' of Peterborough, an account of all the abbot's possessions at this time.

SURVEY OF THE MANOR OF STUKELEY, HUNTS., MADE FOR THE ABBOT OF RAMSEY IN THE REIGN OF HENRY I

At Stukeley are 7 hides.

The village rendered 7 pounds in the time of King Henry. It had then this equipment: 3 ploughs with 30 oxen were then at the court, and each of the oxen was worth 3 shillings. There were then

3 horses, each worth 3 shillings; 100 sheep; and 2 horses for harrowing.

These were the freemen who were enfeoffed in those days:

Jocelyn of Stukeley held 2 hides and 1 virgate. He followed the country and the hundred and the pleas of the abbot.

Robert the knight held 1½ hides and performed the same service.

Fulk of 'Lisures' held 1 hide for which he likewise followed the pleas of the abbot. He also held 2½ virgates in Ripton. In those days these pertained to Stukeley, but now they are not there. One of them used to pay 5 shillings and the rest were held by work.

2 hides and 1 virgate, that is to say, 9 virgates, were then held by work and not by pay. And this is the service which each (holder of a) virgate then performed and now still performs:

From Michaelmas to the beginning of August he works 2 days in each week and ploughs on a third, except at Christmas and Easter and Pentecost. And from the beginning of August until Michaelmas he works the whole week except on Saturdays. He gives 4 hens at Christmas.

To the church there belonged in those days half a virgate quit of service, and it still so belongs.

Henry Lenveise now holds 1 rood.

The house of Henry the archdeacon is on the abbot's demesne.

Thomas, son of Henry, holds 1 virgate which formerly was held by work. Now he gives for it 4 shillings. In the time of Abbot Walter it only paid 2 shillings.

Four cottars dwell on the demesne, and they work every Monday, and 2 days in each week during August.

Adam, son of Henry the archdeacon, now holds this village for 8 pounds and with 2 ploughs.

Cartularium Monasterii de Rameseia (Rolls Series, 1893)

THE FENS, c. 1150

From the flooding of the rivers, or from their overflow, the water, standing on unlevel ground, makes a deep marsh and so renders the land uninhabitable, save on some raised spots of ground, which I think that God set up for the special purpose that they should be the habitations of His servants who have chosen to live there. . . . *Burch* [Peterborough] is founded in the land of the Gyrvii, where the same marsh begins on its eastern side, to extend for sixty miles or more. This marsh, however, is very useful for men; for in it are found wood and twigs for fires, hay for the fodder of cattle, thatch for covering houses, and many other useful things. It is, moreover, productive of birds and fish. For there are various rivers, and very many waters and ponds abounding in fish. In all these things the district is most productive.

Historiae Anglicanae Scriptores Varii, edited by J. Sparke, 1723, including *Historiae Coenobii Burgensis.* Translated by H. C. Darby, *The Medieval Fenland*

FROM BORLEY, A MANOR OF CHRISTCHURCH IN ESSEX, c. 1150

And let it be known that when he, the villein, with other customers shall have done cutting the hay on the meadow in Raneholm, they will receive by custom three quarters of wheat for baking bread, and one ram of the price of eighteen pence, and one pat of butter, and one piece of cheese of the second sort from the lord's dairy, and salt, and oatmeal for cooking a stew, and all the morning milk from all the cows in the dairy, and for every day a load of hay. He may also take as much grass as he is able to lift on the point of his scythe. And when the mown grass is carried away, he has a right to one cart. And he is bound to carry sheaves, and for each service of this kind he will receive one sheaf called "mene-sheaf." And whenever he is sent to carry anything with his cart, he shall have oats, as usual, so much, namely, as he can thrice take with his hand.

P. Vinogradoff, *Villeinage in England*

HUNTING COUNTRY ROUND LONDON

Hard by there stretches a great forest with wooded glades and lairs of wild beasts, deer both red and fallow, wild boars and bulls . . . many of the citizens delight in taking their sport with birds of the air, merlins and falcons and the like and with dogs that wage warfare in the woods. The citizens have the special privilege of hunting in Middlesex, Herefordshire and all Chiltern and in Kent as far as the River Cray.

William FitzStephen, *Descriptio Nobilissimae Civitatis Londonae, c.* 1173. Translated by H.E. Butler

A NOBLE GARDEN, PROBABLY IN SPAIN, Late Twelfth Century

It should be ornamented with roses and lilies, the heliotrope, violets and mandrakes. One should have also parsley, costus, fennel, southernwood, coriander, sage, savory, hyssop, mint, rue, dittany, celery, pyrethrum, lettuce, cress, and peonies. There should be made beds for onions, leeks, garlic, pumpkins, and shallots. A garden is distinguished when it has growing there cucumbers, the soporific poppy, daffodils, and acanthus. There should not be lacking pot vegetables such as beets, dog's mercury, orach, sorrel, and mallows. Anise, mustard, white pepper, and absinthe give usefulness to any garden. A noble garden will show also medlars, quinces, bon chrétien pears, peaches, pears of St Regulus, pomegranates, lemons, oranges, almonds, dates which are the fruit of palm trees, and figs.

U.T. Holmes, Jr., *Daily Living in the Twelfth Century, based on the Observations of Alexander Neckam*

17. Open-field agriculture: Braunton Great Field, Devonshire. Two- or three-field system, leaving part of the arable fallow, was widely used in the eleventh century.

18. Jew's House, Lincoln, *c.*1150

ANNUAL FAIRS OF SAINT-LAZARE AND SAINT-GERMAIN

Barons, be patient, the most expensive things are coming last . . . among the first are inks, sulphur, incense, quicksilver, alum, *graine* [cochineal dye], peppers, saffron, furs, tanned leather, shoe leather, and marten skins.

William Shortnose, *Charroi de Nimes*

STREET CRIES, Twelfth Century

The city was filled with street cries from dawn to dusk. A pedlar, who carries nothing but soap and needles, shouteth and calleth out clamorously what he beareth, and a rich mercer goeth along quite silently.

Ancren Riwle

Family

SOCIAL LIFE

WILLIAM I ON THE NORMANS

The Normans, when under the rule of a kind but firm master, are a most valiant people, excelling all others in the invincible courage with which they meet difficulties, and strive to conquer every enemy. But under the other circumstances they bring ruin on themselves by rending each other. They are eager for rebellion, ripe for tumults, and ready for every sort of crime. They must, therefore, be restrained by the strong hand of justice. But if they are allowed to take their own course without any yoke like an untamed colt, they and their princes will be overwhelmed with poverty, shame and confusion. I have learnt this by much experience. My nearest friends, my own kindred, who ought to have defended me at all hazards against the whole world, formed conspiracies against me, and nearly stripped me of the inheritance of my fathers.

The Ecclesiastical History of Ordericus Vitalis,
translated by T. Forester

NOBLES IN THE TWELFTH CENTURY

Whereupon the nobles, nay rather the traitors of England, arose and discussed terms of peace among themselves. They loved indeed nothing better than discord but were unwilling to commit themselves to battle; for they desired to raise up neither one or the other of the claimants to the throne, lest by vanquishing the one they might become entirely subject to the other. They preferred that each being kept in fear of the other, the royal authority should not be effectively exercised against them. The king

[Stephen] and the duke [Henry of Anjou], therefore, becoming aware of the treachery of their followers were reluctantly compelled to make a truce between themselves.

Henry of Huntingdon, *Historia Anglorum*, *English Historical Documents*, Vol.II

Again, from a party spirit, numerous castles had been erected in the several provinces; and there were now in England, in a certain measure, as many kings, or rather tyrants, as there were lords of castles; each coining his own money, and possessing a power, similar to that of kings, in dictating laws to their dependents.

William of Newburgh, translated by J. Stevenson

ANGLO-SAXONS AND NORMANS IN THE ELEVENTH CENTURY

This was a fatal day [the battle of Hastings] for England, a melancholy havoc of our dear country brought about by its passing under the domination of new lords. For England had long ago adopted the manners of the 'Angles' which had been very various at different times. In the first years after their arrival they were barbarians in their look and manner, warlike in their usages, heathen in their rites; but after embracing the faith of Christ, in process of time and by degrees, owing to the peace which they enjoyed they came to regard arms as only of secondary importance, and gave their whole attention to religion. I say nothing of the poor, whom meanness of fortune often restrains from overstepping the bounds of justice; I omit men of ecclesiastical rank whom respect for their sacred profession, or fear of shame, sometimes restrains from straying from the true path; I speak of princes who from greatness of their power might have full liberty to indulge in pleasure. Some of these in their own country, and some at Rome, changing their habit obtained a heavenly kingdom and a saintly communion; and many during their whole lives, to outward seeming so managed their worldly affairs that they might disperse their treasures on the poor, or divide them among monasteries. What shall I say of multitudes of bishops, hermits, and abbots? Does not the whole island blaze with so many relics that you can scarcely pass a village of any consequence but what you hear the name of some new saint? And of how many have all records perished? Nevertheless, with the lapse of time, the love of learning and of religion decayed, and some years before the coming of the Normans it had declined. The clergy, contented with a very slight measure of learning could scarcely stammer out the words of the sacraments, and a person who understood grammar was an object of wonder and astonishment. The monks mocked the rule of their order with fine vestments and with the use of every kind of food. The nobility, given up to luxury and wantonness, did not go to church in the early morning after the manner of Christians, but merely in a casual manner heard matins and mass from a hurrying priest in their chambers amid the blandishments of their wives. The common people, left unprotected, became a prey to the more powerful who amassed riches, either by seizing the property of the poor or by selling their persons to foreigners. Nevertheless it is the manner of this people to be more inclined to dissipation than to the accumulation of wealth. There was one custom repugnant to nature, which they adopted: namely to sell their female servants when pregnant by them, after they had satisfied their lust, either to public prostitution or to foreign slavery. Drinking in parties was a universal custom, in which occupation they passed entire days and nights. They consumed their whole fortune in mean and despicable houses, unlike the Normans and the French who in noble and splendid mansions live with frugality. The vices attendant upon drunkenness followed in due course and these, as is well known, enervate the human mind. Hence it came about that they engaged William more with rashness and fury than with military skill, and so they doomed themselves and their country to slavery by giving him an easy victory in a single battle. For nothing is less effective than rashness; and what begins with violence is quickly checked. The English at that time wore short garments, reaching to the mid-knee; they had their hair cropped, their beards shaven, their arms laden with gold bracelets, their skin adorned with punctured designs; they were wont to eat until they became surfeited and to drink until they were sick. These latter qualities they imparted to their conquerors; as to the rest they adopted their manners. I would not, however, have these bad propensities ascribed to the English universally. I know that many of the clergy at that time trod the path of sanctity, and I know that many of the laity of all ranks and conditions were well-pleasing to God. Far be it from me to be unjust: my accusation is not indiscriminate. But as in peace the mercy of God often cherishes both the bad and the good together, so also does his severity sometimes include them both in tribulation.

The Normans – that I may speak of them also – were at that time, as they are now, exceedingly particular in their dress, and delicate in their food, but not to excess. They are a race inured to war and can hardly live without it, fierce in attacking their enemies, and when force fails, ready to use guile or to corrupt by bribery. As I have said, they live with economy in large houses; they envy their equals; they wish to vie with their superiors; and they plunder their subjects though they protect them from others. They are faithful to their lords though slight offence gives them an excuse for treachery. They weigh treason by its chance of success, and change their opinions for money. They are the most polite of peoples; they consider strangers to merit the courtesy they extend to each other; and they inter-marry with their subjects. After their coming to England they revived the rule of religion which had there grown lifeless. You might see churches rise in every village, and, in the towns and cities, monasteries built after a style unknown before; you could watch the country flourishing with renewed religious observances; each wealthy man counted the day lost in which he had neglected to perform some outstanding benefaction.

William of Malmesbury, *Gesta Regum Anglorum*

TOOLS FOR THE HOUSEHOLD, Eleventh Century

He should provide many tools for the homestead, and get many implements for the buildings:

An axe, adze, bill, awl, plane, saw, climbe-iron [? spoke-shave], tie-hook [? vice or hook], auger, mattock, prise [lever], share coulter; and also a goad-iron, scythe, sickle, weed-hook, spade, shovel, woad-dibble, barrow, besom, beetle, rake, fork, ladder, horse-comb and shears, fire-tongs, weighing-scales, and many spinning-implements, [such as]: flax-threads, spindle, reel, yarn-winder, stoddle [an unknown weaving tool], weaver's beams, press, comb, carding-tool, weft, woof, wool-comb, roller, slay [?], winder with bent handle, shuttle, seam-pegs [to hold things for sewing], shears, needle, slick-stone.

And if he has skilled workmen, he should provide them with tools. As for the mill-wright, shoe-maker, plumber, and other artisans, each work itself shews what is necessary for each; there is no man that can enumerate all the tools that one ought to have.

One ought to have coverings for wains, ploughing-gear, harrowing-tackle, and many things that I cannot now name; as well as a measure, an awl, and a flail for the threshing-floor, and many implements besides; as, a cauldron, leaden vessel, kettle, ladle, pan, crock, fire-dog, dishes, bowls with handles, tubs, buckets, a churn, cheese-vat, bags, baskets, crates, bushels, sieves, seed-basket, wire-sieve, hair-sieve, winnowing fans, troughs, ashwood-pails, hives, honey-bins, beer-barrels, bathing-tub, bowls, butts, dishes, vessels, cups, strainers, candle-sticks, salt-cellar, spoon-case, pepper-horn, chest, money-box, yeast-box, seats [?], foot-stools, chairs, basins, lamp, lantern, leathern bottles, box for resin [or soap?], comb, iron bin, rack for fodder, fire-guard, meal-ark, oil-flask, oven-rake, dung-shovel.

It is toilsome to recount all that he who holds this office ought to think of; he ought never to neglect anything that may prove useful, not even a mouse-trap, nor even, what is less, a peg for a hasp. Many things are needful for a faithful reeve of a household and a temperate guardian of men.

Duties of a Reeve. *The Growth of English Industry and Commerce*
W. Cunningham, translated by W.W. Skeat

19. Bathing a child in a pot used for many purposes; eleventh century

NORMAN CHARACTERISTICS

They are a most cunning and revengeful race. They leave their native fields for the hope of richer booty; greedy of gain, greedy of dominion; prone to imitate whatsoever they see; evenly balanced between lavishness and greediness [i.e. you never know whether you will find them spendthrifts or robbers]. Their princes are most generous where they hope to earn fame by their generosity. These Normans can flatter when they choose, and are so eager to become accomplished speakers that even the boys argue like trained rhetoricians. They are headstrong to excess unless they be curbed by the stern hand of justice. They are patient of cold if need be, patient of hunger, patient of hard work; they are passionately fond of hawking, of riding, of warlike armour, and of splendid garments.

Geoffrey Malaterra, an eleventh-century Italian chronicler

THE MINGLING OF NORMAN AND SAXON

['By the Conqueror's disposition, whenever a Norman was found dead, and the slayer could not be discovered, it was presumed that he must have been slain by a Saxon; the utility of this provision is obvious for the protection of a small foreign garrison. In virtue of that presumption, a heavy fine was imposed upon the Hundred; i.e. that section of the community in which the corpse was discovered, unless indeed they could clear themselves by producing the murderer and giving him up to vengeance.'

G.G. Coulton]

'Then', asks the pupil in this Dialogue, 'why is there no such disposition when an Englishman is found slain?' To which the master replies: 'There was no such disposition at the first institution of this law, as thou hast heard; but now that English and Normans have lived so long together, and have intermarried, the nations have become so intermingled (I speak of freemen only) that we can scarce distinguish in these days betwixt Englishman and Norman; excepting of course those serfs bound to the land whom we call *villeins,* and who cannot quit their condition without leave of their masters. Wherefore, in these days, almost every secret manslaughter is punished as *murdrum,* except those of whom (as I have said) it is certain that they are of servile condition.'

Dialogue of the Exchequer, c. 1180

WHAT THE ENGLISH FELT AT THE END OF WILLIAM I's REIGN

Alas, how miserable and pitiable a time it was then [1087]. Then the wretched people lay driven very nearly to death, and afterwards there came the sharp famine and destroyed them utterly. Who cannot pity such a time? Or who is so hard-hearted that he cannot weep for such misfortune; but such things happen because of the people's sins, in that they will not love God and righteousness. So it was in those days, there was little righteousness in this country in anyone, except in monks alone where they behaved well. The king and the chief men loved gain much and over-much gold and silver and did not care how sinfully it was obtained provided it came to them. The king sold his land on very hard terms – as hard as he could. Then came somebody else, and offered more than the other had given, and the king let it go to the man who had offered him more. Then came the third, and offered still more, and the king gave it into the hands of the man who offered him most of all, and did not care how sinfully the reeves had got it from poor men, nor how many unlawful things they did. But the more just laws were talked about, the more unlawful things were done. They imposed unjust tolls and did many other injustices which are hard to reckon up.

Anglo-Saxon Chronicle, English Historical Documents, Vol.II

BEDS AND BEDDING

Our fathers and we ourselves have lain full oft upon straw pallets, covered only with a sheet, under coverlets made of dogswain or hop-harlots (I use the very words of the old men from whom I received the accounts), and a good round log under their heads, instead of a boulter. If it were so that our fathers or the good man of the house had a mattress or flock-bed, and thereto a sack of chaff to rest his head upon, he thought himself to be as well lodged as the lord of the town, so well were they contented. Pillows, said they, were meet only for women in childbed.

As for the servants, if they had any sheets above them, it was well, for seldom had they any under their bodies, to keep them from the pricking straws, that ran oft through the canvas, and razed [scratched] their hardened hides.

Raphael Holinshed, *Chronicles*

CONCERNING MARRIAGE

In the reign of Henry I there was a law confirmed by parliament, that no contract, made between man and woman, without witnesses, concerning marriage, should stand good if either of them denied it; and another, that kinsfolk might not contract matrimony, but within the seventh degree of consanguinity; and a third was that a widow should mourn for her husband twelve months, after which time she was at liberty to choose as she would: but if she married within the space of one year, she should forfeit her dowry, and all the wealth she might have enjoyed from her first husband.

Raphael Holinshed, *Chronicles*

A TWELFTH-CENTURY SONG

Yet a second charge they bring:
I'm for ever gaming.
Yea the dice hath many a time
Stripped me to my shaming.
What an if the body's cold
If the mind is burning.
On the anvil hammering
Rhymes and verses turning.

For on this my heart is set:
When the hour is nigh me,
Let me in the tavern die,
With a tankard by me,
While the angels looking down
Joyously sing o'er me
Deus sit propitius
Huic potatori.

From Helen Waddell, *Medieval Latin Lyrics*

BRITAIN IN THE TWELFTH CENTURY

Britain is truly an island of the utmost fertility, abounding in corn and fruit trees, which are nourished by perennial streams. It is diversified by woods, sheltering birds and beasts of chase, affording merry sport to the hunter. Wild fowl of all sorts are exceedingly plentiful, both those which frequent the water, whether the rivers or the sea.

Moreover the island is remarkably adapted for feeding cattle and beasts of burden; insomuch that Solinus remarks that 'in some parts of Britain the herbage of the meadows is so luxuriant that unless the cattle are shifted to poorer pasture there is risk of their suffering from surfeit.' The never failing springs feed rivers abounding in fish. Salmon and eels, especially, are very plentiful. Herrings are taken on the coasts, as well as oysters and other kinds of shell fish. Among these are the mussels, which produce beautiful pearls, of a great variety of colours, red, purple, violet and emerald; principally, however, white. Nor are the cockles wanting from which a scarlet dye is made, whose exquisite tint does not fade by exposure either to the sun or rain, the older it is the brighter the colour becomes. Dolphins and whales are also caught, as Juvenal says

'For as the giant whales of Britain's sea
Exceed the dolphin.'

Britain is also rich in metallic veins of iron, tin, and lead. Some of these contain silver also, though not so commonly. Silver, however, is received from the neighbouring parts of Germany, with which an extensive commerce is carried on by the Rhine in the abundant produce of fish and meat, as well as of fine wool and fat cattle which Britain supplies, so that money appears to be more plentiful there than in Germany itself, and all the coins introduced into Britain by this traffic are of pure silver. Britain, also, furnishes large quantities of very excellent jet, of a black and brilliant hue. Rendered sparkling by fire it drives away serpents; when it becomes heated by friction substances adhere to it, as they do to amber.

The island contains both salt-springs and hot-springs and the streams from which supply baths accommodated to the separate use of persons of every age and of both sexes . . . 'For water,' as St Basil observes, 'acquires the quality of heat by running over certain metals, so that not only it becomes warm, but even scalding hot.'

The cities have for their sites pleasant and fertile banks of rivers. Two of these rivers are more celebrated than the rest, the Thames and the Severn; the two arms, as it were, of Britain, by which it

20. Norman midwife beside woman in bed and a cradle. From *Nativity*, *Psalter*, twelfth century

draws to itself the produce of other countries and exports its own. But it is peculiar to the English that, being much addicted to foreign travel, they are remarkable for that superior style of dress and living, by which they are easily distinguished from other nations. Since, then, Britain abounds in so many things (even vineyards flourish in it, though they are not very common), those who covet its wealth must bring their own in exchange for what they receive. In whose praise someone thus wrote:

> 'Corn, milk and honey, fuller shed their stores
> On Britain's plains, than over all the isles
> Where foaming ocean washes sea-girt shores.'

And a little afterwards:

> 'London for ships, and Winchester for wine,
> Hereford for herds, Worcester for corn renowned,
> Bath for its waters, Salisbury for the chase;
> For fishes Canterbury: York for its woods;
> Exeter boasts its rich metallic ores.
> Narrow the sea 'tween Chichester and France,

While northern Durham fronts the surging waves
On which old Norway launched her conquering sons.
In grace proud Lincoln's children foremost stand,
Ely's high towers the wide champaign command,
Rochester rises bright on Medway's winding strand.'

Nor must it be omitted that the climate of Britain is very temperate and healthy to its inhabitants.

There are four things in England which are very remarkable. One is that the winds issue with such great violence from certain caverns in a mountain called the Peak, that it ejects matters thrown into them, and whirling them about in the air carries them to a great distance. The second is Stonehenge, where stones of extraordinary dimensions are raised as columns, and others are fixed above, like lintels of immense portals; and no one has been able to discover by what mechanism such vast masses of stone were elevated, nor for what purpose they were destined. The third is at Cheddor-hole [Wookey Hole in Cheddar Cliffs, Somerset], where there is a cavern which many persons have entered, and have traversed a great distance underground, crossing subterraneous streams, without finding any end of the cavern. The fourth wonder is this, that in some parts of the country the rain is seen to gather about the tops of the hills, and forthwith to fall on the plains.

Henry of Huntingdon, *Historia Anglorum*,
translated by T. Forester

A FUNERAL PROCESSION, Twelfth Century

The candles and the crosses went first, with the nuns from a convent; then followed the clerics with sacred books and thuribles [censers]. The widow and the vassals followed the bier making very loud and visible grief. When the nuns and the priests had held the service, they returned from the church and came to the grave.

Chrétien de Troyes, *Yvain*

FITTINGS OF AN AVERAGE BEDCHAMBER, Late Twelfth Century

In the bedchamber let a curtain go around the walls decently, or a scenic canopy, for the avoiding of flies and spiders. From the style or epistyle of a column a tapestry should hang appropriately. Near the bed let there be placed a chair to which a stool may be added, and a bench nearby the bed. On the bed itself should be placed a feather mattress to which a bolster is attached. A quilted pad of striped cloth should cover this on which a cushion for the head can be placed. Then sheets of muslin, ordinary cotton, or at least pure linen, should be laid. Next a coverlet of green cloth or of coarse wool, of which the fur lining is badger, cat, beaver, or sable, should be put – all this if there is lacking purple and down.

A perch should be nearby on which can rest a hawk . . . From another pole let there hang clothing . . . and let there be also a chambermaid whose face may charm and render tranquil the chamber, who, when she finds time to do so may knit or unknit silk thread, or make knots of orpheys [gold lace], or may sew linen garments and woollen clothes, or may mend. Let her have gloves with the finger tips removed; she should have a leather case protecting the finger from needle pricks, which is vulgarly called a 'thimble'. She must have scissors and a spool of thread and various sizes of needles – small and thin for embroidery, others not so thin for feather stitching, moderately fine ones for ordinary sewing, bigger ones for the knitting of a cloak, still larger ones for threading laces.

U.T. Holmes, Jr., *Daily Living in the Twelfth Century based on the Observations of Alexander Neckam*

REQUIRED UTENSILS IN A KITCHEN, Late Twelfth Century

In a kitchen there should be a small table on which cabbage may be minced, and also lentils, peas, shelled beans, beans in the pod, millet, onions, and other vegetables of the kind that can be cut up. There should be also pots, tripods, a mortar, a hatchet, a pestle, a stirring stick, a hook, a cauldron, a bronze vessel, a small pan, a baking pan, a meathook, a griddle, small pitchers, a trencher, a bowl, a platter, a pickling vat, and knives for cleaning fish. In a vivarium let fish be kept, in which they can be caught by net, fork, spear, or light hook, or with a basket.

The chief cook should have a cupboard in the kitchen where he may store away aromatic spices, and bread flour sifted through a sieve – and used also for feeding small fish – may be hidden away there. Let there be also a cleaning place where the entrails of ducks and other domestic fowl can be removed and the birds cleaned. Likewise there should be a large spoon for removing foam and skimming. Also there should be hot water for scalding fowl.

Have a pepper mill, and a flour mill. Small fish for cooking should be put into a pickling mixture, that is, water mixed with salt ... To be sure, pickling is not for all fish, for these are different kinds: mullets, soles, sea eels, lampreys, mackerel, turbot, sperlings, gudgeons, sea bream, young tunnies, cod, plaice, herring, lobsters fried in half an egg, sea mullets, and oysters.

In the pantry let there be shaggy towels, tablecloth, and an ordinary hand towel which shall hang from a pole to avoid mice. Knives should be kept in the pantry, an engraved saucedish, a salt-cellar, a cheese container, a candelabra, a lantern, a candlestick, and baskets.

In the cellar or store-room should be casks, tuns, wineskins, cups, cup cases, spoons, ewers, basins, baskets, pure wine, cider, beer, unfermented wine, claret, mead ... clove-spiced wine for gluttons whose thirst is unquenchable.

U.T. Holmes, Jr., *Daily Living in the Twelfth Century based on the Observations of Alexander Neckam*

21. Curtained bed. Twelfth century

A LANGUAGE INVENTED AND APPLIED TO DIFFERENT KINDS OF MEN AND WOMEN

A state of princes; a skulk of thieves; an observance of hermits; a lying of pardoners; a subtiltie of serjeants; an untruth of sompners; a multiplying of husbands; an incredibility of cuckolds; a safeguard of porters; a stalk of foresters; a blast of hunters; a draught of butlers; a temperance of cooks; a melody of harpers; a poverty of pipers; a drunkenship of cobblers; a disguising of tailors; a wandering of tinkers; a malepertness of pedlars; a fighting of beggars; a netful of knaves; a blush of boys; a bevy of ladies; a nonpatience of wives; a gaggle of women; a superfluity of nuns; and a herd of harlots.

DRESS

ELEVENTH-CENTURY HAIR-STYLES

In his twenty-eighth year, the king [Henry I] returned from Normandy; in his twenty-ninth a circumstance occurred in England which may seem surprising to our long-haired gallants, who, forgetting what they were born, transform themselves into the fashion of females, by the length of their locks. A certain English knight, who prided himself on the luxuriousness of his tresses, being stung by conscience on the subject, seemed to feel in

22. This peasant and his superiors show eleventh-century dress. On the left a simple tunic with long sleeves; the woman wears a loose dress with hanging sleeves, the men tunics and banded stockings in the form of puttee-like wrappings.

23. A Cistercian monk

24. Woman's costume with wide sleeves

a dream as though some person strangled him with his ringlets. Awaking in a fright, he immediately cut off his superfluous hair. The example spread throughout England; and, as scant punishment is apt to affect the mind, almost all military men allowed their hair to be cropped in a proper manner, without reluctance. But this decency was not of long continuance, for scarcely had a year expired ere all who thought themselves courtly, relapsed into their former style; they vied with women in the length of locks and wherein they were defective put on false tresses; forgetful, or rather ignorant, of the saying of the apostle, 'If a man nurture his hair, it is shame to him'.

William of Malmesbury, *Gesta Regum Anglorum*
translated by J.A. Giles

25. Short tunics, one embroidered with side vents; eleventh century

DRESS OF A YOUNG GIRL, Twelfth Century

She had a little shirt of linen, a white *pellice* of ermine, and a *bliaut* of silk. Her stockings were embroidered with gladioli designs, and her shoes, by which she was tightly shod, had May flowers.

K. Bartsch, *Altfranzösische Romanzen und Pastourellen*

26. Embroidered super-tunic over kirtle, mantle and coverchief; tenth to the eleventh century

DRESS FOR THE BARON, Late Twelfth Century

Let a man who is not travelling have a *pellice* [fur-lined garment], and a *cote* or *bliaut* provided with sleeves and openings, slit at the crotch. *Braies* are needed to cover the lower limbs, and stockings or *chauces* should be worn around the legs, while covering the feet with laced boots or leather shoes. An undershirt of muslin, silk, or cotton, or linen — the fur of the outer mantle should be gris or vair [grey squirrel], or rabbit, and the mantle's edging can be of sable or marten, or beaver, or of otter, or fox fur.

U.T. Holmes, Jr., *Daily Living in the Twelfth Century based on the Observations of Alexander Neckam*

EMBROIDERY, Eleventh Century

Mahalt she was called and she was a worker; marvellously did she know how to work, to embroider fine gold upon purple silk, to ornament with regal jewels. She knew how to place gems and good stones better than anyone before her. Her fame in this was such that she was sought after by the highest nobles, honoured and demanded for her art.

La vie d'Edouard le confesseur

FOOD AND DRINK

NORMAN MEAL TIMES

Such was his [Hardecanute's] liberality that tables were laid four times a day with royal sumptuousness for his whole court, preferring the fragments of the repast should be removed after those invited were satisfied, than that such fragments should be served up for the entertainment of those who were not invited. In our time it is the custom whether from parsimony, or, as they themselves say from fastidiousness, for princes to provide only one meal-day for their court.

Henry of Huntingdon, *Historia Anglorum*
translated by T. Forester

FOOD AT HARVEST-TIME IN THE ELEVENTH CENTURY

One loaf of second-rate bread, and beer [for carting] [for the first day of harvest-work] bread, beer, pottage [of peas or beans] flesh and cheese, and three loaves for every two men . . . of wheat and rye, with more wheat than rye. [For the second day] bread, pottage, water, herrings and cheese. [On the third day] as on the first, if my lord [abbot] be willing. [For carrying a load on his back to the abbey] one second-rate loaf. [For harvesters] on the first day, sufficient bread, beer, fresh flesh, pottage and cheese; on the other days, fish; and, if the bread be bought, there shall be a three-farthing loaf for every two. [A specially favoured group feed, at harvest time] once a day at my lord's cost, and for supper two billings [small loaves] and cheese, or two herrings.

The Ramsey Cartulary

CHRISTMAS DINNER IN THE BURTON SURVEY, Eleventh Century

In the Burton survey [another Glastonbury manor] there are notices of the Christmas dinner. The tenants cut and carried in the logs for the yule-fire; each brought his faggot of brushwood, lest the cook should serve his portion raw, and each had his own dish and mug, and a napkin of some kind, 'if he wanted to eat off a cloth'. There was plenty of bread and broth, with two kinds of meat, and various savoury messes. At East Pennard the farmer had a right to four places at the yule-feast, and each man was entitled to have a fine white loaf and a good helping of meat, and to sit drinking after dinner in the manorial hall.

HIGH PRICE OF CORN, Eleventh and Twelfth Centuries

In this same year (A.D.1031) the sester [about eight bushels] of wheat went to fifty-five pence, and even further.

In this year (A.D.1043) there was a very great famine over all England, and corn so dear as no man before remembered, so that the sester of wheat went to sixty pence, and even further.

In this same year (A.D.1124) were many failures in England in corn and all fruits, so that between Christmas and Candlemas (February 2nd) the acre seed of wheat, that is, two seedlips [the basket holding the seed when sowing by hand], were sold for six shillings; and that of barley, that is, three seedlips, for six shillings; and the acre seed of oats, that is, four seedlips, for four shillings. That was because there was little corn, and the penny was so bad that the man who had at a market a pound could by no means buy therewith twelve pennyworths.

Anglo-Saxon Chronicle, translated by J.A. Giles

SALT, 1065

In king Edward's time there was . . . a Wich [Nantwich] in which there was a brinepit for making salt, and there were 8 salthouses, so divided between the king and earl Eadwine that of all the issues and renders of the salthouses the king had 2 thirds and the earl a third. But besides these the said earl had a salthouse of his own which belonged to his manor Acatone [Acton by Nantwich]. From this salthouse the earl had sufficient salt for his house throughout the year. If however any was sold from that source, the king had 2 pence of the toll and the earl the third penny.

In the same Wich a number of the men of the country had salthouses, from which there was the following custom. From the Ascension of our Lord to the Feast of St. Martin anyone having a salthouse might carry home [free of toll] his own salt; but if he sold any of it either there or elsewhere in the county of Cheshire, he paid toll to the king and earl. After the Feast of St. Martin anyone who carried salt thence, whether his own or purchased, paid toll, the above-mentioned salthouse belonging to the earl excepted, as having its own custom.

The aforesaid 8 salthouses of the king and earl on the Friday in each week in which they were employed in boiling salt rendered 16 boilings, of which 15 made a horseload of salt. Other men's salthouses did not give these boilings on Fridays between the

27. After-dinner drinking. 'Royal butlers reserved the best wines for the king and for his family and guests: less good wines were served to the lowlier members of the royal household; while royal castles were stocked with the cheapest wine available.'
Ralph Arnold.

Ascension of our Lord and the Feast of St. Martin; but from the Feast of St. Martin to the Ascension of our Lord they all gave the boiling custom like the salthouses of the king and earl.

All these salthouses, both those that were and those that were not in demesne [i.e. held by the king or earl], were surrounded on one side by a certain stream [The Weaver] and on the other by a certain ditch. Anyone incurring a forfeiture within this boundary was allowed to make amends by a fine of 2 shillings or 30 boilings of salt, homicide excepted and theft where the thief was adjudged to die. These offences, if committed here, were amended for as in the rest of the shire.

If a man went from the aforesaid precinct of the salthouses to any part of the county without having paid his toll and was convicted thereof, he had to come back and pay it and to make amends there by a fine of 40 shillings, if he were a free man, 4 shillings, if he were not free. But if he went to some other county, leaving his toll unpaid, he had to pay the fine in the other place where it was demanded . . .

In Mildestvic [Middlewich, now Northwich] Hundred there was another Wich [Middlewich] shared between the king and the earl. There were no demesne salthouses there, however, but the same laws and customs were in force there as have been mentioned under the previous Wich. . . . Now the earl [of Chester] holds it for himself and it is let at farm for 25 shillings and 2 cartloads of salt. . . .

Whoever carried away purchased salt in a cart from these two Wiches, paid 4 pence in toll if he had 4 oxen or more in his cart; if 2 oxen, he paid 2 pence, provided there were 2 horseloads of salt.

A man from any other hundred paid 2 pence for a horseload. But a man from the same hundred paid only a halfpenny for a horseload. Anyone who so loaded his cart that the axle broke within a league of either Wich paid 2 shillings to the king's officer or the earl's, if he could be undertaken within a league. Similarly he who so loaded a horse as to break its back paid 2 shillings. . . . Men on foot from another hundred buying salt there paid 2 pence for 8 men's loads; men of the same hundred paid a penny for 8 loads. . . .

The Domesday Survey of Cheshire, edited by J. Tait

POACHING FISH, 1075

Sir, for God's sake do not take it ill of me if I tell the truth, how I went the other evening along the bank of this pond and looked at the fish which were playing in the water, so beautiful and so bright, and for the great desire I had for a tench I laid me down on the bank and just with my hands quite simply, and without any other device, I caught that tench and carried it off; and now I will tell thee the cause of my covetousness and my desire. My dear wife had lain abed a right full month, as my neighbours who are here know, and she could never eat or drink anything to her liking, and for the great desire she had to eat a tench I went to the bank of the pond to take just one tench; and that never other fish from the pond did I take.

The Court Baron, edited by F.W. Maitland, Selden Society

ONE MEAL A DAY, 1119

Robert, Earl of Mellent, possessed such mighty influence in England, as to change by his single example the long established modes of dress and of diet. Finally, the custom of one meal a day, is observed in the palaces of all the nobility through his means; which he, adopting from Alexius, Emperor of Constantinople, on the score of his health, spread, as I have observed among the rest by his authority. He is blamed, as having done, and taught others to do this, more through want of liberality, than any fear of surfeit, or indigestion; but undeservedly: since no one, it is said, was more lavish in entertainments to others, or more moderate in himself. In law, he was the supporter of justice; in war, the ensurer of victory: urging his lord the king to enforce the rigour of the statutues; himself not only following the existing, but proposing new ones: free from treachery himself towards the king [Henry I], he was the avenger of it in others.

William of Malmesbury, *Gesta Regum Anglorum*,
translated by J.A. Giles

TREATMENT OF UNSOUND FLESH

Some men replace other [sheep] for those which died of murrain. How? I will tell you. If a sheep die suddenly they put the flesh in water for as many hours as are between midday and three o'clock, and then hang it up, and when the water is drained off they salt it and then dry it. And if any sheep begin to fall ill they see if it be because the teeth drop, and if the teeth do not fall out they cause it to be killed and salted and dried like the others, and then they cut it up and distribute it in the household among the servants and labourers, and they shall then yield as much as they cost, for by this means and with the skins they can replace as many. But I do not wish you to do this.

Walter of Henley, *Husbandry*

MONOPOLY OF THE MILL, RAMSEY ABBEY, Early Thirteenth Century

All the tenants owe suit to the mill, whereunto they shall send their corn. And if they cannot, on the first day, grind as much wholemeal as may keep their household in bread for that day, the mill must grind it; and if the peasant cannot grind there that day, then he may take his corn elsewhere at his will. If a man buy his corn, then he may grind it without hindrance at the next mill he comes to. From Aug. 1 to Michaelmas each man may grind where he will, if he be unable to grind at my lord abbot's mill on the day whereon he has sent the corn. Moreover, if it chance that my lord's mill be broken or his milldam burst, so that the tenant cannot grind there, then, as in the former case, he may take it elsewhere at his will. If the tenant be convicted of having failed to

28. Boiling meat, and slaughtering animals. William fitzStephen was impressed by London's 'public cook-shop' on the north bank of the Thames, in the city's wine-selling quarter. We know that roast and boiled meats were always available, and, later in the twelfth century, game and poultry. Many kinds of fish had been long established food, fresh, dried or salted.

render suit to my lord's mill, he shall give sixpence before judgement; or, if he have gone to judgement, he shall give 12d.

Cartulary

FOOD, Late Twelfth Century

'Food was carried up from the kitchen without much respect for distance. Meat was brought in on the spit, while vegetables of different kinds, having been boiled together, were piled on a platter, or perhaps a large flat trencher. It was customary to serve two pieces of bread at a time.' U.T. Holmes

A roast of pork is prepared diligently on a grid, frequently basted, and laid on the grid just as the hot logs cease to smoke. Let condiment be avoided other than salt or a simple garlic sauce. It does not hurt to sprinkle a cut-up capon with pepper. A domestic fowl may be quite tender, having been turned on a long spit, but it needs a strong garlic sauce, diluted with wine or vinegar [green juice of apples]. Flavour a hen which has been cleaned and cut up in pieces, with cumin [fennel], if it is well boiled; but if it has been roasted, let it be treated with frequent drippings of fat.

Let fish that have been cleaned be cooked in a mixture of wine and water; afterwards they should be taken with green 'savory' which is made from sage, parsley, thyme, garlic, and pepper; do not omit salt.

One who takes this is especially exhilarated and restored by a raisin wine which is clear to the bottom of the cup, in its clarity similar to the tears of a penitent, and the colour is that of an oxhorn. It descends like lightning upon one who takes it – most tasty as an almond nut, quick as a squirrel, frisky as a kid, strong in the manner of a house of Cistercians or grey monks, emitting a kind of spark.

U.T. Holmes, Jr., *Daily Living in the Twelfth Century based on the Observations of Alexander Neckam*

Education

CO-EDUCATION

In those days [about 1050] a famous clerk, Barbosus, was at Ireland, and a man of wonderful religion; so much that he held a great school of clerks and lewd [unlearned] men and maidens; but, for he made the maidens adopt the clerical tonsure in manner of scholars, he was put out of Ireland.

ELEMENTARY EDUCATION

Elementary education consisted in reading and writing, and in the rudiments of counting. It is probable that an *eschequir* or counting table was explained, although the fingers made an excellent abacus [calculating frame] if the countings did not go high. Daude de Pradas says that seed pods strung along a stick could be used for adding small sums. Boys who were destined to be clerics received instruction in a nearby monastic school, or from their parish priest.

Teaching began with the alphabet. Then the common beginner's reader was the *Disticha Catonis*, which was read and copied repeatedly. The *Eclogue* of Theodulus was used in the same way, while Donatus was the Latin grammar.

The students carried wax tablets on which they wrote with an ivory, bone, or metal stylus. The tablets were held on the right knee.

At times there were so many boys beginning letters that it was profitable for a clerk to start a small school, and not limit himself to private instruction.

U.T. Holmes, Jr., adapted from *Daily Living in the Twelfth Century based on the Observations of Alexander Neckam*

A PUPIL SUFFERS AT A CLERK'S SCHOOL, Early Twelfth Century

Once I was beaten in school; the school was only one of the rooms in our house. Of those whom the teacher had accepted I alone had been free from discipline. My careful mother had exacted this from the teacher by increasing the fee and conferring the honour of her patronage. Therefore when at one evening hour, the class having been dismissed, I came to my mother's knee soberly, having been beaten harder than I deserved, she began to ask as usual whether I had been whipped on that day. In order not to betray the teacher I denied the fact completely, but she, willy-nilly, lifted up my under-garment, which is called a shirt, and found the ribs somewhat discoloured by the blows of the rod, and the skin covered with welts. When she had grieved over this excessive cruelty endured by my tenderness, she stormed and wept, exclaiming: 'You shall never be a clerk, and you will not endure punishment in order to learn letters.' I answered her as reproachfully as I could: 'I would rather die than to stop learning and not be a clerk.' But she promised me that if I would wish to be a knight she would give me arms when I had reached the proper age.

Guibert de Nogent, *De vita sua*

29. Students from England crossed to the schools of France to learn from William of Champeaux at Notre Dame, or, a little later, from widely famed Peter Abailard, who taught, 'By doubting we come to enquiry, and by enquiring we perceive the Truth'. For his daring spirit, Abailard was excommunicated, but after his death in 1142, his methods of searching and questioning everything became the foundation of thought and of teaching for many years.

30. This seems to be a writing lesson in a twelfth-century schoolroom. It comes from a psalter, *c.*1150, written and illustrated by Eadwine, a monk of Christ Church, Canterbury

STUDENTS QUARTERS, Late Twelfth Century

They dwell in a poor house with an old woman who cooks only vegetables and never prepares a sheep save on feast-days. A dirty fellow waits on the table and just such a person buys the wine in the city. After the meal the student sits on a rickety chair and uses a light, doubtless a candle which goes out continually and disturbs the ideas. So he sits all night long and learns the seven liberal arts. Often he falls asleep at his work and is troubled by bad dreams until Aurora announces the day and he must hasten to the college and stand before the teacher. And he wins in no way the mighty with his knowledge.

Jehan de Hauteville, *Architrenius III,*
translated by Frederick Tupper

The Arts

ELEVENTH-CENTURY HIRELING WRITERS

In the days of Abbot Paul [1077-1093], among other things a certain warlike Norman noble, at the abbot's persuasion, bestowed upon us two-thirds of the tithes of his domain in Hatfield, which he had received at the distribution [of the spoils]; and, at the wish of the Abbot Paul, who loved books, he assigned these tithes for the making of books for the Abbey at St Albans; for the knight himself was a literate man, a diligent hearer and lover of the Scriptures.

To this office were added certain tithes in Redbourne; and the Abbot decreed that certain daily allowances should be given to the scribes from the charities of the brethren and of the cellarer, since such gifts were ready to eat [they were to receive dishes straight from the convent kitchen, instead of uncooked food to prepare for themselves], in order that the scribes might not be hindered in their work. On account of these allowances he gave better endowments by way of reparation to the almoner, that his conscience might not be hurt.

There, then, the Abbot caused such noble volumes as were necessary for the Church [or Abbey] to be written by choice scribes whom he sought from afar; and of pure courtesy (for he was a most courteous man), he bestowed upon the aforesaid Sir Robert, for the use of the chapel in his manor of Hatfield, two sets of vestments, a silver chalice, a missal and other necessary books. Moreover, each forbade that, by reason of the aforesaid gifts of tithes to the scriptorium [room set apart for writing], or of the Abbot's gift, anything else should be written or given henceforward for this knight.

So, after that Paul had thus liberally bestowed upon the said knight his first set of books, he forthwith ordained the writing of choice books in this scriptorium which he had made; and

31. Winchester Psalter. The Crucifixion. Eleventh century

Archbishop Lanfranc lent him archetypes to copy from.

Gesta Abbatum Monasterii St^{ii} Albani,
translated by G.G. Coulton

GERALD OF WALES READS HIS NEW BOOK *TOPOGRAPHIA HIBERNICA* TO MASTERS AND SCHOLARS IN OXFORD, 1184

The following account appears in his autobiography.

In the course of time, when the work was completed and corrected [he wrote], desiring not to hide his candle under a bushel, but to place it on a candlestick so that it might give light, he resolved to read his work at Oxford, where the clergy in England flourished and excelled in clerkship, before that great audience. And as there were three divisions in his work, and each division occupied a day, the reading lasted three successive days.

And on the first day he received at his lodgings all the poor scholars of the whole town; on the second all the Doctors of different Faculties; and on the third the rest of the scholars with many knights, townsfolk and burghers. It was a costly and noble act, for the authentic and ancient times were thus renewed, nor does the present or any past age recall anything like it in England.

From *A Social History of England* by Ralph Arnold

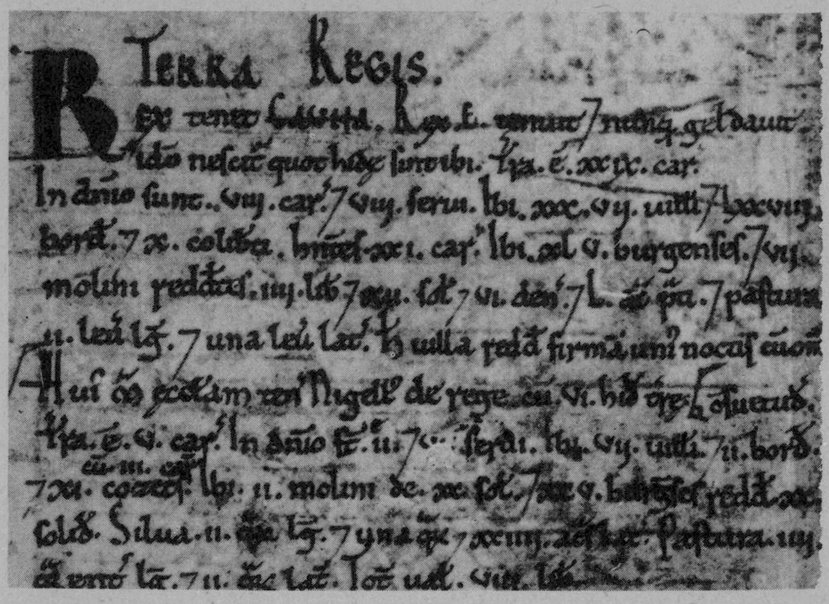

TERRA REGIS.

32. Domesday Book: from the first page of Wiltshire, enlarged.

33. Psalter of St Alban, early twelfth century

34. Wall-painting at Claverley Church, Shropshire, showing Virtue triumphing over Vice. Twelfth century

DOGS AND PRIESTS, Twelfth Century

There are numerous breeds of dogs. Some track down the wild creatures of the woods to catch them. Others guard the flocks of sheep vigilantly against infestation of wolves. Other, the house-dogs, look after the palisade of their masters, lest it should be robbed in the night by thieves, and these will stand up for their owners to the death. They gladly dash out hunting with Master, and will even guard his body when dead, and not leave it. In sum, it is part of their nature that they cannot live without men. . . .

In certain ways, Priests are like watchdogs. They always drive away the wiles of the trespassing Devil with admonishments – and by doing the right thing – lest he should steal away the treasury of God, i.e. the souls of Christians.

The tongue of a dog cures a wound by licking it. This is because the wounds of sinners are cleansed, when they are laid bare in confession, by the penance imposed by the Priest. Also the tongue of a puppy cures the insides of men, because the inside secrets of the heart are often purified by the work and preaching of these learned men.

The dog is said to be very temperate in its diet, because that man only is truly on his guard who excels others in wisdom and studies. . . .

The fact that a dog returns to its vomit signifies that human beings, after a complete confession, often return incautiously to the crimes which they have perpetrated.

Because it leaves the true food in the river out of greed for the shadow, it symbolizes those silly people who often leave that which is peculiarly of the Law out of desire for some unknown thing. . . .

T.H. White, *The Book of Beasts,* being a translation from a Latin Bestiary made in the twelfth century.

UNLIKELY ETYMOLOGIES OF 'CAT' AND 'MOUSE', *c.*1150

She is called Mouser because she is fatal to mice. The vulgar call her Catus the Cat because she catches a thing while others say that it is because she lies in wait *(captat)* i.e. because she watches. So acutely does she glare that her eye penetrates the shades of darkness with a gleam of light. Hence from the Greek comes '*catus*', i.e. 'acute'.

35. The adoration of the Magi, ivory (1104-1113)

Mus the Mouse, a puny animal, comes from a Greek word: although it may have become Latin, it really comes from that. Others say it is 'mice' *(mures)* because they are generated from the dampness of the soil *(enhumore)*. For *'humus'* is *'hu-Mus'*, you see?

The liver of these creatures gets bigger at full moon, just as certain seashores rise and fall with the waning moon.

T.H. White, *The Book of Beasts*, being a translation from a Latin Bestiary made in the twelfth century

36. Seal of Merton Priory. Twelfth century

37. This Gloucester Candlestick made of gilt bell-metal was given to the Benedictine monastery of Gloucester by Abbot Peter about 1110

MATERIALS USED BY SCRIBES, Twelfth Century

The copyist, who is commonly called the scribe, shall have a chair with projecting arms for holding the board upon which the quire of parchment is to be placed. The board must be covered with felt on which a deerskin is fastened, in order that the superfluities of the parchment or membrane may be more easily scraped away by a razor. Then the skin of which the quire is to be formed shall be cleaned with a mordant pumice and its surface smoothed with a light plane. The sheets shall be joined above and below by the aid of a strip threaded through them. The margins of the quire shall be marked on either side with an awl in even measure so that by the aid of a rule the lines may more surely be drawn without mistake. If in writing any erasure or crossing out occurs, the writings shall not be cancelled but scraped off.

C.H. Haskins, translated from the Latin in his *Studies in the History of Medieval Science*

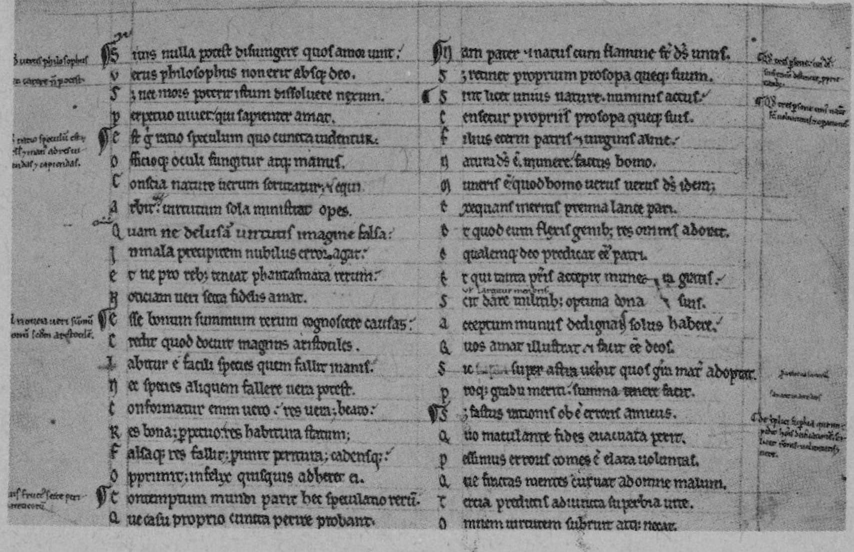

38. The earliest manuscript of John of Salisbury's *Entheticus*. an elegiac poem in praise of Becket. It was probably written in John's lifetime. It belonged to Simon, abbot of St Albans, 1167-1183

39. The marriage of Christ and the Church, from a twelfth-century copy of Commentary on the Song of Songs by the Venerable Bede

ORGAN MUSIC, Late Twelfth Century

Much would you hear the organs play and clerks sing and chant in organum – their voices going up and down, the songs rising and then falling. Much would you hear the knights coming and going in the churches, as much to hear the clerks sing as to view the ladies.

Wace of Jersey, *Roman de Brut*

40. Adam labours.
A twelfth-century
clerestory window
in Canterbury Cathedral

Sports – Pastimes

HUNTING AND HAWKING, Twelfth Century

In our time hunting and hawking are esteemed the most honourable employments, and most excellent virtues, by our nobility; and they think it the height of worldly felicity to spend the whole of their time in these diversions. Accordingly they prepare for them with more solicitude, expense, and parade, than they do for war; and pursue the wild beasts with greater fury than they do the enemies of their country. By constantly following this way of life, they lose much of their humanity, and become as savage, nearly, as the very brutes they hunt.

Husbandmen, with their harmless herds and flocks, are driven from their well cultivated fields, their meadows and their pastures, that wild beasts may range in them without interruption.

If one of these great and merciless hunters shall pass by your habitation, bring forth hastily, all the refreshment you have in your house, or that you can readily buy, or borrow from your neighbours; that you may not be involved in ruin or even accused of treason.

Johannes Sarisburiensis de Nugis Curialium

SUPERSTITIOUS CEREMONIES AFTER A HAWK HAS BEEN ILL

On the morrow tyde, when thou goest oute hauking, say, In the name of the Lord, the birds of Heaven shall be beneath thy feet; also if he be hurt by the heron, say, The Lion of the tribe of Judah, the Root of David, has conquered. Hallelujah; and if he be bitte of any man, say, He that the wicked man doth bind, the Lord at his coming shall set free.

Attributed to Edward the Confessor

A PECULIAR LANGUAGE INVENTED BY SPORTSMEN OF THIS TIME

When animals and birds of the same kind went together there was said to be:

A lepe of leopards; and herd of harts; a bevy of roes; a sloth of bears; a singular of boars; a route of wolves; a harras of horses; a stud of mares; a pace of asses; a baren of mules; a team of oxen; a drove of kine; a tribe of goats; a cete of badgers; a down of

41. Chess was known in England a century before the Norman Conquest. The author of this manuscript makes Ulysses the inventor of chess. Here he is playing with some other Greek hero; the two by-standers are the umpires.

hares; a nest of rabbits; a shrewdness of apes; a labour of moles.

And also a sege of herons; a spring of teels; a covert of cootes; a gaggle of geese; a muster of peacocks; a nye of pheasants; a covey of partridges; a congregation of plovers; a flight of doves; a walk of snipes; a fall of woodcocks; a murmuration of starlings; an exaltation of larks; a watch of nightingales; and a charm of goldfinches.

42. Here men and women are hawking by the river-side. The falconer is frightening the birds to make them rise. The hawk has seized one of them. Eleventh century.

ARCHERY

From *A Mery Geste of Robyn Hode*
The poet tells us that the sherif of Notyngham

Did crye a ful fayre playe
That all the best archyres of the north
Should come upon a daye;
And they that shote, al of the best,
The prize should bear away.
Furthest, fayre and lowe,
At a payre of goodly buttes,
Under the grene wood shawe,
A ryght good arrowe he shal have,
The shaft of sylver whyte,
The head, and fethers of riche red gold,
In Englande is none lyke.
And when they came to Notyngham,
The buttes were fayre and longe.

Thrise Robin shot about,
And alway he cleft the wand.

Black letter without date. Imprinted at London upon the Three Crane Wharfe, by Willyam Copland.
Garrick's Collection of Old Plays, K vol. x

43. Women had hunting parties of their own, rousing the game and pursuing it. They rode astride like men, and were skilful in the use of bow and arrow. Eleventh century.

WRESTLING

From *A Mery Geste of Robyn Hode*

The poet, speaking of a knight who was going to Robin Hood, says,

unto Bernisdale,
As he went, by a bridge was a wrastling,
And there taryed was he,
And there was all the best yemen,
Of all the west countrey.
A full fayre game there was set up;
A white bull, up ypyght;
A great courser with sadle and brydle,
With gold burnished full bryght;
A payre of gloves, a red golde ringe,
A pipe of wyne, good faye:
What man bereth him best, ywis,
The prise shall bear away.

Garrick's Collection of Old Plays, K vol.x

SWIMMING

The poet tells us that every one in the army should learn to swim, and continues 'for commoditie of river and water for that purpose, there is no where better'.

Boys in the country often learned to swim with bundles of bulrushes.

To swymme, is eke to lerne in sommer leson.
Men fynde not a bridge, so often as a flood,
Swymmyng to voyde; and chase an hoste wil eson.
Eke after rayne the rivers goeth wood [wild],
That every man in t'host can swymme, is good:
Knyght, squyer, footman, cook, and cosynere.
And grome, and page, in swymmyng is to lere.

MS. Cotton Titus A. xxiii

HORSE-RACING, Twelfth Century

When a race is to be run by this sort of horses, and perhaps by others, which also in their kind are strong and fleet, a shout is immediately raised, and the common horses are ordered to withdraw out of the way.

Three jockeys, or sometimes only two, as the match is made,

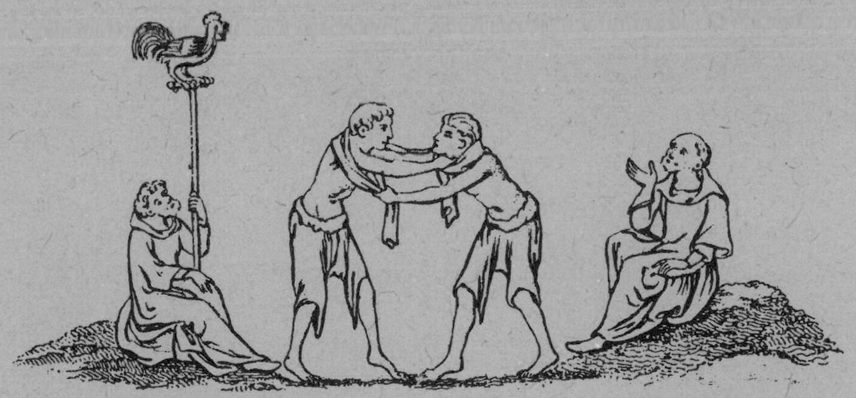

44. Here we see two men wrestling for a cock. In later days the reward was often a ram, as Chaucer says of the Miller
. . . for over-al ther he cam,
At wrastling he wolde have alwey the ram.

prepare themselves for the contest. Such as being used to ride, know how to manage their horses with judgment: the grand point is, to prevent a competitor from getting before them. The horses, on their part, are not without emulation. They tremble and are impatient, and are continually in motion.

At last, the signal once given, they strike, devour the course, hurrying along with unremitting velocity. The jockeys, inspired with the thoughts of applause and the hopes of victory, clap spurs to their willing horses, brandish their whips, and cheer them with their cries.

William FitzStephen, *A Description of London*

SKATING, Late Twelfth Century

It was customary in winter, when the ice would bear them, for the young folk of London to fasten the bones of some animals under their shoes, and taking a stout pole push forward on the ice.

. . . at times, two of them thus furnished agree to start opposite one to the other, at a great distance; they meet, elevate their poles, attack, and strike each other, when one or both of them fall, and not without some bodily hurt; and, even after their fall, are carried a great distance from each other by the rapidity of the motion, and whatever part of the head comes upon the ice, it is sure to be laid bare.

William FitzStephen, *A Description of London*

45. Puppet show, twelfth century

46. Playing bells

DANCING, Late Twelfth Century

In the romances of the middle ages, the character of a hero was incomplete unless he danced excellently. The knights and ladies are often shown dancing together, which in the poem of Launfal is called playing:

The Quene yede to the formeste ende,
Betweene Launfal and Gauweyn the hende [courteous],
  And after her ladyes bryght;
To daunce they wente alle yn same,
To see them playe hyt was fayr game
  A lady and a knyght;
They had menstrelles of moche honours.
Fydelers, sytolyrs, and trompetors,
  And else hyt were unright.

From MS. Cotton marked Caligula, A.2. fol.53

MAY-GAMES, Late Twelfth Century

This custom no doubt, if a relic of one more ancient, was practised by the Heathens, who observed the last four days in April, and the first in May, in honour of the goddess Flora. An old Roman calendar says, on the 30th of April, 'the boys go out to seek may-trees.'

On the calends or first of May, commonly called May-day, the juvenile part of both sexes were wont to rise a little after midnight and walk to some neighbouring wood, accompanied with music and blowing of horns, where they brake down branches from the trees and adorn them with nosegays and crowns of flowers; when this is done, they return with their booty homewards about the rising of the sun, and make their doors and windows to triumph with their flowery spoils. And the after part of the day is chiefly spent in dancing round a tall poll, which is called a may-poll; and being placed in a convenient part of the village, stands there, as it were, consecrated to the Goddess of Flowers, without the least violation being offered to it in the whole circle of the year.

Henry Bourne, *Antiquities of the Common People*

CROSS AND PILE, later called HEADS OR TAILS

This pastime, popular among the lower classes, was later introduced at the court. In one of the wardrobe rolls of Edward II appear the following entries:

Item, paid to Henry the king's barber for money which he lent to the king to play at cross and pile, five shillings.
Item, paid to Pires Barnard, usher of the king's chamber, money which he lent the king, and which he lost at cross and pile; to Monsieur Robert Wattewille eight-pence.

Antiquities Repertorium, vol.ii

47. The performance of mummers or masquerade figures consisted chiefly in dancing, accompanied by minstrels playing on different kinds of musical instruments. Twelfth century.

48. Walrus Ivory Chessmen, found on the Isle of Lewis; Twelfth century.

A TOURNAMENT IN AN OPEN FIELD

Many combatants were engaged at the same time. The champion, unhorsed at the end of the tournament, attained honour and often a large sum of money.

The kyng his sonne a knyght gan make,
And many another for his sake;
Justes were cryed ladyes to see,
Thedyr came lordes grete plente.
Tournementis atyred in the felde,
A thousand armed with spere and shelde;
Knyghtis began togedre to ryde,
Some were unhorsyd on every side,
Ipomydon that daye was victorius,
And there he gaff many a cours;
For there was none that he mette,
But he hys spere on hym woulde sette:
Then after within a lytell stounde,
Horse and man both went to grounde.
The Heraudes gaff the child the gree [reward],
A thousand pound he had in fee;
Mynstrellys had giftes of golde,
And fourty dayes this fest was holde.

From an ancient romance, *Ipomydon,* MS. Harleian 2252

49. This illustration is an example of the ancient balance-master's art. Two men support the large wooden board. The girl has set up three swords, points upward in a triangular form. She indicates them with her right hand, and holds a small trowel-like object in her other hand.

Health

PRAYER TO EARTH, DIVINE GODDESS, MOTHER NATURE, Twelfth Century

'Hear, I beseech thee, and be favourable to my prayer. Whatsoever herb thy power dost produce, give, I pray, with goodwill to all nations to save them and grant me this my medicine. Come to me with thy powers and howsoever I may use them may they have good success, and to whomsoever I may give them. Whatever thou dost grant, may it prosper. To thee all things return. Those who rightly receive these herbs from me, do thou make them whole, goddess, I beseech thee; I pray thee as a suppliant that by thy majesty thou grant this to me.

'Now I make intercession to you, all ye powers and herbs and to your majesty; ye whom earth, parent of all, hath produced and given as a medicine of health to all nations and hath put majesty upon you, be I pray you the greatest help to the human race. This I pray and beseech from you, be present here with your virtues, for she who created you hath herself promised that I may gather you with the goodwill of him on whom the art of medicine was bestowed, and grant for health's sake good medicine by grace of your powers.

B.M. MS. Harley 1585, fols.12v-13r

RULES OF HEALTH OF THE TWELFTH CENTURY

The Salerne Schoole doth by these lines impart
All health to *Englands King,* and doth advise
From care his head to keepe, from wrath his hart,
Drinke not much wine, sup light, and soone arise,

When meat is gone, long sitting breedeth smart;
And after noone still waking keepe your eies;
When moved you find yourself to *Natures Needs*
Forbeare them not, for that much danger breeds;
Use three Physitians still, first Doctor *Quiet*,
Next Doctor *Mery-man*, and Doctor *Dyet*.

50. In a manuscript written at St. Albans about 1120, this is described as *Sugeyethistell* or *Sowethistell*. It is a very good representation of the common *Sonchus oleraceus*, the milk-thistle or sow-thistle. With milky juice it was used as a curative herb

MEDICINAL HERBS, Late Twelfth Century

Colewort and ragwort excite love, but the marvellous frigidity of psyllium seed offers a remedy for that affliction. Myrtle too is a friend of temperance . . . Those who are experienced in such matters distinguish between the heliotrope and our 'heliotrope' which is called calendula, and between mugwort and our native 'mugwort' which is feverfew. It happens that the wool-blade is one shrub and the silver-leaved wool-blade is another. The iris grows a purple flower; the Florentine iris or ireos has a white one. The gladiolus bears a yellow one; but the burweed has no flower. Other noted herbs are horehound, hound's-tongue or *cynoglossa,* parsley, bryony, groundsel, then wild myrrh or angelica, *regina,* coriander – three heaven-gazing species.

U.T. Holmes, Jr., *Daily Living in the Twelfth Century based on the Observations of Alexander Neckam*

51. A cripple with a helpful device. Twelfth century

A 'FRANKISH REMEDY' FOR SCROFULA

Take uncrushed leaves of glasswort, burn them, then soak the ashes in olive oil and sharp vinegar. Treat the scrofula with them until the spot on which it is growing is eaten up. Then take burnt lead, soak it in ghee butter and treat him with it. That will cure him.

Ille et Galeron

52. A trepan operation in the twelfth century. The man in the centre is paying, as he watches his unhappy friend.

LEPROSY, Twelfth Century

We have said nothing about leprosy. The leper was allowed to wander about alone, or in groups of his fellows. He carried a cup or bowl, a *flavel* [clicking apparatus], and often a crutch or staff.

Lepers were called *transportani* because when gathered into special hospitals they were obliged to live outside the walls of the town.

Usamah, *Wistasce li moines*

Work – Wages

RIGHTS AND RANKS OF PEOPLE, Eleventh Century

Thegn's Law. The law of the thegn is that he be entitled to his book-right [land protected by charter], and that he shall contribute three things in respect of his land: armed service, and the repairing of fortresses and work on bridges. Also in respect of many estates, further service arises on the king's order such as service connected with the deer fence at the king's residence, and equipping a guard ship, and guarding the coast, and guarding the lord, and military watch, almsgiving and church dues and many other various things.

Geneat's Right. [Geneat: a riding servant or bailiff] Geneat-right is various according to what is fixed in respect of the estate: in some he must pay rent and contribute a pasturage swine a year, ride and perform carrying service and furnish means of carriage, work and entertain his lord, reap and mow, cut deer hedges and keep up places from which deer may be shot, build and fence the lord's house, bring strangers to the village, pay church dues and alms money, act as guard to his lord, take care of the horses, and carry messages far and near wheresoever he is directed.

Cottar's Right. [A Cottar held about 5 acres, part of the later 'manorial economy'.] The cottar's right is according to the custom of the estate: in some he must work for his lord each Monday throughout the year, or 3 days each week at harvest-time. . . . He does not make land payment. He should have 5 acres: more if it be the custom on the estate; and it is too little if it ever be less; because his work must be frequent. Let him give his hearth-penny [Peter's Pence, an exceptional levy] on Ascension Day even as each freeman ought to do. Let him also perform services on his lord's demesne-land if he is ordered, by keeping watch on the sea-coast and working at the king's deer fence and such things according to his condition. Let him pay his church dues at Martinmas.

Boor's-Right. The boor's [peasant's] duties are various, in some places heavy and in others light. On some estates the custom is that he must perform week-work for 2 days in each week of the year [for the benefit of the lord] as he is directed, and 3 days from the Feast of the Purification to Easter. If he perform carrying service he need not work while his horse is out. At Michaelmas he must pay 10 pence for *gafol* [rent], and at Martinmas 23 sesters of barley, and 2 hens, and at Easter a young sheep or 2 pence. And he must lie from Martinmas to Easter at his lord's fold as often as it falls to his lot; and from the time when ploughing is first done until Martinmas he must each week plough 1 acre, and himself present the seed in the lord's barn. Also [he must plough] 3 acres as boon-work [special services], and 2 for pasturage. If he needs more grass, let him earn it as he may be permitted. Let him plough 3 acres as his tribute land [lord's land scattered in open strip fields] and sow it from his own barn, and pay his hearth-penny. And every pair of boors must maintain 1 hunting dog, and each boor must give 6 loaves to the herdsman of the lord's swine when he drives his herd to the mast-pasture. On the same land to which the customs apply a farmer ought to be given for his occupation of the land 2 oxen, 1 cow, 6 sheep and 7 acres sown on his rood of land. After that year let him perform all the dues that fall to him, and let him be given tools for his work and utensils for his house. When death befalls him let the lord take charge of what he leaves.

The estate-law is fixed on each estate: at some places, as I have said, it is heavier, at some places, also lighter, because not all customs about estates are alike. On some estates a boor must pay tribute in honey, on some in food, on some in ale. Let him who has the shire [sheriff or steward] always know what are the ancient arrangements about the estate and what is the custom of the district.

About the bee-keeper. A bee-keeper if he holds a swarm which is subject to payment must pay what is appointed on that estate. Among us it is appointed that he should give 5 sesters of honey as tax: in some estates a greater tax is due. Also at certain times he must be ready for many sorts of work at his lord's pleasure besides boon-work and the cutting of corn when ordered and the mowing of meadows. And if he will be provided with land he must be provided with a horse so as to give it to supply his lord with a beast of burden or to go with his horse himself, whichever is directed. And many things must a man of such condition do: I cannot recount them all now. When death befalls him let his lord take charge of what he leaves unless there should be anything free.

A swine-herd at pay ought to pay for his animals that are to be slaughtered according to the amount fixed on the estate. On many estates it is fixed that he pay every year 15 swine for killing, 10 old and 5 young. Let him have himself whatever he raises beyond that. On many estates a more severe due is incumbent on the swine-herd. Let each swine-herd take care that after the slaughter of his swine he prepare them properly and singe them: then he will be well entitled to the perquisites. Also he must be – as I said before about the bee-keeper – always ready for every sort of work, and provided with a horse at the lord's need.

A slave swine-herd and a slave bee-keeper after death are liable to one and the same law.

A herdsman slave belonging to his lord who keeps the demesne herd ought to have a young pig kept in a sty, and his perquisites when he has prepared the bacon, and also the dues that belong to a slave.

About men's provisioning. Every slave ought to have as provisions 12 pounds of good corn and 2 carcasses of sheep and 1 good cow for food and the right of cutting wood according to the custom of the estate.

About women's provisioning. For a female slave 8 pounds of corn for food, 1 sheep or 3 pence for winter food, 1 sester of beans for lenten food, whey in summer or 1 penny.

All slaves belonging to the estate ought to have food at Christmas and Easter, a strip of land for ploughing and a "harvest-handful" besides their dues.

About retainers. A retainer [a privileged person] ought to have the use of 2 acres, 1 sown and 1 not sown. Let him sow the latter himself. And he is entitled to his food and shoes and gloves.

About the sower. A sower ought to have a seedlip full of every

January: ploughing with oxen

March: digging and sowing

May: caring for sheep

June: cutting and carting wood

53. Saxon Calendar *c.*1030

kind of seed when he has properly sown every seed throughout the space of a year.

About the ox-herd. The ox-herd must pasture 2 oxen or more with the lord's herd on the common pasture with the cognizance of the overseer. Let him earn thereby shoes and gloves for himself. And his cow for food must go with the lord's oxen.

About the cow-herd. A cow-herd ought to have an old cow's milk for a week after she has newly calved, and the beestings of a young cow for a fortnight. His cow for food is to go with the lord's cow.

About the shepherd. A shepherd's due is that he should have 12 nights' dung at Christmas, and 1 lamb from the year's young ones, 1 bell-wether's fleece, and the milk of his flock for a week after the equinox, and bowl-full of whey or buttermilk all summer.

About the goat-herd. A goat-herd ought to have the milk of his herd after Martinmas, and before that his portion of whey, and 1 kid a year old, if he looks after his herd properly.

About the cheese-maker. 100 cheeses pertain to the cheese-maker, and it behoves her to make butter for the lord's table out of the whey pressed out from the cheese; and let her have all the buttermilk except the shepherd's portion.

About the keeper of the granary. The granary-keeper ought to have the corn spilt at the barn door at harvest-time if his overseer grant it to him, and if he deserves it.

About the beadle. The beadle ought to be more free from work because of his office, since he is bound to be always ready. Also he ought to have some bit of land for his labour.

About the woodward. Every tree blown down by the wind ought to go to the woodward.

It is proper that the hayward should be rewarded for his labour in those parts which lie near the pasture; because if he has neglected his work he can expect . . . (if) he has been granted such a piece of land it must be nearest the pasture by custom; because, if out of laziness he neglects his lord's land his own will not be protected if it is provided in this way. If he makes properly secure what he has to guard he will be well entitled to his reward [that he will not suffer from straying beasts].

The customs of estates are various, as I have said before. Nor do we apply these regulations we have described to all districts. But we declare what the custom is where it is known to us. If we learn better, we will eagerly delight in what we learn and maintain it according to the custom of the district in which we then live.

Wherefore one must delight among the people to learn laws if one does not oneself wish to lose honour on the estate.

There are many common rights: in some districts are due winter provisions, Easter provisions, a harvest feast for reaping the corn, a drinking feast for ploughing, reward for haymaking, food for making the rick, at wood-carrying a log from each load, at corn-carrying food on completion of the rick, and many things which I cannot recount.

This, however, is a memorandum of people's provisions. And all these I have enumerated before.

Rectitudines Singularum Personarum, translated by Miss S.I. Tucker. *English Historical Documents*, Vol.II

FAILURE OF CROPS AND OTHER DISEASES IN ENGLAND

1041. And all that year it was very sad in many and various things, both in tempests and earth fruits. And so much cattle perished in this year as no man before remembered, both through various diseases and through bad weather

1086. And the same year was a very heavy, and toilsome, and sorrowful year in England, through murrain [cattle plague] of cattle, and corn and fruits were at a stand, and so great unpropitiousness in weather, as no one can easily think, so great was the thunder and lightning, that it killed many men and ever it grew worse with men more and more. May Almighty God better it when it shall be His will.

After the birth-tide of our Lord Jesus Christ one thousand and seven and eighty winter, in the one and twentieth year after William ruled and held despotic sway over England, as God had granted him there was a very heavy and very pestilent year in this land. Such a malady came on men that almost every other man was in the worst evil, that is with fever, and that so strongly that many men died of the evil.

Afterwards there came, through the great tempests which came as we have before told, a very great famine over all England, so that many hundred men perished by death through that famine. Alas! how miserable and how rueful a time was then! Who cannot feel pity for such a time? But such things befal for a folk's sins, because they will not love God and righteousness, as it was in those days, that little righteousness was in this land with any man, save with the monks alone, wherever they fared well.

The king and the head men loved much, and over much, coveteousness in gold and in silver, and recked not how sinfully it might be got, provided it came to them. The king gave his land as dearly for rent as he possible could, then came some other and bade more than the other had before given, and the king let it to the man who had bidden him more, then came a third and bade yet more, and the king gave it up to the man who had bidden most of all. And he recked not how very sinfully the reeves got it from poor men, nor how many illegalities they did, but the more that was said about right law, the more illegalities were done. They levied unjust tolls, and many other unjust things they did, which are difficult to reckon.

Also, in the same year, before autumn, the holy monastery of St Paul, the episcopal see of London, was burnt, and many other monasteries, and the greatest and fairest part of the whole city. So also, at the same time, almost every chief town in all England was burnt. Alas! a rueful and deplorable time was it in that year, which brought forth so many misfortunes . . .

1103. This was a very calamitious year in the land, through manifold imposts, and through murrain of cattle, and perishing of fruits both in corn and also in all tree fruits.

1111. In this year was a very long and sad and severe winter; and thereby were the earth-fruits greatly injured; and there was the greatest murrain of cattle that any man could remember.

1112. This was a very good year and very abundant in wood and in field; but it was a very sad and sorrowful one, through a most destructive pestilence.

Anglo-Saxon Chronicle, translated by J.A. Giles

ISABELLA DE SIFREWAST GAVE A MAN AND HIS LAND TO READING ABBEY, Twelfth Century

. . . the half virgate of land in Purley which Osbert son of Godwin the fisherman holds in villeinage with all its appurtenances for ever in pure and perpetual alms, free and quit from all custom and

54. The smith, one of the most important of workmen. Eleventh century

exaction and demand, and immune from all secular service. And so that the abbot and convent of Reading at their will and dispostion may turn the aforesaid Osbert and his offspring either to the work of villeinage or to an annual rent.

British Museum, Harleian MS 1708. f.63

WINTER

Keen is the wind, bare the hill, it is difficult to find
shelter; the ford is marred, the lake freezes, a man
could stand on a single stalk.

Wave after wave covers the shore; very loud are the
outcries before the heights of the hill; scarcely can
one stand up outside.

Cold is the bed of the lake before the tumult of
winter; the reeds are withered, that stalks are
broken, the wind is fierce, the wood is bare.

Cold is the bed of the fish in the shelter of the ice,
the stag is thin, the reeds are bearded, short
is the evening, the trees are bowed.

Snow falls, white is the surface, warriors do not
go to their foray; cold are the lakes,
their colour is without warmth.

Snow falls, white is the hoarfrost; idle is the
shield on the old man's shoulder; very great
the wind, it freezes the grass.

Snow falls on the top of the ice, the wind sweeps
the crest of the close trees; fine is the shield
on the brave man's shoulder.

Snow falls, it covers the valley; the warriors
hasten to battle, I shall not go, a wound
does not allow me.

Snow falls on the hillside, the horse is a prisoner,
the cattle are lean; it is not like a summer
day today . . .

Welsh, author unknown; eleventh century;
translated by Kenneth Hurlstone Jackson

CURIOUS PHENOMENA OF NATURE

Earthquakes

1048. In this year there was a great earthquake widely throughout England.

1049. In this year was also an earthquake on the Kal. of May [May 1st], in many places, at Worcester, at Wick, and at Derby and elsewhere; and there was also a great mortality among men, and a murrain among cattle; and the wildfire [disease affecting sheep] also did much evil in Derbyshire and elsewhere.

1089. There happened all over England a great earthquake, on the day the IIIrd of the Ides of August [August 11th]. And it was a very backward year in corn and fruits of all kinds; so that many men reaped their corn about Martinmas [November 11th] and yet later.

Severe Winters

1046. In this same year, after Candlemas [February 2nd], came the severe winter, with frost and snow, and with all kinds of bad weather, so that there was no man alive who could remember so severe a winter as that was, both through mortality of men, and murrain of cattle; both birds and fishes perished through the great cold and hunger.

High Winds

1039. In this year was the great wind.

1053. In this year was the great wind on Thomas' mass-night [December 21st] ; and also all the midwinter there was much wind.
1103. Also in the morning on the mass day of St. Laurence [August 10th] the wind did so great harm here in the country to all fruits, as no man remembered that it ever did before.
1114. In this year were very great winds in the month of October; but it was excessively great in the night of the octave of St. Martin [November 18th], and that was everywhere manifest in woods and towns.

Comets

1065. Then was seen over all England such a sight in the heavens as no man ever saw before. Some men said that it was the star Cometa, which some men called the haired star; and it first appeared on the eve of Litania Major, the VIII of the Kal. of May [April 24th] and so shone all the seven nights.
1097. Then on St. Michael's mass the IVth of the Nones of October [October 4th] there appeared an extraordinary star, shining in the evening, and soon going to its setting. It was seen in the south-west, and the ray that stood from it seemed very long, shining south-east; and almost all the week it appeared in this wise. Many men supposed that it was a 'comet'.

Anglo-Saxon Chronicle, translated by J.A. Giles

THE FIRST MAKERS OF GLASS IN ENGLAND

For even Britain, which by some is called another world since, surrounded by the ocean, it is not thoroughly known by many geographers, possesses, in its remotest region, bordering on Scotland, the place of his [the Venerable Bede's] birth and education . . .

Here is the River Wear, of considerable breadth and rapid tide; which running into the sea, receives the vessels borne by gentle gales, on the calm bosom of its haven. Both its banks [Jarrow, one of Benedict's monasteries, is really on the River Tyne] have been made conspicuous by one Benedict who there built churches and monasteries; one dedicated to Peter and the other to Paul, united in the bond of brotherly love and of monastic rule. The industry and forbearance of the men, anyone will admire who reads the book which Bede composed concerning his life, and those of the succeeding abbots; his industry in bringing over a multitude of books and being the first person who introduced in England constructors of stone edifices as well as makers of glass windows; in which pursuits he spent almost his whole life abroad; the love of his country and his taste for elegance beguiling his painful labour, in the earnest desire of conveying something to his countrymen out of the common way; for very rarely before the time of Benedict were buildings of stone seen in Britain, nor did the Solar ray cast its light through the transparent glass.

William of Malmesbury, *Gesta Regum Anglorum*
translated by J.A. Giles

COMPLICATION OF SERVICES, Early Twelfth Century

In the year of our Lord 1106 our predecessors, wishing to increase the possessions of this holy place, bought from this Rudolf [the heir of Guntran, a neighbouring tyrant] all that he had there, whether justly or unjustly, acquired, at the price of 200 pounds of silver. For this purpose they broke up here a golden chalice adorned with most precious stones and gems, and two silver crosses which the Countess Richilda of Lenzburg, sister to Count Wernher of Hapsburg, gave to this monastery, and they sold many very profitable farms and despoiled and stripped the monastery of almost all its substance, whether within or without. Here therefore let every man weigh in his own mind what happiness or profit may come to him, soul or body, from possessions so unrighteously gotten; seeing that every man ought to attend to the one question of so nourishing his body as not to lose his soul; and let him consider where is the profit if a robber steals and the monk eats [of his theft]. But let us leave these matters, whether righteously or unrighteously acquired, and let my little book set forth what substance we possess in this village.

There are, then, two courts, an upper and a lower. To the upper belongs so much field as can be rightly ploughed with two teams of oxen, and so also to the lower; in hay, the produce of 32 meadows. The peasants who have day-works are 22; some doing personal service, while others, paying rent, contribute all the rest that we have there as rent. Now this is the constitution of the above-named freemen. The rent is paid only by those who possess dwellings and tofts. For these may do what they will with their fields and meadows; they may sell or give to whomsoever they will as to their peers; yet none pays rent but those who have dwellings. Yet the disposition of the rent is so intricate that scarce any man can get himself clear. So are all things wont to be that arise from evil and from greed. A certain measure of spelt is imposed upon them [as rent], to wit, four bushels by the measure of Zurich and somewhat more. Some pay this rent in full, some the half, some the quarter, and others twofold or threefold or even sixfold, emptying the measure to the very bottom, in order to fulfil his due. This diversity comes to pass whensoever some holding is left, and the heirs divide it among themselves; for each giveth so much for rent as he possesses of the hereditament; and, in proportion as he gives rent, so also he ploughs and mows and reaps and works at the hedges, and gives hens and skeins of flax. When therefore they have to plough, it is measured for them with the rod wherewith the holdings are measured; and this rod is marked according to each man's proportion; and, wheresoever the mark comes, there a peg of wood is fixed in the ground; and yet they [the peasants] plough at the first cutting and sowing. So also is it done in the meadows and the hedges. For he reaps the seed which he has sown; and oftentimes he has to spread out the hay which he mows. So, when he is told beforehand to mow the hay, if he do not cut it forthwith on the morrow, and if rain come, for that he suffers judgement. But if he cut it and the rain come, he suffers no judgement, but cuts the hay and prepares it all through and brings it to our stable with his own oxen. So also with the hens and the flax; the peasant brings all to the monastery. Those who live on this side of the torrent give two [pence?] for wood, and those who live beyond, one [penny?]. On the last day of December they pay a rent of oats, which also some give together, according to the aforesaid proportion of measure. All these dues were originally asked as a favour; now they are compulsory. In the early days there were freemen there, yea, far more than now, because a certain pestilent man of that family [of Guntran], named Gerung, had sorely troubled them, and deceived them with fraud and power, and cast them forth from their hereditaments, and driven them from the district, wherefore also he himself was slain by them in after days.

Muri chronicler, *Origines Murensis Monasterii*

55. The Plough. Eleventh century

COMPLICATED WORKING SERVICES ON THE LORD'S DEMESNE

John Pese (of Lympsham) held a virgate for xxx pence in money and in work on the lord's demesne, from Michaelmas to Martinmas (Nov. 11) to plough one acre for winter corn, and half an acre for spring corn when called upon, and to harrow every Monday in the year one hand-work, except on annual solemnities. To carry loads three times to Glaston [bury], to mow and carry three boon-days, and to go to vineyard. If John Pese preferred to pay his xxx pence in work instead of in cash, his holding then ran as follows: From Michaelmas to Martinmas to plough one acre, besides another whenever called upon, every week. From Martinmas to Hock-day (second Tuesday after Easter) to plough and harrow half an acre every Monday. From Hock-day to Aug. 1st, three "hand-works" every week. After Aug. 1st, in harvest time, to cut half an acre every Monday, Tuesday, Wednesday and Friday. Three Bed-ripes on three Thursdays. To have every day, on leaving off work, his bundle of corn, and to find a sumpter or pack-horse whenever called upon. At Hock-day to subscribe a penny towards a sheep (?). At St Martin's to pay half a day's work as Church-set, and at Michaelmas 5d. land-tax. In some places vexatious services of this kind were already compounded for, "pro omni servitio" etc.

Glastonbury customal, *Lib. H. de Soliaco*

THE COURT AND HOUSEHOLD OF HENRY I

The chancellor shall receive 5 shillings a day, and 1 lord's simnel loaf, and 2 salted simnel loaves, and 1 sextary of clear wine, and 1 sextary of ordinary wine, and 1 fat wax candle and 40 pieces of candle.

The master of the writing office used at first to receive 10 pence a day and 1 salted simnel loaf, and half a sextary of ordinary wine, and 1 fat wax candle and 12 pieces of candle; but King Henry increased the allowance of Robert 'of the Seal' to the extent that on the day when the king died, Robert was receiving 2 shillings and 1 sextary of ordinary wine and 1 salted simnel loaf, and 1 small wax candle and 24 pieces of candle.

The chaplain in charge of the chapel and of the relics shall have the provision of two men; and the four servants of the chapel shall each receive double food, and for each of the two packhorses assigned to the chapel they shall have an allowance of a penny a day, and also a penny a month for shoeing. For their service of the chapel they shall have 2 wax candles on Wednesday, and 2 on Saturday; and 30 pieces of candle; and 1 gallon of clear wine for Mass; and 1 sextary of ordinary wine on Maundy Thursday for the washing of the altar; and on Easter Day 1 sextary of clear wine for Communion, and 1 of ordinary wine.

CONCERNING THE STEWARDS

The steward shall receive the same as the chancellor if they live outside the king's household; but if they live within the king's household, they shall receive each day 3 shillings and 6 pence, and 2 salted simnel loaves, and 1 sextary of ordinary wine and a candle.

The clerk of the issue of bread and wine shall receive 2 shillings a day and 1 salted simnel loaf and 1 sextary of ordinary wine and 1 small wax candle and 24 pieces of candle.

CONCERNING THE DISPENSERS

The master-dispenser of bread who is permanently in office shall receive 2 shillings and 10 pence each day, if he lives outside the king's household, and 1 salted simnel loaf, and 1 sextary of ordinary wine and 1 small wax candle and 24 pieces of candle; but if he lives within the king's household he shall receive 2 shillings and half a sextary of ordinary wine and 1 candle.

CONCERNING THE COOKS

The cook of the king's kitchen shall live in the king's household, and shall receive 3 halfpence a day for his man. The usher of the same kitchen shall have the customary food and 3 halfpence a day for his man. The keeper of the vessels shall live in the king's household and shall receive 3 halfpence a day for his man, and also a packhorse with its allowances. The scullion of the same kitchen shall have the customary food. The cook for the king's private household and the dispenser likewise. Ralph 'de Marchia', who before his death was cook to the king [Henry 1], lived in the king's household and received 3 halfpence for his man.

CONCERNING THE GREAT KITCHEN

Oinus Pochard shall have the customary food and 3 halfpence a day for his man. Two cooks shall likewise have the customary food and 3 halfpence a day for their man. The servants of the same kitchen shall have the customary food. The usher of the turnspit shall have the customary food and 3 halfpence a day for his man. The turnspit likewise. The keeper of the dishes receives the same and also a packhorse with its allowances. The carter of the great kitchen shall have double food and a just allowance for his horse. The carter of the larder likewise. The servant who takes in the beasts killed in the chase shall live in the king's household and shall receive 3 halfpence a day for his man.

CONCERNING THE BUTLERY

The master-butler shall be as the steward, and they shall both have the same allowance. The master-dispenser of the butlery shall be as the master-dispenser of bread and wine. The dispensers of the butlery who serve by turn shall be as the dispensers of issue except that they shall have one candle more, for they have 1 small wax candle and 24 pieces of candle. The usher of the butlery shall have the customary food and 3 halfpence a day for his man. The keepers of the wine barrels shall live in the king's household, and each one of them shall receive 3 halfpence a day for his man. The keeper of the wine-butts shall have the customary food and 3 pence for his man, and half a sextary of ordinary wine and 12 pieces of candle. The cellarman shall have the customary food, but

Sereius shall have besides this 3 halfpence a day for his man, and 2 packhorses with their allowances.

Constitutio Domus Regis
translated by Charles Johnson

56. Illustrations of ploughing, digging and sowing, harvesting, threshing and winnowing, from an eleventh-century English calendar.

PAYMENT OF SERVANTS OF HENRY I

The bearer of the king's bed shall eat in the house and have 1½d. a day for his man and one pack horse. The ewer [waterman] has double diet and when the king goes on a journey 1d. for drying the king's clothes [evidence of the weather hazards of the twelfth-century travel] and when the king bathes 4d. except on the three great feasts of the year. The wages of the washerwoman are in doubt.

Constitutio Domus Regis,
translated by Charles Johnson

HERRING FISHERY AND A CHAPEL AT YARMOUTH, Twelfth Century

There was at that time, however, on the beach at Yarmouth, a certain tiny Chapel built in which divine services were only celebrated during the season of the herring fishery, for there were not there more than four or five small houses [huts] provided for the reception of fishermen. The aforesaid Bishop [Herbert Losinga] besought King Henry [I] for a licence to build on the same sands a church. The desired licence being asked for and secured, he built a church there, placing therein a Chaplain to celebrate divine service always; and he provided the necessary equipment from his own possessions.

And after a time, those coming from the . . . ports turned out the said chaplain by force of arms, thinking to force their will on the same church [in order to have one under their own control.] Hearing which, the aforesaid Bishop directed letters to the king concerning the injury done to him by the men of the harbour in these parts. The king was at that time in Normandy and, having heard the aforesaid, directed letters to Roger Bigot guardian of Norfolk. The latter, desiring to carry out the command of the king directed to him, got together men of the country in order that he might restore to the said Bishop the church of Yarmouth and, if necessary, drive out with force the port men therefrom.

The port men resisted with a force of arms and in the conflict which followed certain were killed by the sword and the remainder put to flight. And the Bishop restored anew to the possession of the said church, then gave . . . to his monks of Norwich the aforementioned church of Yarmouth. . . .

The first Register of Norwich Cathedral Priory,
edited by H. W. Saunders, Norfolk Record Society

ROYAL HUNTSMEN, *c*1136

Each of four *Hornblowers* 3d. a day. Twenty *Serjeants:* Each 1d. a day, *Fewterers* (Keeper of Greyhounds] : Each 3d. a day, and 2d. for their men; and for each greyhound a halfpenny a day. The *King's Pack of Hounds:* 8d. a day. *Knight-Huntsman:* Each 8d. a day. *Huntsmen:* Each 5d. *Leader of the Lime-Hound* [a leashed hound only loosed to kill a stag at bay] and the lime-hound a halfpenny. *Berner* [feeder of hounds] : 3d. a day. *Huntsmen of the Hounds on the Leash:* Each 3d. a day, Of the great leash four hounds 1d. And of the small leashes six should have 1d. For the great leashes two men, each 1d. a day. and for the small, two men, each 1d. a day. *Brach-Keepers* [small hounds hunting by scent] : Each 3d. a day. *Wolf-Hunters:* 20d. a day for horses, men and hounds: and they should have twenty-four running hounds and eight greyhounds, and £6 a year to buy horses; but they say 'eight'. Each of the *Archers* who carried the King's bow 5d. a day; and the other archers as much. Bernard, Ralf the Rober, and their fellows 3d. a day.

Establishment of the Royal Household, translated in *Dialogus de Scaccario, The Course of the Exchequer, and Constitutio Domus Regis*

COOKS, c.1136

Cooks: The Cook of the upper kitchen shall eat in the house, and have three halfpence for his man. The *Usher* of the same kitchen, the customary diet and three halfpence for his man. The *Scullion* shall eat in the house and have three halfpence for his man, and have a sumpter-horse with his livery. The *Sumpterman* of the same kitchen, the like. The *Serjeant of the Kitchen* the customary diet only. *The Cook of the King's personal servants and of the Dispensers,* the like. [Ralf de Marchia, who was cook, died before the King's death.] He shall eat in the house and have three halfpence a day for his man. *Great Kitchen:* Owen Polcheard has the customary diet and three halfpence a day for his man. Two *Cooks,* each the customary diet and three halfpence a day for his man. *Serjeants* of the same Kitchen: The customary diet and three halfpence for his man. *Roaster:* The like. *Scullion:* The like, and a sumpter-horse besides with its livery. *Carter of the Great Kitchen:* Double diet, and the due livery for his horse.

Carter of the Larder: The like.

The Serjeant who received the Venison: Shall eat indoors, and have three halfpence for his man.

Establishment of the Royal Household, *c.* 1136, translated in *Dialogues de Scaccario, The Course of the Exchequer, and Constitutio Domus Regis,* edited by C. Johnson

THE SERVICE AND WORK OF THE HOLDER OF ONE VIRGATE, Late Twelfth Century

From Michaelmas to the beginning of August he works for 2 days in each week and ploughs for a third, except at Christmas and Easter and Pentecost. And from the beginning of August to the Nativity of St. Mary [8 September] he works for 3 days each week. And from the Nativity of St. Mary until Michaelmas he works every day except Saturday. In winter he ploughs half an acre, and sows it with his own seed; and harrows and reaps this, and also another half-acre in August. And he performs carrying services at his own expense. And he makes 2 mitts [about 8 bushels] of malt from the lord's corn and the sixth part of 1 'milla'. He makes payments for rights on the common; and he pays 13 pence as 'heusire'. He pays also 4 pence at Michaelmas, and 1 halfpenny for wool. And he shall go errands: if he goes outside the county he shall be quit of his week's work except for ploughing. And in August he gives 1 carrying service of timber, and 1 work at fencing and he performs 2 carrying services of corn in August. And each 5 virgates give 4 pence for fish, and each 2 virgates give 1 cart of thatch, and they make the thatch. When the winnower comes there, all shall go to the court and thresh the corn from day to day until the 'farm' is made up. And if there is such hard frost in winter that he cannot plough, then he shall work on Fridays instead of ploughing. And when the farmer calls for boon-works in August he shall come to them with his whole household, and he shall then be fed by the farmer.

After the death of King Henry, Ralph of 'Asekirche' received from Abbot Walter [of Ramsey] at a rent of 6 shillings 1 virgate which previously had been held by work.

Richard, son of Rainald, has 2 virgates which Thuri the priest held.

Franceis holds 1 virgate for 6 shillings and by ploughing 6 acres.

Geoffrey of Walsoken holds 1 virgate for 6 shillings and by ploughing 6 acres.

Gilbert of Newton holds 1 virgate for 6 shillings and by ploughing 6 acres.

Gilbert of 'Loituna' holds 1 virgate and 1 toft for 6 shillings, and he ploughs every Friday. And he harrows. He also holds 1 rood for 4 pence.

Godwine the white holds 1 virgate for 5 shillings and by ploughing 3 acres.

This is the equipment in the court of Elton: 4 ploughs with 24 oxen and 8 horses and 10 cows. Each ox and horse is worth 4 shillings; each cow is worth 40 pence. 160 sheep; 26 pigs of more than a year old; and 24 piglets; 16 cocks at work. With this equipment it now renders the full 'farm', and 10 pounds in money; with the mill which gives 100 shillings.

A certain William has half an acre for 2 pence.

Master Ralph has an acre of the demesne.

The men of Elton give 17 pence for a croft.

And this is the sum of the payment of Elton: 6 pounds, besides the 28½ virgates which are held by work.

Robert, brother of Thurkil, holds an acre of land for 16 pence.

57. A master mason discussing building plans with the king

Of 13 acrelands the six better pay 18 shillings, and each of the others gives 20 pence.

There are 2 tofts which Ketelburn and the widows hold for 18 pence.

THE EXCHEQUER, AND THE REASON FOR ITS NAME, *c.*1177

Disciple. What is the Exchequer?

Master. The Exchequer is a quadrangular board about ten feet in length and five in breadth placed before those who sit around it in the manner of a table. Running round it there is a raised edge about the height of four fingers. Above the board is placed a cloth purchased at the Easter term – not an ordinary cloth, but a black one marked with stripes which are the space of a foot or a hand's breadth distant from each other. Within the spaces counters are placed according to their value, and of this we shall speak elsewhere. But although such a board is called an 'exchequer', nevertheless this name is applied also to the court which sits with the Exchequer so that if anyone obtains anything through its judgment, or anything is determined by common counsel, this is said to have been done "at the Exchequer" of such-and-such a year. Thus as men say today "at the Exchequer", so the formerly said "at the tallies".

Disciple. What is the reason for this name?

Master. No truer one at present occurs to me than that it has a shape similar to that of a chess-board.

Disciple. Would the ancients in their wisdom have so named it for its shape alone? For it might for a similar reason have been called a draught-board.

Master. I was right to call thee conscientious. There is another but less obvious reason. For just as in a game of chess there are certain classes of pieces and they move or stand still by definite rules or within certain limits, some being first in dignity and others in place, so in this, some preside while others sit in virtue of their office and none is free to depart from the established rules, as will be manifest from what follows. Again, as in chess the battle is joined by the kings, so in this it is chiefly between two men that the conflict takes place and the battle is waged, namely, the treasurer and the sheriff who sits there to render his account, while the others sit by like umpires to watch and judge the proceedings.

Disciple. It is then the treasurer who receives the account, although there are many others present who are of higher rank?

Master. That the treasurer should receive the account from the sheriff is manifest from the fact that the said account is required from him whenever it shall please the king: for what he had not received could hardly be demanded of him. Nevertheless, there are some who say that the treasurer and the chamberlains are only answerable for what is entered in the rolls as being "In the Treasury", and for this alone an account may be demanded of them. But the more correct view is that they should answer for all that is written in the roll, as will be readily understood from what follows.

Dialogus de Scaccario

THE DUTIES OF THE CHANCELLOR

Master. In that order the chancellor is first; he is as great a man at the Exchequer as he is at court, so that nothing important is done, or ought to be done, without his consent and advice. But this is his office when he sits at the Exchequer; to him pertains the custody of the royal seal, which is kept in the Treasury and is not removed therefrom, except when by order of the justiciar it is taken by the treasurer and then only for the purpose of discharging Exchequer business. This accomplished, it is put in its case, which is then sealed by the chancellor and handed over to the treasurer for safe keeping. When it is needed again, it is presented to the chancellor before the eyes of all in a sealed condition; it should never be removed either by the chancellor or anyone else on any other occasion. Likewise to him, through his deputy, belongs the custody of the roll of Chancery, and, as seemed good to these great men of the State, the chancellor is held equally responsible with the treasurer for all that is written on the roll, save only what is recorded as having been received "in the Treasury". For although he may not dictate what the treasurer writes, nevertheless he writes together with him, and if the latter makes a mistake, it is permissible for the chancellor or his clerk to rebuke him in moderation and to suggest what he ought to write. But if the treasurer shall persist in his error and refuse to alter it, the chancellor may, if he is fully confident in his opinion, argue the point before the barons, so that the latter may give judgment as to what ought to be done.

Disciple. It seems probable that the keeper of the third roll is also bound by the same rule in respect of his entries.

Master. It is not only probable but actually the case, for the authority of the third roll is equal to that of the other two in respect of their entries, because it so pleased the author of the system.

Dialogus de Scaccario

THE DUTIES OF THE TREASURER

Master. The duties of the treasurer, and his cares and anxieties, can hardly be expressed in words, though mine were "the pen of a ready writer". For in everything which is done, either in the Lower or the Upper Exchequer, he must show careful diligence. From what has been said before, however, it will be fairly clear where his chief care lies, namely in receiving the accounts of the sheriffs and in the writing of the roll, so much so that he cannot be released from these duties while the Exchequer is still sitting. According to the nature of the business he dictates the words for the writing of his roll, from which afterwards the same words are copied on to the other rolls, as mentioned above. He must take care that there be no mistake in the amount, the occasion or the person, lest anyone be discharged who is not quit of payment, or one who ought to have been acquitted be summoned again. For so great is the authority of his roll that no one is allowed to dispute or alter it, unless perchance the mistake is so glaring that it is manifest to all. Nor even then may it be changed except by the common counsel of the barons and in their very presence, so long as the Exchequer of that roll shall last. But the writing of the roll of the previous year, or even of the current year, once the Exchequer has risen, may not lawfully be changed by anyone save the king, whose will is law in these matters. Likewise it is the treasurer's right to associate himself with his superiors in all great affairs, and to let nothing be hidden from him.

Dialogus de Scaccario

THE DUTIES OF THE MELTER

Taking the coins in his own hand, the melter counts them and arranges them in a bowl of burnt cinders which is in the furnace. Then, following the rules of the melter's art, he reduces them to a

58. The smith at work for a baron making weapons and armour. Twelfth century

lump, melting and purifying the silver. But he must be careful not to stop before the process is complete nor to injure and reduce the silver by unnecessary melting, since in the former case the king, in the latter the sheriff, would suffer loss. He should, however, take every precaution and exercise all diligence that the silver be not damaged but only thoroughly refined; moreover, those who have been sent there by the barons should pay heed to this very thing. When the test-piece has been made, the silverer takes it to the barons, accompanied by the others, and then weighs it in the sight of all against the pound weight mentioned above. Moreover, he then makes good what the fire has consumed by adding coins out of the purse until the test-piece balances the pound weight. Next, the test-piece is marked with chalk in these words, "Yorkshire. The pound lost in the fire so many or so many pence", and then it is called an 'assay'; for it is not marked unless it has been previously agreed that it should be so marked. But if the sheriff whose 'assay' it is shall challenge it on the ground that too much has been consumed, perhaps by over-heating, or by the melting of the silver into lead; or if the melter himself shall admit that for some reason or other the test has failed, another twenty shillings shall be counted out from the remainder left in the purse in the presence of the barons, as described above, and the test shall be repeated in the same manner. Hence it must be clear to thee for what reason, out of the huge pile of coins placed there, forty-four shillings were originally put aside in the purse on which the sheriff's seal has been fixed. It must be noted indeed that the melter receives two pence for the 'asssay', as mentioned above. But if by chance the test shall be made twice, or even a third time, he shall receive nothing more, but shall remain content with the two pence already received.

Disciple. I marvel that such care should be shown by so many great men in the testing of a single pound, since neither great gain nor grievous loss can result therefrom.

Master. This is done, not only for the sake of this particular pound, but also of all those which are paid in together with it by the same sheriff under the same account, that of the 'farm'. For, according to the amount which this pound has lost through the refining fire, the sheriff will know how much is to be subtracted from his total for every other pound; so that if he should pay a hundred pounds 'by tale' and the test-pound shall be twelve pence short, only ninety-five pounds shall be credited to him.

Dialogus de Scaccario

THE MANY DUTIES OF THE SHERIFF, Twelfth Century

All sheriffs and bailiffs, therefore, to whom summonses are directed, are bound by the same legal sanction, that is to say, by the authority of a royal mandate, to the effect that on the day named and at the place appointed they shall gather together and discharge their debts. In order that this may be clearer to thee, consider more carefully the wording of the summons itself. For it reads: "See to it, as thou lovest thyself and all that is thine, that thou attend at the Exchequer at such-and-such a time and place, that thou hast with thee whatsoever thou owest for the old 'farm' and for the new, as well as the debts written below." Give heed, then, for two things are said which fit in respectively with the two which follow; for this, "See to it, as thou lovest thyself", relates to "That thou attend there at such-and-such a time and place", but the other, "As thou lovest all that is thine", seems to refer to this, "And that thou have there with thee all these debts written below", as if it were openly said, "Whosoever thou art that receivest a summons, thy absence, unless it can be excused by unavoidable and legitimate causes, will rebound to the peril of thine own head. For thou wilt appear thus to have spurned the royal mandate and to have acted disrespectfully and in contempt of the king's majesty if, when thou hast been summoned concerning the business for which thou art bound to him, thou hast neither come nor sent anyone to make an 'essoin' for thee. But if it is thy fault that the undermentioned debts have not been paid, then the other debts for which thou has been summoned shall be taken from the 'farm' due from thee, and the latter shall be made good from thy chattels and the revenues of thy estates. Thou thyself, in the meantime, if the barons have so decreed, shall be lodged in a safe place under liberal surveillance." When, therefore, the aforesaid summons has been received by the sheriff, on the day named let him come and present himself to the president, if the latter chance to be there, or if he be absent, to the treasurer. Then, having paid his respects to the greater barons, let him have that day free on the understanding that he will return to the Exchequer on the following day and every day thereafter. But if perchance he neither comes nor sends in advance a valid excuse, on the first day he shall be condemned to pay to the king a hundred shillings of silver for each county, on the next, ten pounds of silver, on the third, as we have learnt from our predecessors, whatsoever movables he possesses shall be at the mercy of the king. But on the fourth day, because he is now by this convicted of contempt towards the king's majesty, he shall lie at the sole mercy of the king, not only in respect of his property, but also of his person. There are some, however, who believe that for the whole total a pecuniary penalty alone will suffice, namely, that on the first day absentees should be amerced to the extent of a hundred shillings, on the second, likewise a hundred shillings, and so thereafter for each day another hundred shillings. With them I do not disagree; that is, however, provided that the king, who is wronged thereby, has given his consent thereto. Moreover, it is likely enough that the king will be willing to allow a sentence of this kind, since his singular indulgence "is slow to punish and swift to reward".

Disciple. It is the lot of an imprudent and an impudent listener to interrupt the flowing pen before the appointed end of the narrative, and so I have thus far forborne, revolving in my mind the while a question which somewhat troubles me. For thou didst say that if it was the sheriff's fault that the debts recorded were not paid, then they ought to be deducted from the 'farm' [yearly sum payable as rent, tax or the like] which he is about to pay. If then the sheriff has disbursed the whole sum due from him through the king's writ, either in public works of otherwise, what is to be done?

Master. When by the king's order he has expended the 'farm' of the county on the king's private household, or on public works or on any other undertaking, if he is then found remiss in paying his debts, he shall be detained on oath, wherever the barons shall decide, until he shall make good his debts, as he would have done for his 'farm'.

Disciple. Since a grievous loss, both to his movable and immovable property, and also to his own person, befalls a sheriff who has been summoned, but has neither come nor sent an 'essoin', unless he explains his absence as involuntary and unavoidable; I beg thee to disclose without delay what reasons he can put forward as sufficient excuse for his absence once he has been summoned.

Dialogus de Scaccario

A WEAVER AT WORK, Late Twelfth Century

The weaver has a breast roller to which the cloth to be rolled up is fastened. Let there be beamlike strips marked with holes and facing each other from opposing sides, with wires shaped like a shepherd's crook and the strips going the same way as the warp threads. Also [let there be] linen threads as slender as those that are properly associated with fringes [tied to] rods in the heddles, these threads at set intervals; let the weaver draw the warp threads [with such a heddle], the upper series of threads and then the lower. When the weft has been passed through by means of a shuttle, let him beat down the work accomplished, and let the shuttle have an iron or wooden bobbin between open spaces. The bobbin should be filled from a spool, and this spool should be covered in the manner of a clew of yarn with a weight. Let the material of the weft thread be pulled from this weighted spool, so that the one hand of the weaver tosses the shuttle to the other, to be returned vice versa.

But in vain does one weave a cloth unless previously iron combs, working upon the wool, to be softened by flame, have carded the strands in long and reciprocal endeavour. Thus the better and finer parts of the combed wool may be reserved for the thread, with the woolly dregs like coarse tow being left over. Afterwards let the wool thread be aided by the application of madder or woad such as is done in Beauvais, or let the material to be dyed be saturated in frequent dipping in *graine* [scarlet]. Then let the weaver reclaim it; but before it makes its appearance in the form of clothing, it should be subjected to the care of the fuller, demanding frequent washing.

U.T. Holmes, Jr., *Daily Living in the Twelfth Century based on the Observations of Alexander Neckam*

THE IDEAL DAIRYMAID, Twelfth Century

The dairymaid should be chaste and honest and faithful, laborious in her dairy duties, wise and neat-handed; not lavish but of a thrifty nature. For she must not suffer any man or woman to come to her dairy and carry aught away which might make her render the less perfect account. Now it is her work to receive the vessels proper to her office with a written indenture from the Reeve, and to restore them according to the same indenture when she leaves, and in this record it must be noted on what day she began work. She must receive the milk by tallies, and make cheese and butter according to the tale of the gallons; she must keep ward over the poultry, and render to the Bailiff and Reeve frequent account of the profits arising therefrom; nor will some Auditors allow her to account for less than twelve pence a year for every goose and four pence for every hen. Moreover it is her duty to winnow or sift, to cover up the fire, and to do such like petty works when she can find time for them.

Fleta, edited by J. Selden, 1647

THE TRIALS OF A PEASANT HOUSEWIFE, Twelfth Century

And what if I ask besides, though it may seem silly, how the wife stands, that heareth, when she cometh in, her child scream, sees the cat at the bacon, and the dog at the hide? Her cake is burning on the stone, and her calf is sucking up all the milk. The pot is boiling over into the fire and the churl her husband is scolding. Though this be a silly tale, maiden, it ought to deter thee more strongly from marriage, for it seems not silly to her who trieth it.

From *Hali Meidenhad*

CARPENTERS WORKING IN THE FORESTS, Eleventh Century

They had the lumber brought from the forests. The carpenters of the district were summoned to assemble. Every peasant envied his fellow who knew something of carpentry . . . Most of them went to the forest. They felled seven large oak trees. They split out the boards, and when the time came for eating, the carpenters sat down; they ate and drank gaily. When they had eaten they began their labour again. The hot sun and the long day hampered their work greatly. They went to rest in the shade, and when they had slept a bit they went merrily back to work.

La vie d'Edouard le confesseur

UPSTAIRS MAID AND DOWNSTAIRS OR KITCHEN MAID, Late Twelfth Century

Now let the upstairs maid exclude the intemperate air with a *cote.* A band or a hair net should restrain her flowing hair. She should have a necklace, and a brooch by which she can fasten the neck opening of her *cote,* or fustian, or shirt. She may have bracelets and earrings.

There should also be a kitchen maid who will place eggs under the sitting hens, and will give maslin [mixed rye and wheat] to the geese, and who will feed the ailing lambs with milk from a ewe other than the mother, in her gentleness. She will keep the calves to be weaned, whose teeth are few, in an enclosure near the barn. On holidays her clothing should be a cast-off *pellice* and a wimple. It is her practice to give the swineherd, ploughmen, and other herdsmen whey, but to the master and his friends, clabber [curds], in cups, and to offer in the evening bran bread to the dogs in the pen.

U.T. Holmes, Jr., *Daily Living in the Twelfth Century based on the Observations of Alexander Neckam*

A POOR WIDOW SWEEPING HER HOUSE, Twelfth Century

When the poor widow would cleanse her house, she gathereth into a heap, first of all, all the largest sweepings, and then shovelleth it out. After that she cometh again and sweepeth together all that was left before, and shovelleth it out also. Again, upon the small dust, if it is very dusty, she sprinkleth water, and sweepeth it out away after all the rest.

From *Ancren Riwle* (The rule for religious women)

REQUIREMENTS OF AN AVERAGE PEASANT, Late Twelfth Century

A peasant spending his life in the country, wishing to provide for poverty and old age, should have many kinds of baskets and beehives of willow wands. He should have also a fishing fork shaped like a hook that he may get himself fish. Nor should he be without a willow basket for pressing clabber, in which milk saved from the milking, pressed frequently, may be transformed into cheese with the whey well extracted. The whey should be kept for young children to drink.

Afterwards the cheese in its fresh state should be kept in a cheese-box of paper or of marsh reeds, wrapped in leaves and covered against the attacks of flies, mice, stinging flies and such.

Also he should have straw and coarse grains, which are fed to hens, ducks, and geese. He must also have bolting cloth and a strainer, so that he can sift flour with them; he can clarify beer with them too. He must possess a sword, a spade, a threshing sledge, a seed bucket for sowing, a wheelbarrow, a mousetrap, and a wolf trap. He should have also stakes or pales, frequently sharpened and tested in the fire. He should have also a two-headed axe for removing thorns, thistles, brambles, spines, and bad shoots, and holly wood for tying and renewing hedges in order that, taking advantage of carelessness, no thieves may enter into the livestock enclosure and take animals. He should have a large knife also by which he may cut grafts and insert them into trees if there should be need. He may have hoes for removing tares, chicory and bennet grass, vetch, darnel, thistles, and avens [herb bennet]. Some of these, however, are eradicated better with a curved implement than with a hoe.

He needs a herdsman and a shepherd because of the treachery of wolves, and he must be provided with a fold in order that the sheep placed there may render richer the land with the wealth of their dung. The shepherd must have a hut in which a faithful dog shall pass the night with him. Our peasant should have also a cow barn and mangers: one manger for horses, one for cattle, and if prosperity smiles a bit and Fortune is kind, he should get an ass and a stallion for a stud. He will need also sheep, goats, oxen, cows, heifers, bullocks, bull calves and mules. He must have boxes, nets, and long lines to trap hares, does, kids, stags, hinds, and young mules. This is the equipment of the peasant. He will require also brachet hounds, and mastiffs.

U.T. Holmes, Jr., *Daily Living in the Twelfth Century based on the Observations of Alexander Neckam*

TRADESMEN OF PARIS, Late Twelfth Century

He [Gwain] looks at the entire town peopled by many fine people, at the changers of gold and silver moneys, all under cover; he sees the open places, the streets completely filled with good workmen who are practising their different trades. This man is making helmets, this one mailed coats; another makes saddles, and another shields. One man manufactures bridles, another spurs. Some polish sword blades, others full cloth, and some are dyers. Some prick the fabrics and others clip them, and these are melting gold and silver. They make rich and lovely pieces: cups, drinking vessels, and eating bowls, and jewels worked in with enamels; also rings, belts, and pins. One could certainly believe that in that town there was a fair every day, it was so full of wealth. It was filled with wax, pepper, cochineal dye, and with vair and gris [fine furs], and every kind of merchandise.

Chretien de Troyes, *Conte del Graal*

59. Dyeing cloth, twelfth century

TWELFTH CENTURY CARPENTERS DID THE WORK OF HOUSEBUILDERS, SHIPBUILDERS, COOPERS, WHEELWRIGHTS CARTWRIGHTS. . . .

The carpenters who came there had great axes dangling from their necks, plainers and adzes draped at their sides . . . they brought timber from the ships and dragged it to the spot . . . already bored and smoothed off. They brought, in large casks, the joining pegs completely dressed. Before it was evening they had constructed a wooden castle; they made a ditch around it.

Wace of Jersey, *Rou*

Religion

THE BEGINNING OF HOLY CHURCH AND AFTER

Sir William Dugdale in his Antiquities of Warwickshire *(1656) gives us the following quotation from an old Ms. Legend of St John the Baptist:*

And ye shall understand and know how the *evens* were first found in old time. In the beginning of holy church, it was so that the people came to the church with candles burning, and would *wake,* and come with light toward the church in their devotions. And after they fell to lechery and songs, dances, harping, piping; and also to gluttony and sin; and so turned the holiness to cursedness. Wherefore holy fathers ordained the people to leave that *waking,* and to fast the *even.* But it is called *vigilia,* that is *waking* in English, and it is called *even* for at *even* they were wont to come to church.

EADMER DESCRIBES CANTERBURY'S ANCIENT CATHEDRAL, c.1060

This was that very church which had been built by Romans, as Bede witnesses in his history, and which was duly arranged in some parts in imitation of the Church of the blessed Prince of the Apostles, Peter, in which his holy relics are exalted by the veneration of the whole world. The venerable Odo had translated the body of the blessed Wilfrid, Archbishop of York, from Ripon to Canterbury, and had worthily placed it in a more lofty receptable, to use his own words – that is to say, in the great altar which was constructed of rough stones and mortar, close to the wall at the eastern part of the prebytery. Afterwards another altar was placed at a convenient distance before the aforesaid altar, and dedicated in honour of our Lord Jesus Christ, at which altar the divine mysteries were daily celebrated. In this altar the blessed Elphege had solemnly deposited the head of St. Swithun, which he had brought with him when he was translated from Winchester to Canterbury, and also many relics of other saints. To reach these altars, a certain crypt which the Romans call a confessionary had to be ascended by means of several steps from the choir of singers. This crypt was fabricated beneath in the likeness of the Confessionary of St. Peter, the vault of which was raised so high that the part above could only be reached by many steps. Within this crypt had at the east an altar, in which was enclosed the head of the blessed Furseus, as of old it was asserted. Moreover, the single passage [of entrance], which ran westward from the curved part of the crypt, reached from thence up to the resting-place of the blessed Dunstan, which was separated from the crypt itself by a strong wall; for that holy father was interred before the aforesaid steps at a great depth in the ground, and at the head of the saint stood the matutinal [morning] altar. Thence the choir of singers was extended westward into the body of the church, and shut out from the multitude by a decent enclosure.

In the next place, beyond the middle of the length of the body, there were two towers which projected beyond the aisles of the church. The south tower had an altar in the midst of it, which was dedicated to the blessed Pope Gregory. At the side was the principal door of the church, which of old by the English and even now is called the Suthdore, and is often mentioned by this name in the law-books of the ancient kings. For all disputes from the whole kingdom, which cannot legally be referred to the King's Court or to the hundreds or counties, do in this place receive judgment. Opposite to this tower and on the north there was another tower in honour of the blessed Martin, and had about it cloisters for the use of the monks. And as the first tower was devoted to legal contentions and judgments of this world, so in the second the younger brethren were instructed in the knowledge of the offices of the church, for the different seasons and hours of the day and night.

The extremity of the church was adorned by the oratory of Mary, the blessed Mother of God, which was so constructed that access could only be had to it by steps. At its eastern part there was an altar consecrated to the worship of that Lady, which had within it the head of the blessed virgin Austroberta. When the priest performed the divine mysteries at this altar he had his face turned to the east, towards the people who stood below. Behind him to the west was the pontifical chair, constructed with handsome workmanship and of large stones and cement, and far removed from the Lord's table, being contiguous to the wall of the church which embraced the entire area of the building. And this was the plan of the church of Canterbury.

Eadmer, *De reliquiis S. Audoeni,* translated in
Willis, *Architectural History of Canterbury Cathedral*

60. Pilgrimage to the shrine of St Edmund, King of East Anglia, Bury St Edmunds. Domesday Book tells us that the needs of the pilgrims were ministered to by 'eighty less five bakers, brewers, tailors, washerwomen, shoemakers, robemakers, cooks, porters, *dispensatores.* All these wait daily upon the Saint, the Abbot, and the Brethren.'

BRIEF SURVEY FROM THE ABBEY OF BURY ST EDMUNDS, 1045-1098

At the anniversary of the burial of King William [died 9 September 1087] the lord abbot, Baldwin, has appointed that every year on the same day 10 shillings shall be given as a charitable gift, and on the day of the death of his queen, namely Maud, he has decreed that the same amount, namely 10 shillings, shall be paid to us in addition as a perpetual obligation. And in order that it may be established whence this money, namely 20 shillings, shall be paid for the sake of the brethren, the same lord abbot has decreed in full chapter in the presence of all, that it should be paid from the manor of Warkton which the said King William gave to St. Edmund for the soul of the aforesaid queen [died 2 November 1083], since the abbot judges it proper that the brethren should enjoy something better as food on the anniversaries of those whose names they do not hesitate to repeat in their prayers before God frequently and, so to say, without intermission. At the anniversary of the burial of King Edward the above-mentioned abbot has appointed 10 shillings as a charitable gift for his brethren that they may remember his soul with greater devotion, whoever comes after me as abbot that 10 shillings shall be given on my behalf on the anniversary of my coming as abbot, namely on 19 August.

Anglo-Saxon Documents, A.J. Robertson

RELIGIOUS EDUCATION

Geoffrey of Auxerre, St Bernard's pupil, private secretary and biographer, speaks of him in this memorial sermon on his master.

It is true that, comparing spiritual things with spiritual, he spake sublimely; yet did he not shrink from condescending to untaught and simple folk. But that which in him seemed the more humble was perchance more wonderful then, and is now the sweeter to our taste. For how often were we delighted then to hear, and are delighted now to recall, how he was wont to spur on those rustic men and poor simple women to duties of humanity which became their station. For he taught them that, when one of their neighbours, as often happens – *uti assolet* – lacks bread, they should cheerfully lend unto him until he could repay; or when another

61. The Western Doorway, Llandaff Cathedral, Glamorganshire. The see is regarded as the oldest in Great Britain with a religious community here in the sixth century. The cathedral itself was begun about 1120, erected by Bishop Urban.

neighbour, perchance otherwise busied, had prepared no food, that they should generously send him a few vegetables and share with him their scanty pulse. So also he taught them to keep the faith of lawful wedlock, nor transgress (as men ungrateful to God's gift), the bounds of wholesome indulgence. Moreover, he bade them pay their dues, or give their tithes without fraud, to Him who could more justly claim for himself nine-tenths than the husbandman could claim even one-tenth. For it was He who both made the earth and gave unto the labourer his arms and his strength; it is He also who sends His frost to lock in the seed that has been sown, His rains to water it, His vernal warmth to cherish it, and His summer suns to ripen it; so that, unless He gave the increase, the plougher would lose his labour. Moreover, he would studiously warn them to beware of magicians and their sacrilegious charms; and that, being unable to pursue with swords those who harmed them, they should not attack them with their tongues; nor should they, by cheating each other, follow after scanty gains to their own grievous destruction; but let them remember Him who, being rich, was made poor for our sake; and let them bear in mind that the poor man is left unto Him.

Patrologia Latina, Migne

AN EARLY ENFEOFFMENT ON THE LAND OF THE ABBEY OF BURY ST EDMUNDS, 1066-1087

Be it known to all of you that Peter, a knight of King William, will become the feudal man of St. Edmund and of Baldwin the abbot, by performing the ceremony of homage. He will do this by permission of the king and with the consent of the monks, and in return for the service which will here be stated, saving always the fealty which he owes to the king, the fief having been freely received except for the six royal forfeitures. Peter promises that he will serve on behalf of the abbot within the kingdom with 3 or 4 knights at their own expense if he has been previously summoned by the king and the abbot to take part in the earlier or later levies of the king's host. If he is bidden to plead on the abbot's behalf at any place within the kingdom, they shall likewise bear their own expense. But if the abbot shall take him anywhere else, then the expense of his service shall be borne by the abbot. Besides this, he shall equip a knight for service without or within the kingdom where and when the abbot shall require to have this knight as his own retainer. This is the description of the fee. The land of Edric the blind [probably Edric of Axfield] with 14 freemen and as many peasants; Wulfmaer the priest and his land with 3 freemen; Thorkill with his wife and land; and Guthred and his land; Grimbald the priest; Leofstan; Gunnulf; Osfrith; Acwuf; Wlfgive; Leofgeat; Wlfgife; Lufe; Wlfricus; Tonhardus; Thurstan; Oslac; Thurstan 'Cati'; Thurstan 'Rumpe'; Godwine the priest; Glupus with the following 7 freemen who are his neighbours: Thurkeda; Brother; Brunstan; Wulfmaer; Godgive; Deorun; Stubhart. All these and their lands are free. Witnesses on behalf of the abbot.

Robert Blunt; Frodo; Robert 'de Vals'; Arnulf; Fulcher; Burgard; Jocelyn. Witnesses on behalf of Peter: Rannulf; Richard; Herdwin; Philip; Ralph 'fachiez'; William, son of Robert; Thorold 'papilio'.

62. Winchester Cathedral: west wall of north transept, eleventh century

LANFRANC'S CANTERBURY CONSTITUTIONS

Lanfranc was archbishop of Canterbury from 1070 to 1089 and worked in close accord with William the Conqueror. He had been prior of Bec in Normandy.

On the second day in Lent, before the brethren enter the Chapter House, the keeper of the books should have the volumes collected in the said Chapter House and spread out upon a carpet, save only such as shall have been given out for reading during the past year, which must be brought in by the brethren, each bearing his own volume in his own hands, according to the warning which the aforesaid keeper shall have given in the Chapter of the day before.

Then let the sentence of St Benedict's Rule be read concerning the observance of Lent, and let a sermon be made upon this theme; after which the keeper shall read his list of the books borrowed by the brethren for the year past.

Each monk, hearing his name pronounced, shall render back the book which had been committed to him for reading during the year; and, if he be conscious of not having read it to the end, he shall fall down and confess his fault and beseech indulgence. Then shall the said keeper give unto each of the brethren some other book to read, distributing them in order and writing down on the spot both the titles of the books and the names of the readers.

Lanfrance, *Opera,* edited by J.A. Giles

WULSTAN, BISHOP OF WORCESTER, PROFESSES OBEDIENCE TO LANFRANC, ARCHBISHOP OF CANTERBURY, *c.* 1070

By 1087, Wulstan was the only English-born and pre-Norman Conquest bishop to survive.

This custom of holy religious observance prevails: when a bishop is consecrated he should reverently go to the metropolis [of his province] and there make profession of obedience to the metropolitan; he should also leave a written profession of the same obedience to the metropolitan and his successors. But at the time when I, Wulfstan, was ordained bishop of the Hwiccas in the city of Worcester, Stigand had seized the holy church of Canterbury to which all my predecessors had been subjected; by force and guile he had expelled the metropolitan from his see; and in contempt of

63. The Norman tower, Tewkesbury Abbey, Gloucestershire

the apostolic see he had rashly presumed to wear the *pallium* which he had seized. For this reason he was summoned, excommunicated and condemned by the Roman pontiffs, Leo, Victor, Stephen, Nicholas and Alexander. Nevertheless, in the hardness of his heart he persisted in his obduracy. During this time therefore orders were given throughout England by the popes forbidding anyone to reverence him as bishop; further, no one was to go to him for ordination. For this reason some bishops of the English at that time went for consecration to Rome, and others to France, whilst others again had recourse to their fellow-bishops at home. But I went to Aldred, bishop of the church of York, and I have put off making my profession of canonical obedience down to this day. Now, therefore, I, a bishop, and according to the canons, offer to you, Lanfranc, metropolitan of the holy church of Canterbury, my profession of obedience to your orders and to those of your successors. And as God is my witness I promise to keep my pledge.

SEPARATION OF SPIRITUAL AND LAY JURISDICTION, 1072

William, by the grace of God king of the English, to R. Bainard, and G. de Magneville, and Peter de Valoines, and all my liege men of Essex, Hertfordshire, and Middlesex greeting.

Know ye and all my liege men resident in England, that I have by common council, and by the advice of the archbishops, bishops, abbots and chief men of my realm, determined that the episcopal laws be mended as not having been kept properly nor according to the decrees of the sacred canons throughout the realm of England, even to my own times.

Accordingly I command and charge you by royal authority that no bishop nor archdeacon do hereafter hold pleas of episcopal laws in the Hundred, nor bring a cause to the judgment of secular men which concerns the rule of souls. But whoever shall be impleaded by the episcopal laws for any cause or crime, let him come to the place which the bishop shall choose and name for this purpose, and there answer for his cause or crime, and not according to the Hundred but according to the canons and episcopal laws, and let him do right to God and his bishop.

But if any one, being lifted up with pride, refuse to come to the bishop's court, let him be summoned there several times, and if by this means, even, he come not to obedience, let the authority and justice of the king or sheriff be exerted. And he who refuses to come to the bishop's judgment shall make good the bishop's law for every summons.

This too I absolutely forbid that any sheriff, reeve, or king's minister, or any other layman, do in any wise concern himself with the laws which belong to the bishop, or bring another man to judgment save in the bishop's court. And let judgment be nowhere undergone but in the bishop's see or in that place which the bishop appoints for this purpose.

Ancient Laws and Institutes of England, I, 213

64. The choir of Canterbury Cathedral in the Early English style, 1150-1250

65. The Norman gatehouse of the Benedictine abbey of Bury St Edmunds, 1120-1148

RELIGIOUS SCHOOL AT CANTERBURY FOR OBLATES AND NOVICES, c.1075

Monasteries were the centre of an outstanding revival in religious life in England during the late eleventh century and the whole of the twelfth.

When a boy is to be offered [i.e. made an oblate], let a round tonsure be made on his head, and carrying the host in his hands and the cup with the wine, as the custom is, let him be offered by his parents after the Gospel to the priest who celebrates mass. When the priest has accepted the offering, the aforesaid parents should wrap the boy's hands in the pall with which the altar is covered and part of which hangs down in front, and then the abbot shall receive him. After which the said parents . . . should immediately promise that . . . the boy will never leave the order he has accepted. . . . This promise they should make beforehand in writing in the presence of witnesses and afterwards place it on the altar.

The prior ought to make a noise to waken the brethren at such hour in the morning as the boys when they have said their several prayers can see to read in the cloister, and when they begin to read let them for some time read aloud, sitting separate from each other, so that one cannot touch another with his hands or clothes. No child shall dare to make a sign or say a word to another except in the sight and hearing of the master; nor get up from the place in which he sits unless told or given leave to do so. Wherever the children go there should be a master between every two of them. When they pass in front of the brethren they should bow to them, and the brethren remaining seated should do the same. One lantern should serve for two; if there are three, the third should carry a second lantern; if there are more, the same arrangement should be observed. They should not put anything into anyone's hand or take anything from anyone's hand, except in the case of the abbot, the senior prior, or their own master, and that not everywhere but only in proper places, where it cannot or ought not to be otherwise. The precentor, too, when he is in their school may give or take from them a book from which to sing or read. If they are serving at the altar, too, they can give or take as their orders require. They should be flogged in a chapter of their own, as their elders are in the great chapter. When they go to confession they should go to the abbot or prior or those specially assigned for the purpose by the abbot. While one confesses another should sit on the steps, and the master should sit close by outside the chapter-house. If they go into the refectory after the verse which is said before food, or into choir at the hours after the Gloria of the first psalm, they are to go to their places and bow as usual, while their master is to go to the place set apart for those who are tardy: but the boy who waits at the abbot's table is not to have any abstinence from food or drink imposed on him except by the abbot's orders. But if by his orders it is imposed, either he must be pardoned or he must be removed from the abbot's table. In choir, if the abbot is there, no one may strike them, no one order them out except by his direction. When he is away, the precentor may chastise them for things to do with his office, and the prior for other things, in which they behave childishly. Wherever they are, no one except the persons above-mentioned may make signs to them, no one may smile at them.

No one shall go into their school, no one shall speak to them anywhere, unless leave to go in or to talk to them has been given by the abbot or prior. They are never to read or do anything else

66. Crypt of Worcester Cathedral (1084-1092)

in bed at midday but to cover themselves up and keep quiet. A monk of more than ordinary gravity and discretion shall be master over the other masters, one who may know how, when he has heard any charge against them, to inflict punishment in moderation on those who are at fault or to let them off. When they go to bed the master shall stand by them at night with lighted candles until they are covered up.

Young men, whether those who have been brought up in the monastery or those coming in from the outside world who are given in charge to masters, shall be looked after in most things as is before provided with regard to the boys. They shall, as is above said, sit separate from each other; shall never leave the place where they go to bed, the masters shall stand by them at night with lighted candles until they are covered up.

Lanfranc's *Constitutions*, translated from Wilkins, *Concilia*, by A.F. Leach, *Educational Charters and Documents 598 to 1909*

CLUNIACS, 1077

Much of the intellectual activity and of the new learning came from France to the religious life of England.

. . . I William de Warren and Gundreda my wife were going on a pilgrimage to St. Peter's at Rome, and in passing through France we visited various monasteries to pray. We learnt in Burgundy that we could not go forward safely because of the war between the Pope and the Emperor so we stopped at the great and holy monastery of St. Peter at Cluny and there prayed to St. Peter. We found the holiness, piety and devotion there very great as also the respect which the good prior paid to us with the whole convent, and they received us into their fraternity. We thus began to have more love and devotion towards that house and that order than towards any of the other houses which we had seen. But Hugh, the holy abbot, was not then at home. It had long been our wish and intention, as advised by Archbishop Lanfranc to found some religious house for our sins and the safety of our souls; and we then thought that we should not get any greater happiness than by making one of any order than that of Cluny. So we sent and asked Hugh the abbot and all his holy congregation that they would let us have two, or three, or four monks out of their holy flock and we would give them a church which we had built of

stone in place of a wooden church under the castle of Lewes. This had of old been dedicated to St. Pancras and this we would give them with, at the first, as much land and beasts and goods as would keep twelve monks there. But the holy abbot at first was stern towards us in hearing our request because of the distance of a foreign land and especially because of the sea. But after we had obtained licence from our lord, King William, to bring monks from Cluny to English land, and after the abbot on his part had sought the king's wish, at last he granted and sent to us four of his monks, Lanzo and three companions. To them we gave at first all that we had promised them and confirmed this by a writing which we sent to the abbot and convent of Cluny, for they refused to send us monks before they had confirmation from us and from the king . . .

Lewes cartulary, extract in Sir W. Dugdale, *Monasticon Anglicanum, A History of the Abbies and other Monasteries, Hospitals, Frieries and Cathedral and Collegiate Churches,* edited by J. Caley, H. Ellis and Rev. Bulkeley Bandinel

WRIT OF WILLIAM I IN FAVOUR OF THE ABBEY OF BURY ST EDMUNDS, 1077

William (by the grace of God), king of the English, to Lanfranc, archbishop of Canterbury, and Geoffrey, bishop of Coutances, and Robert, count of Eu, and Hugh of Montfort-sur-Risle, and to his other magnates of England, greeting. I command and order you that you cause St. Augustine and Abbot Scotland to be repossessed of the borough of Fordwich, which Haimo the sheriff

---

67. Fountains, the Cistercian Abbey of St Mary, named after the hillside springs, *ad fontes.* Some Benedictine monks left their abbey, St Mary's at York, in 1132, encouraged to do so by Archbishop Thurstan. They received help from St Bernard of Clairvaux, who sent one of his monks to advise them. They became Cistercians, and built this famous abbey, standing in wide expanses, three miles from Ripon. It shows the typical Cistercian arrangement of the church, presbytery, cloisters and conventual buildings, and a certain plain and unadorned austerity. Its chancel was enlarged and rebuilt in the thirteenth century. The most notable feature of the church is the eastern transept or Nine Altars, which inspired its only English counterpart at Durham.

Fountains Abbey, a blending of beauty and strength, shows also boldness in its complex of buildings, and ingenuity in making good use of the swiftly flowing waters of the River Skell. It has been called an architectural triumph 'characterised by what is almost a fastidious elegance'.

[of Kent] now holds, and also of all the other lands which Aethelsige, whom I sent into exile, either by carelessness or fear or greed gave away or allowed to be alienated. And if anyone has taken away anything of them by violence, you are to compel him willy-nilly to restore it.
Farewell.

Witness: Odo, bishop of Bayeux, at the dedication of Bayeux.

WILLIAM I AND POPE GREGORY VII, 1080, 1081

To Gregory [VII], most excellent shepherd of holy Church, William, king of the English and duke of the Normans, greeting and friendship. Your legate, Hubert, most holy father, coming to me on your behalf, has admonished me to profess allegiance to you and your successors, and to think better regarding the money which my predecessors were wont to send to the Church of Rome. I have consented to the one but not to the other. I have not consented to pay fealty, nor will I now, because I never promised it, nor do I find that my predecessors ever paid it to your predecessors. The money has been negligently collected during the past three years when I was in France; but now that I have returned by God's mercy to my kingdom, I send you by the hands of the aforesaid legate what has already been collected, and the remainder shall be forwarded by the envoys of our trusty Archbishop Lanfranc when the opportunity for so doing shall occur. Pray for us and for the state of our realms, for we always loved your predecessors and it is our earnest desire above all things to love you most sincerely, and to hear you most obediently.

Letter of William I (1080)
English Historical Documents Vol.II

The king of the English, although in certain matters he does not comport himself as devoutly as we might hope, nevertheless in that he has neither destroyed nor sold the Churches of God; that he has taken pains to govern his subjects in peace and justice; that he has refused his assent to anything detrimental to the apostolic see, even when solicited by certain enemies of the cross of Christ; and that he has compelled the priests on oath to put away their wives and the laity to forward the tithes they were withholding from us – in all these respects he has shown himself more worthy of approbation and honour than other kings. . . .

Letter of Gregory VII (1081
English Historical Documents Vol.II

ARGUMENTS OF BOTH SIDES, 1084

I have received and read your letter which you sent me by the bearer of mine, and some things in it have displeased me. I do not approve of your vituperation against Pope Gregory, or of your calling him Hildebrand and his legates bad names, or of your advocacy of Clement. For it is written that a man should neither be praised nor condemned in his lifetime nor his neighbours disparaged. What men are now is as yet unknown to mankind, and also what they will be in the sight of God. Yet I do not believe that the emperor would have ventured to take so grave a step without good reason, nor do I think that without the help of God

68. Chapter House, Wenlock Abbey, twelfth century

he would have been able to achieve so great a victory. I do not recommend your coming to England unless you first obtain permission from the king of the English. For our island has not yet rejected the former [Pope] nor pronounced judgment as to whether it should obey the latter. When the arguments on both sides have been heard, if it so happen, it will be possible to see more clearly what ought to be done.

Letter of Lanfranc to Hugh the Cardinal (1084)
English Historical Documents, Vol.II

CONCERNING THE DEATH OF WILLIAM, DUKE OF THE NORMANS AND KING OF THE ENGLISH, WHO CAUSED HOLY CHURCH TO LIVE IN PEACE

In the year of our Lord 1087, King William of most pious memory, when returning from the sack and burning of Mantes, began to be afflicted with weakness. His stomach rejected food and drink, his breathing became difficult, and he was shaken with sobs. Thus his strength began to ebb away. He therefore ordered a little dwelling to be prepared at the church of St. Gervase, which is in the suburbs of Rouen, and there in his weakness he betook himself to bed. Who shall reveal the anxiety then felt for the state of the Church, and for its impending afflictions, and who shall describe the tears then poured out to hasten the divine pity? The king did not grieve so much by reason of his approaching death, as because he knew the future. He declared that after his death disasters would visit his Norman homeland, and subsequently events were to show that he spoke the truth [Allusion to disturbances in Normandy, time of Duke Robert II]. Then there came to console the king venerable prelates and many other servants of God. Among these were William [William 'Bonne Anne', archbishop of Rouen, 1079-1110], archbishop of the aforesaid city, and Gilbert, bishop of Lisieux, and John, the doctor, and Gerard, the chancellor, and also Robert, count of Mortain, the king's brother, in whom the king reposed great confidence because he was his close kinsman. Wherefore the king ordered the same Robert, who was then advanced in years, to summon to his side the officials of his household and he commanded them to enumerate one by one all the things which were in his household, to wit crowns and arms, vessels and books,

69. Winchester Cathedral; the treasury in the south transept, mid-twelfth century

and ecclesiastical vestments. And, as it seemed good to him, he declared what ought to be given to churches, to the poor, and finally to his sons. He allowed William, his son, to have his crown, his sword, and his gold sceptre studded with gems. Wherefore Archbishop William and others who were present were afraid lest the king should be too harsh to his first-born son, Robert, since they knew that a wound frequently cut and cauterized may cause a greater pain to him who bears it. For this reason trusting in the invincible patience which the king had always shown they gently urged him through Archbishop William that he would not disdain their counsel. At first the king showed some bitterness at this intervention, but, after a little, somewhat rallying his strength, he seemed to consider the great injuries he had received from Robert, and then he spoke: "Since he has disdained to come here himself, it is with your witness and with the witness of God that I shall act. With such testimony I declare that I forgive him all the sins he has committed against me and I grant him the whole duchy of Normandy. This, before God and in the presence of the magnates of my court, I previously promised him. It will be your duty however to admonish him. I have pardoned him so often that he has learnt to take advantage of my leniency, and now he has brought down his father's grey hairs in sorrow to the grave. By so doing he has broken the commands of God and incurred the wrath of him who is our common Father." Having spoken thus, the king asked that the Visitation and the Unction of the Sick should be celebrated, and Holy Communion was administered to him in due form by the hand of the archbishop. Thus he departed this life, and, as we believe, went happily to his rest. He died on 10 September [more correctly 9 September] in the fifty-ninth year of his age, having reigned over England for twenty-two years.

This king excelled in wisdom all the princes of his generation, and among them all he was outstanding in the largeness of his soul. He never allowed himself to be deterred from prosecuting any enterprise because of the labour it entailed, and he was ever undaunted by danger. So skilled was he in his appraisal of the true significance of any event, that he was able to cope with adversity, and to take full advantage in prosperous times of the false promises of fortune. He was great in body and strong, tall in stature but not ungainly. He was also temperate in eating and

70. The south porch, Malmesbury Abbey, Wiltshire, twelfth century. The medallions on the outer arch depict scenes from the New Testament; the medallions on two other arches depict scenes from the Old Testament.

drinking. Especially was he moderate in drinking, for he abhorred drunkenness in all men and disdained it more particularly in himself and at his court. He was so sparing in his use of wine and other drink, that after his meal he rarely drank more than thrice. In speech he was fluent and persuasive, being skilled at all times in making clear his will. If his voice was harsh, what he said was always suited to the occasion. He followed the Christian discipline in which he had been brought up from childhood, and whenever his health permitted he regularly, and with great piety, attended Christian worship each morning and evening and at the celebration of Mass. And so, at last, it seemed to everyone that he could be given no more honourable grave than in the church which out of love he had built at Caen to the honour of God and of St. Stephen, the first martyr. This, indeed, he had previously arranged. Therefore in that church he was buried, and a monument of gilded silver was erected over his tomb by his son, William, who succeeded him as king of England.

Written by a monk of St. Stephen's, Caen,
within a few years of the death of William the Conqueror.

WRIT OF WILLIAM II GRANTING A HUNDRED COURT TO BE HELD IN FEE-FARM BY THE ABBEY OF THORNEY, 1087-1100

William, king of the English, to all the sheriffs and barons of Huntingdonshire, greeting. Know that I have granted the hundred of Normancross to the abbot and monks of Thorney to be held in fee-farm for an annual rent of 100 shillings which I order them to pay to my sheriff at Huntingdon. And I forbid any of my officers to do them injury or insult in respect of this.

WRIT OF HENRY I ADDRESSED TO GILBERT, SHERIFF OF SURREY, 1100

Henry, king of the English, to Gilbert, sheriff of Surrey, greeting. I order and command you to give quittance to the land of St. Peter of Westminster and of Abbot Gilbert which is in my demesne within the park and the forest of Windsor, and particularly 8 hides of the manor of Pyrford which my father granted to the same church to be for ever quit from all geld [national land tax] and scot [assessed contribution] and all other things. And in particular

71. The South Doorway of Kilpeck Church, Herefordshire, 1150-1175

I call them quit of the new geld on account of hidage and of all other gelds, as my father and my brother granted it by their writs.

Witness: R. Bigot at Bushley.

WIVES OF PRIESTS, 1093

Boso, a knight of the Bishop of Durham, ill for three days, had many visions, and described a guide who led him through pleasant and disturbing experiences. He recognized monks of Durham, and heard that they were on the verge of destruction.

So they led me to where I could observe all the inhabitants of this province assembled in a field of immense extent; they were mounted on very fat horses, and (according to their usual custom) were carrying long spears; and as they tilted with these the one against the other, the shivering of the lances occasioned a considerable noise, and the riders swelled with pride. Hereupon my guide asked me if I knew who these persons were; and my reply was, that I recognised first one, then another; and, lastly, that I could distinguish every single individual of their number. Whereupon he added, 'All these persons are on the very verge of destruction'; and immediately as he spoke the words, the whole multitude vanished away like smoke from before my eyes.

. . . Casting my eyes over the field once more, I saw it covered, for some miles, with a large body of women; and while I was in astonishment at their number, my guide informed me that they were the wives of priests. He spoke thus: 'These wretched women, and those persons also who are consecrated for sacrificing to God, but who, unworthy, have become enchained in the pleasures of the flesh, are awaiting the eternal sentence of condemnation, and the severe punishment of the fires of hell.'

A Vision of the Dead, 1093, Simeon of Durham, translated by Rev. J. Stevenson in *The Church Historians of England*

CHAPTER AT CANTERBURY, Late Eleventh Century

When each day the smallest bell begins to ring for chapter, all the brethren sitting in choir shall at once rise and stand facing the east and waiting, while the brethren elsewhere in the monastery shall enter the choir. No one at that time shall hold a book, nor read nor look at a book; no one shall for any reason whatever remain seated in the cloister; but when the bell ceases to ring all in order shall follow their leader out of church.

When the brethren are seated in chapter the superior gives a sign, and the reader, after asking a blessing, reads and gives out the customary lesson and notices. Then, after the sermon, the superior says, 'Let us now speak of matters of discipline.' If anyone is accused who bears a name common to one or more others, and the accuser does not make it absolutely definite beyond doubt, then all of that name shall at once arise and humbly offer themselves for penance, until the accuser says clearly whom he means to accuse. This he shall do by specifying, if possible, the dignity in order or office, as follows: 'Dom Edward the priest,' or 'deacon,' or 'subdeacon,' or 'sacristan,' or 'master of the children or juniors,' or something of that sort. . . .

The accuser shall not, during the chapter in question, inflict punishment on him he accuses. The brother who is lying prostrate shall, when questioned in the usual way, answer *mea culpa* . . .

He who is to undergo punishment shall be scourged either with a single stout rod while he lies in his shift on the ground, or with a bundle of finer rods while he sits with his back bare. In each case he is punished at the discretion of the superior, who should consider the degree and the magnitude of the fault. While he is being scourged all the brethren should bow down with a kindly and brotherly compassion for him. No-one should speak, and no-one look at him save the seniors who may make intercession for him. No-one who is accused may in the same chapter accuse his previous accuser. The abbot or prior shall appoint him who is to administer punishment, taking care that neither child, nor junior, nor novice is bidden.

The Monastic Constitutions of Lanfranc,
translated by D. Knowles

MONKS AND MONASTERIES

The Abbey of Abingdon

'When beggars die there are no comets seen.'

Abbot Ordric who had returned to his own monastery . . . died after a long illness on the Feast of St Vincent. Then two men were promoted: Earl Harold became king of England; and Ealdred who

had been in charge of the abbey's external property became abbot of the monks at Abingdon.

At the next Eastertide [1066] an unusual star, called a comet [Halley's Comet, 'the long-haired star, and it first appeared on the eve of the Greater Litany, that is 24 April, and so shone all the week'.], appeared during a whole week, and this was taken to be an omen of great and untoward misfortune. Nor was this opinion falsified, for, in the month of September, the king of Norway, who bore the same same as the king of England, to wit, Harold, arrived in England and sought to gain the kingdom for himself as booty. He had the support of Earl Tostig, brother of Harold, our king. King Harold, however, meeting them outside the walls of York, destroyed both of them in battle with their followers.

Scarcely was this victory won, when Harold learnt from a messenger that William, count of Normandy, was threatening him, being prepared to offer him battle at Hastings unless the Kingdom was speedily yielded. William alleged that he had the better right to rule in England because Edward, the late king, had solemnly bequeathed the kingdom to him on the grounds of their kinship. Harold treated this message with scorn; placing too much confidence in his own strength, he advanced against the count with less than proper caution. Having been taunted as the weaker, he thought himself the stronger, and so, rushing into battle, he perished, together with all his companions.

William obtained the crown of England. Some submitted to him and swore fealty, but not a few departed into exile, hoping that they might find for themselves homes in other lands....

In those days not only was the abbey thus robbed of its estates, but the ornaments of the Sanctuary itself were stolen. An order came that the most precious of these should be sent to the queen....

---

72. The Cistercian Abbey of Rievaulx, in North Yorkshire near Helmsley, stands in a valley beside the River Rye from which comes its name. It was founded by the monks of St Bernard of Clairvaux about 1131. Henry I was its patron, and Thurstan, archbishop of York, and its third abbot, St Aildred, known as 'Bernard of the north', raised it to be the premier abbey of its order in England.

As with so many abbeys it has magnificent views, 'rivalled among monastic sites only by Fountains, which indeed it may be judged to surpass in the beauty of its architecture'

Meanwhile many plots were hatched in the kingdom of England by those who resented the unaccustomed yoke of foreign rule. Some of them hid in woods and islands, living like outlaws and plundering and attacking those who came their way. Others besought the Danes to come to England. And when the Danes came in answer to this call, they in their turn plundered the land and laid it waste by fire, and took away many into captivity. But they were not strong enough to wage a pitched battle or to subdue the kingdom, and so with their task unaccomplished they returned to their own land. . . .

While the lord abbot, Ealdred, was in captivity . . . Athelhelm was raised to the place of abbot by the express order of King William. He was a monk from the monastery of Jumiéges which is in Normandy. . . .

Thus the causes of strife and unrest in England were diminished, and the blessings of peace were enjoyed. Wherefore the abbot, turning his mind from secular affairs studied the needs of the church. He supervised the instruction in letters of those who were under his care, and watched over their practice of the religious life. He also added to the ornaments of the church, and sought to arrange for the future good conduct of its affairs. Besides all this he made plans to rebuild the Church from its foundations, and set aside money for that purpose. He died suddenly in the midst of these activities on 10 September 1084.

Abingdon Chronicle, *English Historical Documents,* Vol.II

THE MONASTIC BATH AT CANTERBURY, *c.* 1080

On the vigil of Thomas the apostle, if it be not a Sunday, the brethren shall be shaved and let those who will take a bath, in such wise that all shall have taken it two days before Christmas Day. If need be, they may take their bath even on the feast of the apostle. Let the bathing be ordered as follows. On the previous day the abbot or superior should appoint a devout and prudent senior and order him to take charge of the matter, to warn the brethren when to bathe, and to see that they conduct themselves in an orderly way. This senior shall see that all is ready, and that the right attendants are provided – mature men, neither children nor youths. If he see anything unfitting, let him tell the chamberlain, who shall at once remedy it. Then the senior shall return to the

73. The choir of Rievaulx Cistercian Abbey in Yorkshire, founded in Ryedale in 1132. 'It colonized the wilderness around, and later in its outlying granges.'

cloister and give notice to as many of the brethren as can be accommodated. Let him take care that the youths and novices go not all together, but with their elders. The brethren whom he has notified shall, when shaved, take their change of clothes and go to the place where the baths are prepared and there, taking off their clothes in due order as they are wont to do in the dormitory, they shall enter the bathing place as directed, and letting down the curtain that hangs before them they shall sit in silence in the bath. If anyone needs anything let him signal for it quietly, and a servant lifting the veil shall quickly take him what he wants and return at once. When he has finished washing himself, he shall not stay longer for pleasure but shall rise and dress and put on his shoes as he does in the dormitory, and having washed his hands shall return to the cloister. The young monks in ward shall go and return with their masters.

The Monastic Constitutions of Lanfranc,
translated by D. Knowles

EARLY ENFEOFFMENTS, 1083

i. In the year of the Incarnation of our Lord, one thousand and eighty-three. We Gilbert, the abbot, and the convent of Westminster have given to William Baynard a certain farm in the township of Westminster, by name 'Totenhals' to house him, and to be held by him for the whole of his life by the service of 1 knight. This is to be held by him with all things that pertain to it, as well and freely as ever Wulfric the thegn surnamed 'Bordewayte' held it from the church. Therefore William shall himself have the customs and the liberties which we have in the same, always excepting the aids which we shall receive from our knights as is done on the other lands of the church, and always excepting the tithes of this land which are assigned to our house in alms. We have granted these things to be held by him because of the love and service he has shown to our church; but on the condition that after his death the aforesaid land may remain bound to our church and quit of obligations. And in respect of this, the aforesaid William has pledged us that he will neither sell this land nor place it in pawn nor alienate it to anyone to the loss of our church. Witness: Robert the prior; William and Herbert, monks; Ralph Bainard; Herluin, brother of Cunzo; and many others.

ii. This privilege Robert, bishop of the church of Hereford, ordered to be recorded as agreed between him and Roger, son of Walter, concerning certain land which is called 'Hamme', and those things which pertain to it. This land belongs to the church of Holy Mary, the Mother of God, and of St. Ethelbert the martyr; and previously the said bishop held this land as his own demesne and for the sustenance of the church. This land the aforesaid knight, to wit, Roger, asked from the bishop through his friends, and he offered money in respect of it. But the bishop, by the counsel of his vassals, gave him this same land in return for a promise that he would serve the bishop with 2 knights as his father did whenever the need arose. This also was part of the contract: that the men of the bishop belonging to King's Hampton and Hereford, and to the estates pertaining thereto, should be at liberty to take timber from the wood for the use of the bishop as often as it should be needed for fuel or for repairing houses; and the pigs of these manors should feed in the same wood. This refers to the men belonging to the bishop. And this contract further enjoins that if Roger becomes a monk, or dies, neither his mother nor his wife nor his sons nor his brothers nor any of his kinfolk shall have rights in the aforesaid land, but let the bishop receive whatever in the estate may be to the profit of holy Church, and his men shall receive the same without any contradiction whatsoever. This instrument was executed in the year of the Incarnation of our Lord 1085, it being the eighth Indiction.

English Historical Documents, Vol.II

SOME CONSTITUTIONS AFFECTING PRIESTS, 1102

Anselm, archbishop of Canterbury, held a council at Westminster . . . Divers constitutions were made by authority of this council. . .

1. That priests should no more be suffered to have wives.
2. That no spiritual person should have the administration of any temporal office or function, nor sit in judgment of life and death.
3. That priests should not haunt ale houses, and further, that they should wear apparel of one manner of colour, and shoes after a comely fashion: for a little before that time, priests used to go very unseemly.
4. That no archdeaconries should be let to farm.

74. Durham Cathedral: nave, eleventh century. The standard of building now changed to reach the high level of Norman and Continental churches.

7. That no priests' sons should succeed their fathers in their benefices.
10. That no tithes should be given but to the church.
11. That no benefices should be bought or sold.
14. That abbots should not be made knights or men of war, but should sleep and eat within the precinct of their own house . . .
16. That no monks should be godfathers, nor nuns godmothers to any man's child.
19. That contracts made between man and woman without witnesses concerning marriage should be void if either of them denied it.
20. That such as did wear their hair long should be nevertheless so rounded, that part of their ears might appear.
22. That the bodies of the dead should not be buried but within their parishes.
24. That there should be no more buying and selling of men used in England, which was hitherto accustomed, as if they had been kine or oxen.

Holinshed, *Chronicles,* Vol.II

MILITARY MONKS KNOWN AS KNIGHTS TEMPLARS TOOK PART IN THE CRUSADES

'The templars became known as "the poor soldiers of Jesus Christ", and they always formed the right wing of the crusading army.'

Obedience is the first rule of life of the Knights Templars. There is no superfluity in diet or dress; necessity only is consulted. They live a common life, in sobriety and pleasant conversation, without the distraction of wives and children. Like the early Christians, the whole company have one purse, one heart, and one soul, and study nothing so much as to submit their individual wills to that of their superior. They neither sit idle nor wander for their pleasure, they earn their bread by mending their arms and clothes.

No insolent, or immoderate laughter, is heard among them. They abhor chess and dice; they neither hunt nor hawk. They detest actors, sorcerers, jongleurs, licentious songs and gay spectacles as vanities, falsehoods and follies. They cut their hair short, never adorn, seldom wash themselves; they pride themselves on neglected hair, soiled with dust and burnt by the sun and the

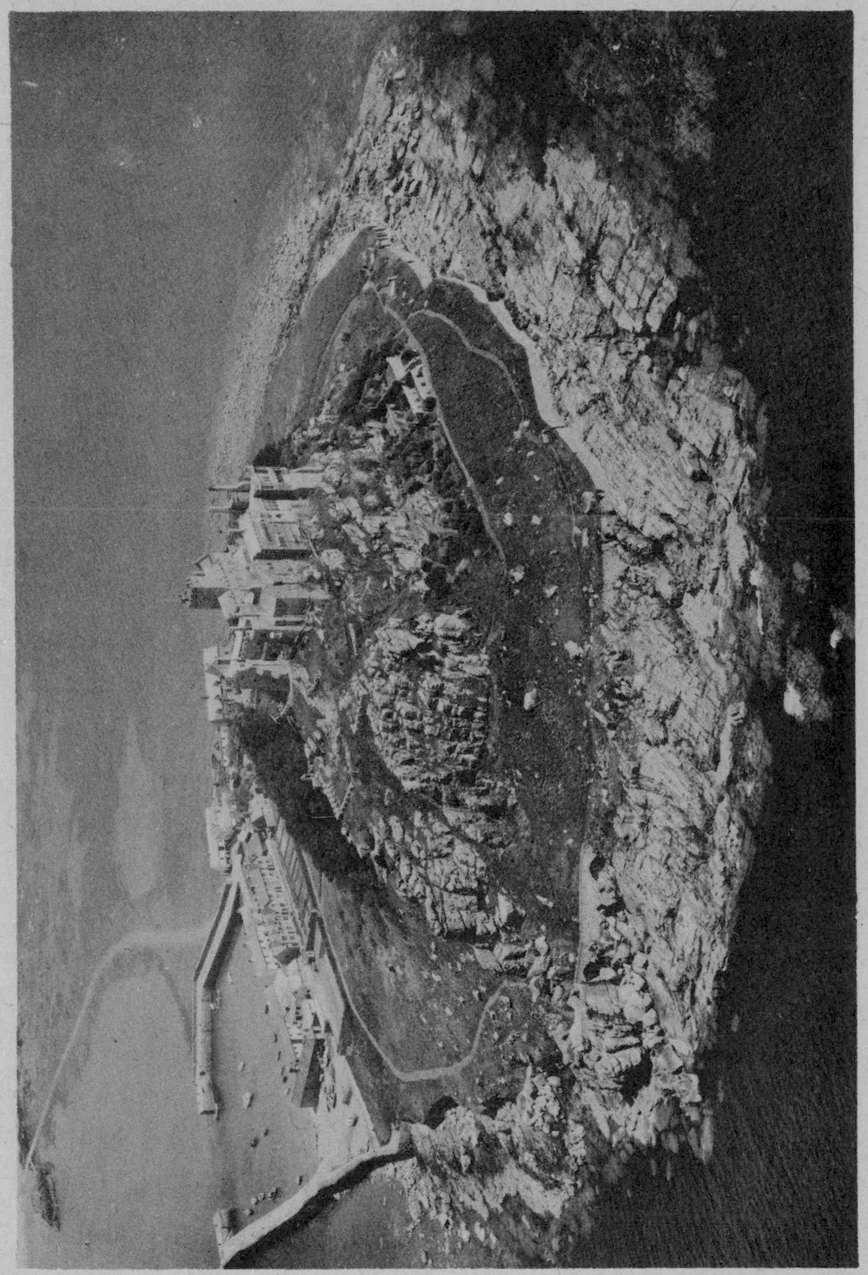

hauberk . . . Wonderful and strange it is to see them at once as gentle as lambs and as bold as lions. I hardly know whether to call them monks or knights – wanting as they do neither the meekness of the monk nor the courage of the knight.

St Bernard of Clairvaux, *Exhortatio ad milites Templi*

THE STATUES OF THE CISTERCIANS, *c.*1117

They rejected what was contrary to the Rule, namely wide cucullas [hoods], furs, linen, shirts, cowls and breeches, combs and blankets, mattresses, a wide variety of dishes in the refectory as well as fat and everything else which is opposed to the Rule. . . . And since they could not find either in the Rule or in the life of St Benedict that this teacher ever possessed churches, altars or offerings, burial places or tithes of other people, or bakeries or mills or farmhouses or serfs and that women had ever entered his monastery, nor was buried there anybody with the exception of his sister, they renounced all of that. . . . And behold, after the new soldiers of Christ, poor themselves as Christ was poor, had denounced the riches of this world, they began to consult with one another, how, with what work or occupation, they should provide in this world for themselves as well as for their arriving guests, rich and poor alike, who after the Rule were to be welcome as Christ. Since they realized that without their help they would be unable to fulfil perfectly the precepts of the Rule day and night, they decided to admit unlettered men as lay-brothers with the approval of the bishop and to treat them in life and death as their own, except for the rights reserved for choir monks. For the same reason they resolved to employ hired hands. They also wanted to take on landed properties which lay removed from human dwellings as well as vineyards and meadows and woods and waters in order to install mills, but only for their own use, and because of the fishing, also to keep horses and cattle and various

---

75. St Michael's Mount, a Benedictine priory, some years before the Conquest. The priory was established by about 1087. The island in Mount's Bay, two and a half miles by water from Penzance and connected with Mazarion at low water by a causeway of a third of a mile, belonged to the abbey of Mont St Michel till *c.*1415. After the Dissolution the priory was converted into a mansion. The tower faces the Atlantic:

'Where the great vision of the guarded Mount
Looks towards Namancos and Bayona's hold.'

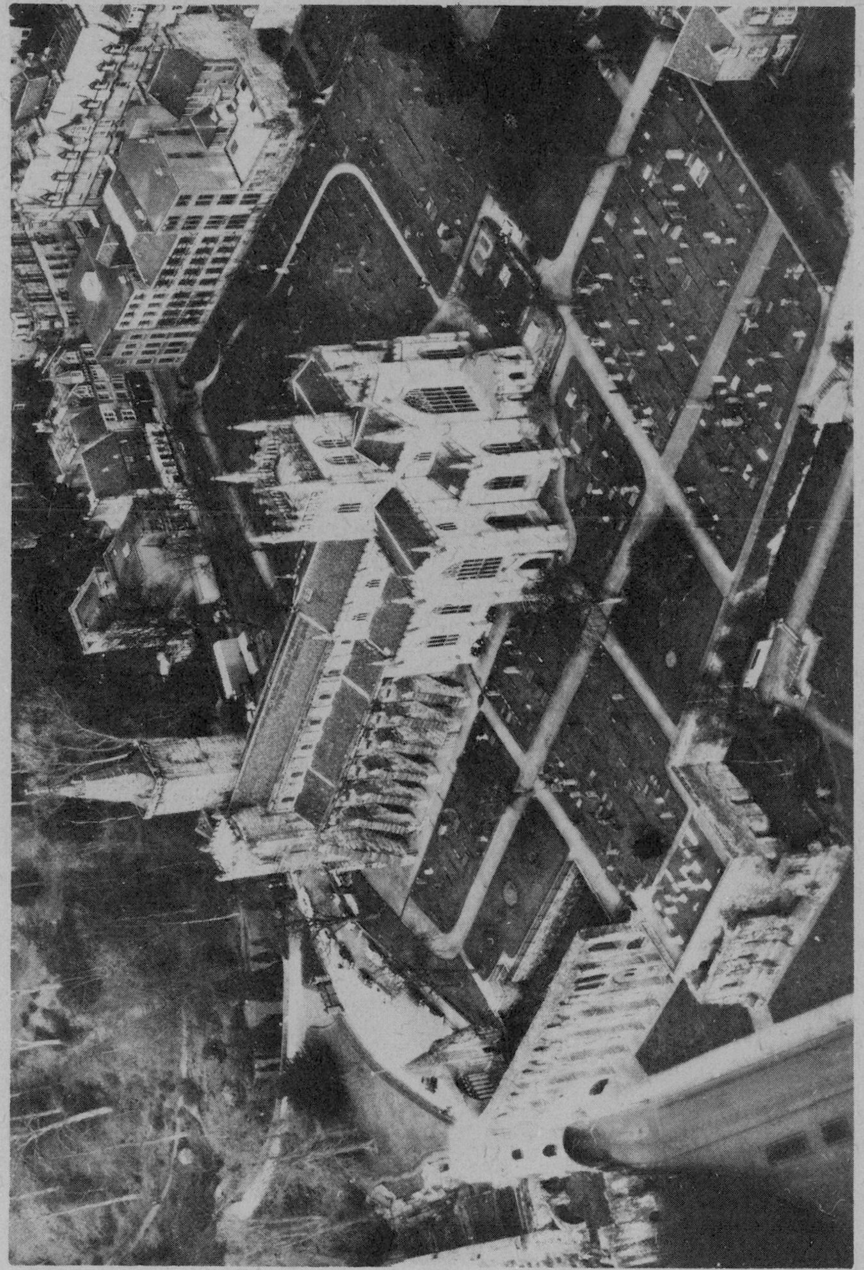

things that are needed and useful to men. They also decided that when they would have established farmhouses for the practice of agriculture, the said lay brothers should manage those houses and not monks, whose residence according to the Rule should be within their cloister. Since it was also known to those holy men that Saint Benedict had built the monasteries not in towns or in fortified places or in villages, but in places removed from the traffic of men, they promised to follow the same, and as he installed twelve monks together with a father abbot in each of the newly-erected monasteries, so they declared their wish to proceed in the same manner. . . .

Exordium Parvum, *The White Monks,* L.J. Lekai

THE WILD MAN COMES TO THE MONASTERY

. . . There was a time when I thought sweeter than
the quiet converse of monks, the cooing of the
ringdove flitting about the pool.

There was a time when I thought sweeter than
the sound of the little bell beside me, the
warbling of the blackbird from the gable and
the belling of the stag in the storm.

There was a time when I thought sweeter than
the voice of the lovely woman beside me, to hear
at matins the cry of the heath-hen of the
moor.

There was a time when I thought sweeter the
howling of wolves, than the voice of a
priest indoors, baa-ing and bleating.

There you like your ale with ceremony in the
drinking-halls, I like better to snatch a
drink of water in my palm from a spring.

---

76. The Benedictine Abbey of Dunfermline in Fife, three miles from the Firth of Forth. Monks from Christ Church, Canterbury, founded it about 1120. Their church had been erected by Queen Margaret, *c.*1070. Building was extended when King David I, in 1128, appointed Geoffrey, prior of Canterbury, to be the abbot. It became renowned throughout Scotland, and was the recognised place of royal sepulture. Alexander III and Robert Bruce are buried there. The guest-house was turned into a royal place in the sixteenth century; here Charles I was born in 1600.

Though you think sweet, yonder in your
church, the gentle talk of your students,
sweeter I think the splendid talking the
wolves make in Glenn mBolcáin.

Though you like the fat and meat which are
eaten in the drinking-halls, I like better
to eat a head of clean water-cress in a
place without sorrow . . .

Irish; author unknown; twelfth century.

From *A Celtic Miscellany,* translated
by Kenneth Hurlstone Jackson

LIFE AT RIEVAULX ABBEY, 1135

Our food is scanty, our garments rough; our drink is from the stream and our sleep often upon our book. Under our tired limbs there is but a hard mat; when sleep is sweetest we must rise at a bell's bidding. . . . Self-will has no scope; there is no moment for idleness or dissipation. . . . Everywhere peace, everywhere serenity, and a marvellous freedom from the tumult of the world, such unity and concord is there among the brethren, that each thing seems to belong to all, and all to each. . . . To put all in brief, no perfection expressed in the words of the gospel or of the apostles, or in the writings of the Fathers, or in the sayings of the monks of old, is wanting to our order and our way of life.

Ailred of Rievaulx, *The Monastic Order in England,* M.D. Knowles

ST COLUMBA'S ISLAND HERMITAGE, IONA

Delightful I think it to be in the bosom of an isle, on the
peak of a rock, that I might often see there the
calm of the sea.

That I might see its heavy waves over the glittering
ocean, as they chant a melody to their Father on
their eternal course.

That I might see its smooth strand of clear
headlands, no gloomy thing; that I might hear the
voice of the wondrous birds, a joyful tune.

That I might hear the sound of the shallow waves
against the rocks; that I might hear the cry of
the graveyard [island cemetery], the noise of the
sea.

That I might see its ebb and its flood-tide in their
flow; that this might be my name, a secret I
tell, 'He who turned his back on Ireland,'

That contrition of heart should come upon me as
I watch it; that I might bewail my many
sins, difficult to declare.

That I might bless the Lord who has power over all,
Heaven with its pure host of angels, earth, ebb,
flood-tide.

That I might pore on one of my books, good for my
soul; a while kneeling for beloved Heaven, a
while at psalms.

A while gathering dulse from the rock, a while
fishing, a while giving food to the poor, a
while in my cell.

A while meditating upon the Kingdom of Heaven,
holy is the redemption; a while at labour
not too heavy. it would be delightful!

Irish; author unknown; twelfth century

From *A Celtic Miscellany*, translated
by Kenneth Hurlstone Jackson

CANTERBURY CHURCH DORMITORY, Late Twelfth Century
. . . he [a brother] goes to the dormitory and there rest in absolute silence and quiet, so that neither by sound of voice nor by movement of any object does anyone make a noise nor do anything that may be heard by his neighbour or may in any way be a nuisance to his brethren. Let him place his habit tidily before his bed so that he may find it to hand in the morning, and similarly let him put his footwear at the foot of the bed. If anything is done or shifted or placed untidily or awkwardly, the watchman, that is, the monk who remains awake in the dormitory and goes round often in the night to see if there be anything needing correction,

shall tell of it in the morning at chapter in the presence of all, and satisfaction shall be made. Therefore we must take care that nothing be done at night that will be shameful to hear in the morning. . . .

When day has dawned he should rise straightway when the signal is heard and take his night shoes and go to the church, and there say the *Miserere* at the desks until *Deus in adjutorium* is said. After Prime the seven penitential psalms are straightway said with the litany and prostration – that is, we prostrate ourselves after the seven psalms. After the litany and the collects that follow he goes forthwith to the dormitory and then taking his book, descends into the cloister, and there sits and studies in his book, each in his appointed place, until the signal known as the 'shoe-signal' is heard. Then, shod and carrying knife and comb, he descends again to the cloister, and putting the books on the seat goes to the washing-place, and having washed his hands stands again by his book and combs his hair. Then, book in hand, he goes in order to church for Terce. . . .

The Monastic Constitutions of Lanfranc,
translated by D. Knowles

BENEDICTINE MONKS, Twelfth Century

An Abbot who is worthy to rule over the monastery ought always to remember what he is called, and correspond to his name by his works. For he is believed to hold the place of Christ in the monastery, since he is called by His name, as the Apostle says: 'Ye have received the spirit of the adoption of sons, in which we cry: Abba, Father.'

And therefore the Abbot ought not [God forbid] to teach, or ordain, or command anything contrary to the law of the lord; but let his bidding and his doctrine be infused into the minds of his disciples like the leaven of divine justice.

Let the Abbot be ever mindful that at the dreadful judgment of God, an account will have to be given both of his own teaching

77. The Cistercian Abbey of St Mary in Furness on the peninsula near Barrow. It was founded at Tulketh near Preston in 1123, moved to Furness in 1126 by Stephen, who later became king. With large estates the abbey became wealthy and claimed highest rank in its order. It is a fine example of the transition period, Norman and Early English architecture.

and of the obedience of his disciples. And let him know that lack of profit which the father of the household may find in his sheep, shall be imputed to the fault of the shepherd. Only them shall he be acquitted, if he shall have bestowed all pastoral diligence on his unquiet and disobedient flock, and employed all his care to amend their corrupt manner of life: then shall he be absolved in the judgement of the Lord, and may say to the Lord with the prophet: 'I have not hidden thy justice in my heart, I have declared thy truth and thy salvation, but they condemned and despised me.' So at the last to those disobedient sheep may their punishment come, overmastering death.

Therefore when anyone takes the name of Abbot, he ought to govern his disciples by a two-fold doctrine: that is, he should show forth all that is good and holy by his deeds, rather than his words: declaring to the intelligent among his disciples the commandments of the Lord by words: but to the hard-hearted and the simple-minded setting forth the divine precepts by the example of his deeds. And let him show by his own actions that those things ought not to be done which he has taught his disciples to be against the law of God; lest, while preaching to others, he should himself become a castaway, and God should say to him in his sin: 'Why doest thou declare my justice, and take my covenant in thy mouth? Thou hast hated discipline, and hast cast my words behind thee.' And again, 'Thou sawest the mote in thy brother's eye, didst thou not see the beam in thine own?'

Let him make no distinction of persons in the monastery. Let not one be loved more than another, unless he be found to excel in good works or in obedience. Let not one of noble birth be put before him that was formerly a slave, unless some other reasonable cause exist for it. If upon just consideration it should so seem good to the Abbot, let him advance one of any rank whatever; but otherwise let them keep their own places; because whether bond or free, we are all one in Christ, and bear an equal burden in the army of one Lord: for 'with God there is no respecting of persons'. Only for one reason are we to be preferred in His sight,

---

78. The Cistercian Abbey of Calder near Egremont, three miles from the sea in Cumberland. It was founded about 1140. The view is taken from the west of the church, showing parts remaining as they were built.

if we be found to surpass others in good works and in humility. Let the Abbot, then show equal love to all, and let the same discipline be imposed upon all according to their deserts.

For the Abbot in his doctrine ought always to observe the rule of the Apostle, wherein he says: 'reprove, entreat, rebuke': suiting his action to circumstances, mingling gentleness with severity; showing now the rigour of a master, now the loving affection of a father, so as sternly to rebuke the undisciplined and restless, and to exhort the obedient, mild, and patient to advance in virtue. And such as are negligent and haughty we charge him to reprove and correct. Let him not shut his eyes to the faults of offenders; but as soon as they appear, let him strive, as he has the authority for that, to root them out, remembering the fate of Heli, the priest of Silo.

Those of good disposition and understanding let him correct, for the first or second time, with words only; but such as are forward and hard of heart, and proud, or disobedient, let him chastise with bodily stripes at the very first offence, knowing that it is written: 'Strike thy son with the rod, and thou shalt deliver his soul from death.'

The Abbot ought always to remember what he is, and what he is called, and to know that to whom more is committed, from him more is required; and he must consider how difficult and arduous a task he has undertaken, of ruling souls and adapting himself to many dispositions. Let him so accommodate and suit himself to the character and intelligence of each, winning some by kindness, others by reproof, others by persuasion, that he may not only suffer no loss in the flock committed to him, but may even rejoice in their virtuous increase.

Above all let him not, overlooking or undervaluing the salvation of the souls entrusted to him, be more solicitous for fleeting, earthly, and perishable things; but let him ever bear in mind that he has undertaken the government of souls, of which he shall have

---

79. The Cistercian Abbey of Forde in Dorset, near a ford on the upper Axe. Founded in 1141 by monks, who came from Brightley near Okehampton, it developed under Baldwin, archdeacon of Exeter, later to be Archbishop of Canterbury. Building was extended under Abbot Chard before the Dissolution. In 1649 Sir Edmund Prideaux took possession, and the work of either Inigo Jones or John Webb, his pupil, made it one of the remarkable buildings in the West Country.

to give an account. And that he may not complain for want of wordly substance, let him remember what is written: 'Seek first the kingdom of God and his justice, and all these things shall be added unto you.' And again: 'Nothing is wanting to them that fear him.'

And let him know that he who has undertaken the government of souls, must prepare himself to render an account of them. And whatever may be the number of the brethren under his care, let him be certainly assured that on the Day of Judgement he will have to give an account to the Lord of all these souls, as well as of his own. And thus, being ever fearful of the coming judgement of the shepherd concerning the state of the flock committed to him, while he is careful on other men's accounts, he will be solicitous also on his own. And so, while correcting others by his admonitions, he will be himself cured of his own defects.

The ideal Abbot, *The Rule of St. Benedict*, by the Right Rev. Dom Paul Delatte, Abbot of Solesmes and Superior-General of the Congregation of the Benedictines of France, translated by Dom Justin McCann, Monk of Ampleforth

CLOTHES OF MONKS, Twelfth Century

Let clothing be given to the brethren suitable to the nature and climate of the place where they live; for in cold regions more is required, in warm regions less. It shall be the Abbot's duty, therefore, to consider this.

We think, however, that in temperate climates a cowl and a tunic should suffice for each monk; the cowl to be of a thick stuff in winter, but in summer something worn and thin: likewise a scapular [short cloak] for work, and shoes and stockings to cover their feet.

Of all these things and their colour or coarseness let not the monks complain, but let them be such as can be got in the region where they live, or can be bought most cheaply. Let the Abbot be

---

80. The Augustinian Priory of Twynham, soon called Christchurch, on the bank of the River Avon in Hampshire. First a house of secular canons, it was refounded about 1150 for Austin canons. The priory church, a cruciform building with now no central tower, has majestic length, fine interior decoration and architectural variety – nave and transepts mainly Norman, in part Romanesque, a late Perpendicular tower at the western end.

careful about their size, that these garments be not short for those who wear them but fit well.

When they receive new clothes let them always give back the old ones at once, to be put by in the clothes-room for the poor. For it is sufficient for a monk to have two tunics and two cowls, as well for night wear as for convenience of washing. Anything beyond this is superfluous and ought to be cut off. In the same way let them give up their stockings, and whatever else is worn out, when they receive new ones.

Let those who are sent on a journey receive drawers from the clothes-room, and on their return restore them washed.

Let their cowls and tunics also be a little better than those they usually wear; they must receive these from the clothes-room when setting out on their journey, and restore them on their return.

For their bedding let a mattress, blanket, coverlet, and pillow suffice. These beds must be frequently inspected by the Abbot because of private property, lest it be found therein. And if anyone be found to have what he has not received from the Abbot, let him be subjected to the most severe discipline.

And in order that this vice of private ownership may be cut off by the roots let the Abbot supply all things that are necessary: that is cowl, tunic, stockings, shoes, girdle, knife, style, needle, handkerchief, and tablets; so that all plea of necessity may be taken away.

Yet let the Abbot always be mindful of those words of the Acts of the Apostles: 'Distribution was made to everyone, according as he had need.' Let him, therefore, consider the infirmities of such as are in want, and not the ill-will of the envious. Nevertheless, in all his decisions, let him think of the judgement of God.

The Rule of St. Benedict, by the Right Rev. Dom Paul Delatte Abbot of Solesmes and Superior-General of the Congregation of the Benedictines of France, translated by Dom Justin McCann, Monk of Ampleforth

---

81. The Augustinian Priory of Bolton six miles from Skipton in Yorkshire, known as Bolton Abbey. It lies in open country beside the River Wharfe. Founded in 1121 at Embsay near Skipton, it was moved to its more splendid site in 1154. Master-masons, in the church, showed Gothic at its best.

THE INVESTITURE CONTROVERSY ENDS IN A COMPROMISE

On the first of August an assemble of bishops, abbots, and nobles of the realm was held at London in the king's palace. And for three successive days, in Anselm's absence, the matter was thoroughly discussed between king and bishops concerning church investitures, some arguing for this that the king should perform them after the manner of his father and brother, or according to the injunction and obedience of the pope. For the pope in the sentence which had been then published, standing firm, had conceded homage, which Pope Urban had forbidden, as well as investiture, and in this way had won over the king about investiture, as may be gathered from the letter which we have quoted above. Afterwards, in the presence of Anselm and a large concourse, the king agreed and ordained that henceforward no one should be invested with bishopric or abbacy in England by the giving of a pastoral staff or the ring, by the king or any lay hand: Anselm also agreeing that no one elected to a prelacy should be deprived of consecration to the office undertaken on the ground of homage, which he should make to the king. After this decision, by the advice of Anselm and the nobles of the realm, fathers were instituted by the king, without any investiture of pastoral staff or ring, to nearly all the churches of England which had been so long widowed of their shepherds.

Eadmeri Monachi Cantuariensis
Historiae Novorum

'REPSELVER' THE CELLARER'S DUE, Late Twelfth Century

Many wondered at the changes in ancient customs that were made by order of the Abbot or with his permission. From the time when the town of St. Edmund received the name and liberty of a borough, men used at the beginning of August to give the Cellarer one penny for each house towards the cutting of our corn, which due was called 'repselver'. And before the town received its liberty, all of them used to reap as though they had been serfs: only the dwellings of knights, chaplains, and servants of the court were exempt from such a due. But in process of time the Cellarer spared some of the richer men of the town, demanding nought of them; wherefore the other burgesses seeing this said openly that no man, who had a messuage of his own, should pay that penny, but only those who hired houses that belonged to others. And afterwards they all in common demanded this liberty, speaking to the Lord Abbot on the matter and offering him a yearly payment in lieu of this exaction. And noting how the Cellarer went through the town to collect the repselver without regard to his dignity, and how he caused security for payment to be taken in the houses of the poor, sometimes three-legged stools, sometimes doors and sometimes other utensils, and how old women came out with their distaffs, threatening and abusing the Cellarer and his men, the Abbot ordered that twenty shillings should be given to the Cellarer every year at the next portmanmoot [meeting of burgesses to administer affairs of the town] before August, this sum to be paid through the town reeve by burgesses who assigned a revenue for the payment of this due. This was done and confirmed by our charter.

The Chronicle of Jocelin of Brakelond concerning the Acts of Samson, Abbot of the Monastery of St Edmund, translated by H.E. Butler

MONKS OF THE CLUNIAC AND CISTERCIAN ORDERS, Twelfth Century

With respect to the two Orders, the Cistercian and the Cluniac, this may be relied upon; although the latter are possessed of fine buildings, with ample revenues and estates, they will soon be reduced to poverty and destruction. To the former, on the contrary, you would allot a barren desert and a solitary wood; yet in a few years you will find them in possession of sumptuous churches and houses, and encircled with an extensive property. The difference of manners (as it appears to me) causes this contrast. For as without meaning offence to either party, I shall speak the truth, the one feels the benefits of sobriety, parsimony, and prudence, whilst the other suffers from the bad effects of gluttony and intemperance: the one, like bees, collect their stores into a heap, and unanimously agree in the disposal of one well-regulated purse; the others pillage and divert to improper uses the largesses which have been collected by divine assistance, and by the bounties of the faithful; and whilst each individual consults solely his own interest, the welfare of the community suffers; since, as Sallust observes, 'Small things increase by concord, and

the greatest are wasted by discord.' Besides, sooner than lessen the number of one of the thirteen or fourteen dishes which they claim by right of custom, or even in a time of scarcity or famine recede in the smallest degree from their accustomed good fare, they would suffer the richest lands and the best buildings of the monastery to become a prey to usury, and the numerous poor to perish before their gates.

The first of these Orders, at a time when there was a deficiency in grain, with a laudable charity, not only gave away their flocks and herds, but resigned to the poor one of the two dishes with which they were always contented. But in these our days, in order to remove this stain, it is ordained by the Cistercians, 'That in future neither farms nor pastures shall be purchased; and that they shall be satisfied with those alone which have been freely and unconditionally bestowed upon them.' This Order, therefore, being satisfied more than any other with humble mediocrity, and, if not wholly, yet in a great degree checking their ambition; and, though placed in a worldly situation, yet avoiding, as much as possible, its contagion; neither notorious for gluttony or drunkenness, for luxury or lust; is fearful and ashamed of incurring public scandal, as will be more fully explained in the book we mean (by the grace of God) to write concerning the ecclesiastical Orders.

Gerald the Welshman, Itinerary through Wales,
translated by Sir R.C. Hoare

CISTERCIAN MONKS, 1138 to 1177

. . . While Abbot Gerold and his monks were travelling from Furness to the Archbishop of York with nothing except the books and gear which they could take on a wain drawn by eight oxen, they were getting near Thirsk when they happened to meet the steward of the lady Gundrea, widow of Nigel de Albini and mother of Roger de Mowbray then a minor and a ward of King Stephen, but soon due to come into his estate. The steward

82. Lacock, an abbey of Augustinian nuns, near Chippenham in Wiltshire. It was founded in 1232 by the Lady Ela Longespee, countess of Salisbury, who became abbess in 1238. Sir William Sharingtom bought this property in 1540 and turned the abbey into a family mansion, though medieval buildings were retained including the cloister, the chapter-house, and a Lady Chapel added in the fourteenth century.

83. Whitby Abbey, from the Monks' Fishpond. Dating from the middle of the thirteenth century; the abbey rests upon Anglo-Saxon foundations.

wondered at the movement of such men and asked Abbot Gerold about his troubles. When informed about them, the steward humbly begged the abbot to dine with his lady, then at Thirsk Castle in the vicinity. The Abbot agreed, trusting to God's will. The steward went on ahead to the castle and told his lady about the visit of those whom piety had impelled him to ask to dinner in his lady's name. The Abbot and monks drew near with the wain behind them, and the lady took a private look at their distress from a window in an upstairs room. The sight reduced her to tears. She was very glad that they came and was impressed by their humble demeanour, so she kept them all, supplying their wants. She would not let them leave her and promised to help their board and lodging. The Abbot and convent could not possibly or decently follow the lady round from manor to manor in different counties, so she sent them to her kinsman, Robert de Alneto, a Norman, once a monk at Whitby and then a hermit at Hode, and there she kept them supplied until her son Roger de Mowbray came into estate.

. . . The monks migrated from Hode to a place by the River Rye in Byland and built a little cell where their tilery now is, not far from the abbey which the noble lord Walter le Spek of Helmslet had founded 12 years before, called Rievaulx. And thus Abbot Roger [successor of Gerold] and his monks remained by the Rye for five years.

It had been the intention of Roger de Mowbray that if practicable the abbey should have been built on the south bank of the Rye with all the advantages which Rievaulx enjoyed on the north bank. But the lie of the land made this impossible and the convents were too close together for each could hear the bells of the other at each hour of the day and night and this was improper and altogether intolerable.

On getting possession of the vill of Byland, Abbot Roger and his monks decided to reduce it to a grange [outlying farm]. With this in view they allotted some land to the inhabitants at Stutekelde where they could build a new vill . . . Roger de Mowbray gave more land out of waste at Cukewald under Blakhow-hill . . . and there they industriously built a little stone church, a cloister, buildings and workshops as can be clearly seen on the ground and there they remained for 30 years. . . . While Abbot Roger and his monks dwelt in the western part of Cukewald they began an energetic clearance of the wood and drew the water out of the bogs by means of long wide dykes. When the land was drained they prepared a broad, suitable and worthy site in the eastern part of Cukewald between Whitaker and Cambe-hill near Burtoft and Berslive and there they built a beautiful great church as may still be seen which may God preserve and fulfil for ever. Thither they moved from Stockyng on the eve of All Saints, 1177.

Byland Cartulary, translated from W. Dugdale, *Monasticon Anglicanum, A History of the Abbies and other Monasteries, Hospitals, Frieries and Cathedral and Collegiate Churches.*

84. Corn brought to the mill. From *Bestiary*, late twelfth century.

THE MEANING OF MATINS, c.1150

To the antiquity of Matins the prophet David is once more the witness when he says, *O God, my God, early do I watch unto Thee*, and again, *Early in the morning will I think of Thee*. But the reason for praying at daybreak is to celebrate Christ's resurrection. For in the early morning Christ, rising from death and saving His people, condemned the devil and his satellites to everlasting chains. It was assuredly at the first ray of dawn that the Lord rose from Hades, when the light began to rise for the faithful which had set for sinners when he died. By the Morning Office is recalled also the baptism of the People of Israel, which typified our own. Exodus narrates that this took place in the morning watch, when the children of Israel crossed the Red Sea, after their enemies had been destroyed by the power of God. And, lastly, we believe that the hope of the future general resurrection, when all men, just and unjust, will awake, arising from this temporal death as from the stupor of sleep, will come at that time too.

Robert of Bridlington, *The Bridlington Dialogue, An Exposition of the Rule of St. Augustine for the Life of the Clergy, Given through a Dialogue between Master and Disciple*, translated and edited by a Religious of C.S.M.V., A.R. Mowbray & Co.

ST MARGARET'S BOOK OF THE GOSPELS

She had a book of the Gospels beautifully adorned with jewels and gold, and ornamented with the figures of the four Evangelists, painted and gilt. The capital letters throughout the volume were also resplendent with gold. For this volume she had always a greater affection than she had for any others she was in the habit of reading. It happened that while the person who was carrying it was crossing a ford, he let the volume, which had been carelessly folded in a wrapper, fall into the middle of the stream, and, ignorant of what had occurred, he quietly continued his journey. But when he afterwards wished to produce the book, he, for the first time, became aware that he had lost it. It was sought for a long time, but was not found. At length it was found at the bottom of the river, lying open, so that its leaves were kept in constant motion by the action of the water, and the little coverings of silk which protected the letters of gold from being injured by the contact of the leaves, were carried away by the force of the current. Who would imagine that the book would be worth anything after what had happened to it? Who would believe that even a single letter would have been visible in it? Yet of a truth it was taken up out of the middle of the river so perfect, uninjured, and free from damage, that it looked as though it had not even been touched by the water. For the whiteness of the leaves, and the form of the letters throughout the whole of the volume remained exactly as they were before it fell into the river, except that on the margin of the leaves, towards the edge, some trace of the water could with difficulty be detected. The book was conveyed to the Queen, and the miracle reported to her at the same time, and she having given thanks to Christ, esteemed the volume much more highly than she did before. Wherefore let others consider what they should think of this, but as for me I am of opinion that this miracle was wrought by our Lord because of his love for this venerable Queen.

Turgot, *Life of St Margaret* in *Ancient Lives of Scottish Saints*, translated by W.M. Metcalfe

FISHPONDS AT BURY, Late Twelfth Century

There is also another strain of evil-doing which, God willing, the Abbot will wash out with tears of penitence, that one transgression should not blacken such a multitude of good deeds. He raised the level of the fish-pond of Babwell by the new mill to such a height, that owing to the holding up of the waters, there is no man rich or poor, having lands by the waterside, from the Towngate to Eastgate, but has lost his garden and orchards. The Cellarer's pasture on the other side of the bank is destroyed, the arable land of neighbours is spoilt. The Cellarer's meadow is ruined, the Infirmarer's orchard is drowned owing to the overflow of water, and all the neighbours complain of it. Once the Cellarer spoke to him in full Chapter concerning the greatness of the loss, but the Abbot at once angrily replied that he was not going to lose his fish-pond for the sake of our meadow.

The Chronicle of Jocelin Brakelond concerning the Acts of Samson, Abbot of the Monastery of St Edmund, translated by H.E. Butler

85. Shepherds at Bethlehem with sheep, goats, pig, and a dog with collar. *Psalter*, late twelfth century.

ST ANSELM, ARCHBISHOP OF CANTERBURY, 1093-1109, REPEATS THE WORDS OF LANFRANC, WHEN HE WRITES TO THE KING OF IRELAND

We hear that marriages, in your kingdom, are dissolved and changed without any reason . . . It is said that men exchange their wives for those of other men as freely and publicly as any one changes one horse for another.

PETRUS CANTOR, *c.* 1200, ON THE SAME POINT CONDEMNS THE CHURCH

See also how that most holy Sacrament of Church, viz. Matrimony, by reason of traditions concerning the third degree of affinity, and certain other traditions, becomes at one moment invalid, at another sound and firm, through the chatterings of advocates, who rely upon the nets of tradition in order thus to fill their own purses and empty those of other people, so that the Sacrament of Martrimony is turned to derision among the layfolk, for they say, 'I will marry this woman and grow rich [with her money], for I will leave her whenever I wish and let her be in the third degree of affinity to me.

CRITICISM OF CLUNIAC IDEALS BY ST BERNARD OF CLAIRVAUX, 1090-1153, FAMOUS CISTERCIAN MONK

I will not speak of the immense height of the churches, of their immoderate length, of their superfluous breadth, costly polishing, and strange designs, which while they attract the eyes of the worshipper, hinder the soul's devotion, and somehow remind me of the old Jewish ritual.

However, let all this pass; we will suppose it is done as we are told, for the glory of God. But, as a monk myself, I do ask other monks . . . 'Tell me, O ye professors of poverty, what does gold do in a holy place? . . . By the sight of wonderful and costly vanities men are prompted to give rather than to pray. Some beautiful picture of a saint is exhibited, and the brighter the colours the greater the holiness attributed to it. Men run, eager to kiss; they are invited to give, and the beautiful is the more admired than the sacred is revered.

'In the churches are suspended not coronae [circular chandeliers], but wheels studded with gems, and surrounded by lights, which are scarcely brighter than the precious stones which are near them. Instead of candlesticks we behold great trees of brass, fashioned with wonderful skill and glittering as much through their jewels as their lights . . . If we cannot do without the images, why can we not spare the brilliant colours?'

THE CONTENTS OF A CHURCH, Late Twelfth Century

The furnishings are these: a baptismal font, a crucifix, a Little Mary, and other images; a lectern of some kind, a ewer, a small ewer, basins, a chair, the chancel, an elevated seat, a stool, candlesticks, the piscina or lavabo [stone basin for carrying away water used in rinsing the chalice], the altar stone, a case for images, cruets, and pyxides [vessel to contain the consecrated bread of the Sacrament]. Let there be a bier for the dead, a hand towel, a face towel, and a fine cloth on the altar. There should be gilded vessels, a thurible [censer], gilded columns and bronze veneering with silver and marble bases . . .

There should be books: Missal, Breviary, Antiphonal, Gradual,

86. Christ and two disciples in the dress of twelfth-century pilgrims

Processional, Manual, Hymnal, Psalter, and Ordinal [Service-book used on ordinations]. The priest's vestments are surplice, silk cap, cincture [girdle], headband, baldric, stole, maniple [strip hanging from left arm], and chasuble.

In the ceiling there should be beams of maplewood or oak, crosspieces where the roof adheres to the beams or to the leads. Wooden pegs and iron nails are required where the tiles and roof siding are suspended. Small bells, immense bells, and little bells must be hung in the tower. A cupola, tower, and bell tower are the same thing. A weathercock can be placed on top. Bent bars, bolts, hinges, and locks should be there on the doors. There should be an entry vestibule for temple, or church, or monastery, or oratory, or chapel . . . Let there be a tabernacle in which the Eucharist may be kept most worthily, the salvation of faithful souls, for he who does not believe cannot be saved.

U.T. Holmes, Jr., *Daily Living in the Twelfth Century based on the Observation of Alexander Neckam*

87. St George and the Dragon; tympanum of the twelfth-century church of St George, Brinsop, Herefordshire.

HOW HERMITS AND SOME MONKS DIFFER, Late Twelfth Century

The monks drink in violence and strife of the best wines which God has established. They eat bread as white as hail; of all flesh do they eat also, so that their bellies are full and stuffed and they almost burst through the middle. But holy men, the hermits, do not act so. They have bread of barley, kneaded with water, and wild fruit which they have gathered in the woods, and various herbs and roots also. When Bauclus had been in the abbey to the point that he had his fill of ease and bread and wine, he realized that he would not be saved in this way. In a wood that was some seven hundred yards away he became a hermit, for fourteen or fifteen years. He did not eat of bread or flour, or anything which was not a root. His back became so thin from fasting that he could hardly stand upon his feet.

Anseÿs de Mes

Travel

TRAVEL IN THE ELEVENTH CENTURY

At the same time there had also come to Rome at the king's command two royal priests, Giso and Walter, men most suitably and excellently trained in their office, so that they might be ordained bishop by the lord pope. After their business had been successfully completed according to their desire, they all to Rome together, and on the same day fell among thieves; and, robbed and plundered, some even to nakedness, they were compelled to turn back again.

On that occasion a young man named Gospatric, a kinsman of King Edward, a knight who accompanied Earl Tostig on his journey, bore himself courageously in his service to his lord. For as he rode clad in garments suited to his noble rank in the very van of the pilgrims, he was asked by the robbers which of them was Earl Tostig. Realizing immediately what was their trade, he said that he was, and signalled the earl with all possible signs to ride away. He was believed because of the luxury of his clothes and his physical appearance, which was indeed distinguished; and so he was taken away, in vain hope indeed, with the rest of the booty. When, however, he thought the earl far enough away to be safe, during his interrogation on various matters he confessed at length that he was not the man they thought they had captured. Although when the robbers first understood the case they put his life in jeopardy, finally, however, some of them treated his behaviour more generously, and not only was he allowed to depart, but, marked with these soldiers' great esteem and praise, and restored to possession of his own things, he was escorted back in peace, followed by the good wishes of all.

Life of King Edward the Confessor, edited by F. Barlow

JOURNEYS OF HENRY I CAREFULLY PLANNED

He arranged with great precision, and publicly gave notice of, the days of his travelling and of his stay, with the number of days and the names of the vills, so that everyone might know without chance of a mistake the course of his living month by month. Nothing was done without preparation or without previous arrangement or in a hurry. Everything was managed as befitted a king and with proper control. Hence there was eager sailing from beyond the seas to his court, of merchants with wares and luxuries for sale, and likewise from all parts of England, so that nowhere save about the king, wherever he went, were there plentiful markets.

Walter Map, *De Nugis Curialium*,
translated by M.R. James; Cymmrodorion Record Series, No.9

CLOTHING FOR THE TRAVELLER, *c*.1150

Let one who is about to ride have a *chape* [long cloak] with sleeves, of which the hood will not mind the weather, and let him have boots, and spurs that he may prevent the horse from stumbling, jolting, turning, rearing, resisting, and may make him *bien amblant*, 'possessed of a good gait', and easily manageable. Shoes should be well fastened with iron nails.

U.T. Holmes, Jr., *Daily Living in the Twelfth Century, based on the Observations of Alexander Neckam*

Law – Crime

ADMINISTRATION OF JUSTICE

William the Conqueror was the first in England who instituted the jury of twelve men, by whom justice might be rendered, and a fair trial given to every man obnoxious to the penal law.

William the Conqueror ordained also that the terms should be kept four times in the year, in such places as he should nominate, and that the judges should sit in several places, to judge and decide causes and matters in controversy betwixt party and party in manner as is used unto this day. He decreed, moreover, that there should be sheriffs in every shire, and justices of the peace to keep the countries in good quiet, and to see offenders punished.

Furthermore, he instituted the court of the exchequer, and the offices of the same, as barons, the clerks, and such other, also the high court of the chancery.

Raphael Holinshed, *Chronicle*

THE ADMINISTRATION OF WILLIAM I

After his coronation in London, King William ordered many affairs with prudence, justice, and clemency. Some of these concerned the profit and honour of that city, others were for the advantage of the whole nation, and the rest were intended for the benefit of the church. He enacted some laws founded on admirable principles. No suitor ever demanded justice of this king without obtaining it: he condemned none but those whom it would have been unjust to acquit. He enjoined his nobles to comport themselves with grave dignity, joining activity to right judgment, having constantly before their eyes the Eternal King who had given them victory. He forbade their oppressing the conquered, reminding them that they were their own equals by their Christian profession, and that they must be cautious not to excite revolt by their unjust treatment of those whom they had fairly subdued. He prohibited all riotous assemblages, murder, and robbery, and as he restrained the people by force of arms, he set bounds to arms by the laws. The taxes and all things concerning the royal revenues were so regulated as not to be burdensome to the people. Robbers, plunderers, and malefactors had no asylum in his dominions. Merchants found the ports and highways open, and were protected against injury. Thus the first acts of his reign were all excellent, and eminent for the great benefits flowing from good government conferred on his subjects, which were confirmed by perseverance in a right course, with plain indications of a successful result.

Ordericus Vitalis, *Historia Ecclesiastica*,
translated by T. Forester

THE LAWS OF WILLIAM THE CONQUEROR

Here is set down what William, king of the English, established in consultation with his magnates after the conquest of England:

1. First that above all things he wishes one God to be revered throughout his whole realm, one faith in Christ to be kept ever inviolate, and peace and security to be preserved between English and Normans.

2. We decree also that every freeman shall affirm by oath and compact that he will be loyal to King William both within and without England, that he will preserve with him his lands and honour with all fidelity and defend him against all his enemies.

3. I will more-over, that all the men whom I have brought with me, or who have come after me, shall be protected by my peace and shall dwell in quiet. And if any one of them shall be slain, let the lord of his murderer seize him within five days, if he can; but if he cannot, let him begin to pay me 46 marks of silver so long as his substance avails. And when his substance is exhausted, let the whole hundred in which the murder took place pay what remains in common.

4. And let every Frenchman who, in the time of King Edward, my kinsman, was a sharer in the customs of the English, pay what

they call "scot and lot" according to the laws of the English. This decree was ordained in the city of Gloucester.

5. We forbid also that any live cattle shall be bought or sold for money except within cities, and this shall be done before three faithful witnesses; nor even anything old without surety and warrant. But if anyone shall do otherwise, let him pay once, and afterwards a second time for a fine.

6. It was also decreed there that if a Frenchman shall charge an Englishman with perjury or murder or theft or homicide or 'ran', as the English call open rapine which cannot be denied, the Englishman may defend himself, as he shall prefer, either by the ordeal of hot iron or by wager of battle. But if the Englishman be infirm, let him find another who will take his place. If one of them shall be vanquished, he shall pay a fine of 40 shillings to the king. If an Englishman shall charge a Frenchman and be unwilling to prove his accusation either by ordeal or by wager of battle, I will, nevertheless, that the Frenchman shall acquit himself by a valid oath.

7. This also I command and will, that all shall have and hold the law of King Edward in respect of their lands and all their possessions, with the addition of those decrees I have ordained for the welfare of the English people.

8. Every man who wishes to be considered a freeman shall be in pledge ['System of compulsory collective bail fixed for individuals, not after their arrest for crime, but as a safeguard in anticipation of it'] so that his surety shall hold him and hand him over to justice if he shall offend in any way. And if any such shall escape, let his sureties see to it that they pay forthwith what is charged against him, and let them clear themselves of any complicity in his escape. Let recourse be had to the hundred and shire courts as our predecessors decreed. And those who ought of right to come and are unwilling to appear, shall be summoned once; and if for the second time they refuse to come, one ox shall be taken from them, and they shall be summoned a third time. And if they do not come the third time, a second ox shall be taken from them. But if they do not come at the fourth summons, the man who was unwilling to come shall forfeit from his goods the amount of the charge against him – 'ceapgeld' as it is called – and in addition to this a fine to the king.

9. I prohibit the sale of any man by another outside the country on pain of a fine to be paid in full to me.

10. I also forbid that anyone shall be slain or hanged for any fault, but let his eyes be put out and let him be castrated. And this command shall not be violated under pain of a fine in full to me.

English Historical Documents, Vol.II

FOREST LAW

'The law of the forest . . . was not the slow growth through centuries of settled government, but the Norman innovation due to the love of hunting which in William I and his successors amounted to almost a passion.' D.M. Stenton

The forest has its own laws, based not on the common law of the realm, but on arbitrary legislation by the king . . .

In the forests are the secret places of the kings and their great delight. To them they go for hunting, having put off their cares, so that they may enjoy a little quiet. There, away from the continuous business and incessant turmoil of the court, they can for a little time breathe in the grace of natural liberty, wherefore it is that those who commit offences there lie under the royal displeasure alone . . .

The king's forest is the safe dwelling place of wild beasts, not of every sort, but of the sort that dwell in the woodlands, not in any sort of place, but in certain places suitable for the purpose.

Richard fitz Nigel, *Dialogus,* from
English Society in the Early Middle Ages, D.M. Stenton

WILLIAM I SHOWS HIS ATTITUDE REGARDING THE INTERNAL ORGANIZATION OF THE ESTATES OF WEALTHY MEN, 1085

. . . in the Christmas council of 1085 the king had very deep speech with his wise men about this land, how it was peopled and by what sort of men. Then he sent his men into every shire all over England and caused it to be found out how many hundred hides were in the shire and what land the king had, and what stock on the land, and what dues he ought to have each year from the shire.

Also he caused it be written how much land his archbishops,

bishops, abbots, and earls had, and, though I may be somewhat tedious in my account, what and how much each landholder in England had in land or in stock, and how much money it might be worth. So minutely did he cause it to be searched out that there was not one hide or yard of land, nor even (it is shameful to write of it, but he thought it not shameful to do it) an ox, or a cow, or a swine that was not set down in his writ. And all the writings were brought to him afterwards.

Peterborough Chronicle, *sub anno* 1085 from *English Society in the Early Middle Ages,* D.M. Stenton

ROYAL SUPREMACY

Eadmer says, 'Some of those novel points I will set down which he [William I] appointed to be observed:

1. He would not then allow any one settled in all his dominion to acknowledge as apostolic the pontiff of the City of Rome, save at his own bidding, or by any means to receive any letter from him if it had not first been shown to himself.

2. The primate also of his realm, I mean the Archbishop of Canterbury or Dorobernia, presiding over a general Council assembled of bishops, he did not permit to ordain or forbid anything save what had just been ordained by himself as agreeable to his own will.

3. He would not suffer that any, even of his bishops, should be allowed to implead publicly, or excommunicate, or constrain by any penalty of ecclesiastical rigour, any of his barons or ministers accused of incest, or adultery, or any capital crime, save by his command.

Eadmeri Monachi Catuariensis Historiiae Novorum, I, vi

FIRST CHARTER OF THE CITY OF LONDON

William the king friendly salutes William the bishop, and Godfrey the portreve, and all the burgesses within London, both French and English: And I declare, that I grant you to be all law-worthy, as you were in the days of King Edward; and I grant that every child shall be his father's heir, after his father's days; and I will not suffer any person to do you wrong. God keep you.

Historical Charters and Constitutional Documents of the City of London

THE CURFEW BELL, 1068

Moreover to reduce the English people the more unto obedience and awe, he [William the Conqueror] took from them all their armour and weapons. He ordained also that the master of every household about eight of the clock in the evening, should cause his fire to be raked up in ashes, his lights to be put out; and then go to bed. Besides this, to the end that every man might have knowledge of the hour to go to rest, he gave order, that in all cities, towns and villages, where any church was, there should a bell be rung at the said hour, which custom is still used even unto this day, and commonly called by the French word, 'Couvre feu,' that is, 'Rake up the fire.'

Holinshed, *Chronicles*, II

SUMMONS TO THE KING, 1072

William, king of the English, to Aethelwig, abbot of Evesham, greeting. I order you to summon all those who are subject to your administration and jurisdiction that they bring before me at Clarendon on the Octave of Pentecost all the knights they owe me duly equipped. You, also, on that day shall come to me, and bring with you fully equipped those 5 knights which you owe me in respect of your abbacy. Witness Eudo the steward. At Winchester.

English Historical Documents, Vol.II

THE NEW FOREST, 1070

Whereupon greater burdens were laid upon the English, insomuch that after they had been robbed and spoiled of their goods, they were also debarred of their accustomed games and pastimes. For where naturally (as they do unto this day) they took great pleasure in hunting of deer, both red and fallow, in the woods and forests about without restraint, King William seizing the most part of the same forests into his own hands, appointed a punishment, to be executed upon all such offenders: namely, to have their eyes put out.

And to bring the great number of men in danger of those his penal laws (a pestilent policy of a spiteful mind and savouring altogether of his French slavery) he devised means how to breed, nourish and increase the multitude of deer, and also to make room for them in that part of the realm which lieth between Salisbury and the sea southward. He pulled down towns, villages and churches and other buildings for the space of 30 miles to make thereof a forest, which at this day is called the New Forest. The people as then sore bewailed their distress, and greatly lamented that they must leave house and home to the use of savage beasts.

Holinshed, *Chronicles*, II

WILLIAM I AND HIS SHERIFFS

William (by the grace of God), king of the English, to Lanfranc, archbishop of Canterbury, and Geoffrey, bishop of Coutances, and Robert, count of Eu, and Richard, son of Count Gilbert, and Hugh of Montfort-sur-Risle, and to all his other magnates of England, greeting. Summon my sheriffs by my order and tell them from me that they must return to my bishoprics and abbacies all the demesne, and all the demesne-land which my bishops and abbots, either through carelessness or fear or greed, have given them out of the demesne of my bishoprics and abbacies; which they have consented to hold; or which they have seized by violence. And unless they return those things belonging to the demesne of my churches which they have up to now wrongfully held, you are to compel them willy-nilly to make restitution. And if anyone else, or if any one of you [Richard fitz Gilbert, and Hugh of Montfort-sur-Risle, had both 'despoiled' the church of Canterbury], to whom I have addressed this instrument of justice, is liable to the same accusation, let him likewise make restitution of whatever he holds of the demesne of my bishoprics and abbacies, lest any one of you holding anything by a similar wrong might be the less able to coerce any sheriff or any other person who in like manner possesses the demesne of my churches.

Writ of William I, 1077,
English Historical Documents, Vol.II

DOMESDAY SURVEY

'The survey was the greatest fiscal work England had ever known, nor did she for several centuries know another of equal importance. The survey furnished the basis of taxation and military service, as well as that for the establishment and maintenance of the English feudal system. The utility of the return was established at the national gathering, or Gemot, on Salisbury Plain. There William exacted from every landholder oaths of homage, fealty,

and allegiance, binding each man directly to the king instead of to the mesne lord – the great difference between English and Continental feudalism.'
G.C. Lee

A. 1085. . . . At midwinter the king was at Gloucester with his witan; and held his court there five days; and afterwards the archbishop and clergy held a synod during three days; and Maurice was there chosen to the bishopric of London, William to that of Norfolk, and Robert to that of Cheshire; they were all clerks of the king. After this the king had a great consultation, and spoke very deeply with his witan concerning this land, how it was held and what was its tenantry. He then sent his men over all England, into every shire, and caused them to ascertain how many hundred hides of land it contained, and what lands the king possessed therein, what cattle there were in the several counties, and how much revenue he ought to receive yearly from each. He also caused them to write down how much land belonged to his archbishops, to his bishops, his abbots, and his earls, and, that I may be brief, what property every inhabitant of all England possessed in land or in cattle, and how much money this was worth. So very narrowly did he cause the survey to be made, that there was not a single hide nor a rood of land, nor – it is shameful to relate that which he thought no shame to do – was there an ox, or a cow, or a pig passed by, and that was not set down in the accounts, and then all these writings were brought to him.
Anglo-Saxon Chronicle

THE OATH OF SALISBURY, 1086

A. 1086. This year the king wore his crown and held his court at Winchester at Easter, and he so journeyed forward that he was at Winchester during Pentecost, and there he dubbed his son Henry a knight. And afterwards he travelled about, so that he came to Salisbury at Lammas; and his witan, and all the landholders of substance in England, whose vassals soever they were, repaired to him there, and they all submitted to him, and became his men, and swore oaths of allegiance, that they would be faithful to him against all others.

From there he went into the Isle of Wight, because he meant to go to Normandy. But all the same he first acted according to his custom, that is to say he obtained a very great amount of money from his men where he had any pretext for it either justly or otherwise. He afterwards went into Normandy. And Prince Edgar, Edward's kinsman, left him because he did not have much honour from him, but may Almighty God grant him honour in the future. And Christina, the prince's sister, sought refuge in the convent at Romsey and took the veil.

Anglo-Saxon Chronicle

DOMESDAY BOOK. ACCOUNT OF THE LAWS OBSERVED IN THE CITY OF CHICHESTER, 1085

If any freeman, breaking the king's peace which had been given, killed a man in a house, all his land and chattels were forfeit to the king, and he became an outlaw. The earl exacted the same penalty, but only when his own man incurred this forfeiture. Nobody, however, could give back peace to any outlaw except by the will of the king.

A man who shed blood from the morning of Monday to noon on Saturday paid a fine of 10 shillings. But from noon on Saturday until the morning of Monday 20 shillings was the amount of the fine for bloodshed. A like 20 shillings was paid as a fine by the man who shed blood in the 12 days Nativity, on Candlemas Day, on the first day of Easter, and the first day of Pentecost, on Ascension Day, on the day of the Assumption or of the Nativity of Holy Mary, and on the day of the Feast of All Saints.

He who killed a man on these holy days paid a fine of 4 pounds; but on other days 40 shillings. So too he who committed 'hamfare' [breaking in to commit robbery] or 'forsteal' [violence in the street] on these feast days and on Sunday paid 4 pounds; on other days 40 shillings.

He who incurred 'hengwite' [failure to start hue and cry after thief] in the city paid 10 shillings; but a reeve of the king or earl incurring this forfeiture paid a fine of 20 shillings.

He who was guilty of robbery or theft, or assaulted a woman in a house, paid a fine of 40 shillings.

If a widow had unlawful intercourse with any man, she paid a fine of 20 shillings; a young girl paid 10 shillings for this offence.

A man who seized the land of another in the city and could not prove it to be his, paid a fine of 40 shillings. He who made the claim paid a like fine if he could not prove the land to be his by right.

He who wished to take up his land or the land of his kinsman gave 10 shillings; and if he could not or would not pay this, the reeve took his land into the king's hand.

88. An execution. In Norman times criminals were executed, outlawed, or made to pay fines. A new form of justice was trial by battle, often used to settle a personal feud.

He who did not pay his 'gafol' at the term when it was due paid 10 shillings as a fine.

If a fire broke out in the city, the man from whose house it came paid a fine of 3 ounces of pennies, and to his next-door neighbour he gave 2 shillings.

Two-thirds of all these forfeitures were the king's and one-third the earl's.

If ships arrived at the port of the city, or departed therefrom without the permission of the king, the king and the earl had 40 shillings from each man who was on the ships.

If a ship came against the king's peace, and despite his prohibition, the king and the earl had the ship, and the men, and all that was in the ship.

But if the ship came in the king's peace, and with his leave, then those on board might sell what they had undisturbed. When it left, however, the king and the earl took 4 pence from each last. If the king's reeve ordered those who had martens' pelts not to sell to anyone until the king had seen them and been given the opportunity of buying, then he neglected to do this paid a fine of 40 shillings.

A man or a woman giving false measure in the city paid a fine of 4 shillings. Likewise the maker of bad beer was either set in the cucking-stool, or paid 4 shillings to the reeves. The officers of the king and the earl took this forfeiture in the city in whosoever's land it arose, whether the bishop's or that of any other man. In like manner did they take toll and anyone who delayed paying it beyond three nights paid a fine of 40 shillings.

There were in this city *T.R.E.* 7 moneyers who, when the coinage was changed, paid 7 pounds to the king and earl over and above the 'farm'.

There were then 12 'judges' of the city and these were taken from the men of the king and the bishop and the earl. If any of them absented himself from the hundred court on the day of its session without proper excuse, he paid a fine of 10 shillings to the king and the earl.

For the repair of the city wall the reeve was wont to call up one man from each hide in the county. The lord of any man who failed to come paid a fine of 40 shillings to the king and the earl. This forfeiture was not included in the 'farm'.

This city then rendered a 'farm' of 45 pounds and 3 'timbres' of martens' pelts. A third of this was the earl's and two-thirds the king's.

When Earl Hugh received it, it was not worth more than 30 pounds for it was greatly wasted; there were 205 houses less than there had been *T.R.E.* There are now the same number as he found there.

Mundret held the city from the earl for 70 pounds and 1 mark of gold. The same Mundret had at 'farm' for 50 pounds and 1 mark of gold all the earl's pleas in the shire court, and in the hundred courts, except Englefield.

The land on which the church of St. Peter stands, which Robert of Rhuddlan claimed as thegn-land, never belonged to a manor outside the city, and this was proved by witness of the county. It belongs to the borough and always paid dues to the king and the earl like the lands of the other burgesses.

RECORD OF THE JUDGMENT GIVEN BY WILLIAM I IN HIS COURT IN A PLEA BETWEEN THE ABBEY OF FECAMP AND WILLIAM OF BRIOUZE, c.1086

King William held a court at Laycock, a manor of William of Eu, and there decided a plea concerning the claims which William of Briouze had made respecting the possessions of the abbey of Holy Trinity [Fécamp]. The trial lasted one Sunday from morning until evening, and there were present with the king his sons and all his barons. There it was decided and agreed, as to the wood of Hamode, that it should be divided through the middle, both the wood and the land in which the villeins had lived and which belongs to the wood; and by the king's command a hedge was made through the middle of the wood, and our part remained to us and William's to him. As to St. Cuthman's rights of burial, it was decreed that they should remain inviolate; and by the king's command the bodies which had been buried in William's church were exhumed by William's own men and taken to St. Cuthman's church for lawful burial. And Hubert the dean restored the money which he had received for burials and wakes and for tolling the bells, and for all dues for the dead; and he swore first through the mouth of a relative that he had not taken more. As to the land at 'Udica' which William had claimed from Holy Trinity for his park, it was adjudged that the park should be destroyed; and it was destroyed. As to the warren which he had made on the land of Holy Trinity, it was adjudged that it ought not to be paid, because it was never paid in the time of King Edward; and by the king's command what had there been taken in toll was returned, the toll collector swearing that he had not taken more. As to the ships which go up [the river] to St. Cuthman's harbour, it was adjudged that they should be quit for 2 pence for each ascent and descent [of the river], unless they should make another market at William's castle. As to the road which William had made on the land of Holy Trinity, it was adjudged that it should be destroyed; and it was destroyed. As to the ditch which William had made to bring water to his castle, it was adjudged that it should be filled up; and it was filled up; and the land remained the abbot's. As to the marsh, it was decreed that it should be the abbot's as far as the hill and the salt pits; and it was so. As to the eighteen gardens it was adjudged that these should belong to Holy Trinity. As to the weekly toll, it was adjudged that the whole should belong to the saint but that William should have half on Saturday. All these things remained free and quit to the church at Fecamp; and in respect of them William placed his pledge in the king's hand, he being in the king's mercy.

English Historical Documents, Vol.II

DOMESDAY BOOK, 1086

Instructions for taking the Survey

The King's barons enquire by oath of the sheriff of each shire and of all the barons of the French born of them and of the whole hundred, of the priests, the reeve, and six villeins [feudal tenants] from each town . . . the name of the manor, who held it in the time of King Edward the Confessor and who held it now [1086], how many hides [about 100 acres] there were in each manor, how many ploughs on the domain, how many men, how many villeins, how many cottars [cottagers], how many bondsmen, how many freeman, how many soc-man [holding land by virtue of service in the lord's soke or court], how much wood, how much meadow, how much pasture; what mills, what fish or ponds; what had been added or taken away; what it was worth in the time of King Edward the Confessor, and how much it was worth now; how much each free-holder held; and whether more could be got out of it than now.

Inquisitio Elinesis, Domesday Book: Additamenta

DOMESDAY BOOK SHOWS HOW SAXONS SUFFERED IN TAXATION AND LOSS OF DWELLINGS

'At Shrewsbury the Survey describes how the English burgesses of the town took it very hard that they had to pay as much to the king in taxation as was paid from the whole town in King Edward's day.'

D.M. Stenton

The earl's castle [in Shrewsbury] occupies the site of 51 dwellings and another 50 are waste, and the French burgesses hold dwellings that used to pay in the old days, and the earl has given 39 burgesses, whose predecessors used to share in the payment, to the abbey he has founded.

At Lincoln there are 240 dwellings of which 166 have been

destroyed on account of the castle. The remaining 74 are waste outside the castle boundary, not because of the oppression of the sheriffs and officers, but by reason of misfortune and poverty and the ravage of fires.

Anglo-Saxon Chronicle

EXACTIONS OF WILLIAM RUFUS

While these events were occurring in Normandy, beyond sea, and enormous sums were prodigally spent in useless armaments, Ranulph Flambard, now bishop of Durham, and the other minions and officers of the king, were robbing England, and, worse than thieves, pillaged without mercy the granaries of the farmers and the stores of the merchants, not even restraining their bloody hands from plundering the church. On the death of the prelates, they immediately intruded themselves into their places by a violent exercise of the royal authority, and seized without decency whatever they found in their treasuries. They took into the king's hands the domains of the monasteries and the revenues of the bishoprics, and exacted from the abbots or bishops who still survived enormous sums of money.

Thus amassing, by fair means or foul, an immense amount of contributions, they remitted it to the king beyond sea, to be employed on his own occasions whether good or bad. Vast sums, accumulated by these taxes, were presented to the king who used them ostentatiously to enrich foreigners. But the native inhabitants, unjustly spoiled of their goods, were in great distress and cried lamentably to God, who delivered Israel from the hand of Moab, when Eglon the corpulent king was slain by Aoth, the left-handed.

Ordericus Vitalis, X, viii

AN 'ADULTERINE' OR ILLEGAL MILL, Twelfth Century

Herbert the dean erected the windmill upon Haberdon. When the abbot heard of this, his anger was so kindled that he would scarcely eat or utter a single word. On the morrow, after hearing Mass, he commanded the sacrist that without delay he should send his carpenters thither and overturn it altogether, and carefully put by the wooden materials in safe keeping. The dean hearing this came to him saying that he was able in law to do this upon his own frank fee, and that the benefit of the wind ought not to be denied to anyone. He further said that he only wanted to grind his own corn there, and no one else's, lest it should be imagined that he did this to the damage of the neighbouring mills. The abbot, his anger not yet appeased, answered, "I give you as many thanks as if you had cut off both my feet. By the mouth of God I will not eat bread until that building be plucked down. You are an old man, and you should have known that it is not lawful even for the king or his justiciar to alter or appoint a single thing within the banlieue, without the permission of the abbot and the convent; and why have you presumed to do such a thing? Nor is this without prejudice to my mills, as you assert, because the burgesses will run to you and grind their corn at their pleasure, nor can I by law turn them away, because they are free-men. Nor would I endure that the mill of our cellarer, lately set up, should stand except that it was erected before I was abbot. Begone," he said "begone: before you have come to your house, you shall hear what has befallen your mill." But the dean, being afraid before the face of the abbot, by the counsel of his son Master Stephen, forestalled the servants of the sacrist, and without delay caused that the very mill which had been erected by his own servants to be overthrown. So that when the servants of the sacrist came thither, they found nothing to be pulled down.

Jocelin of Brakelond, *Chronicle*

THE FOREST CHARTER, Twelfth Century

[The forest charter promised that] in future no one shall lose life or limb for our venison. But if anyone shall be taken and convicted of stealing venison he shall redeem himself by a heavy payment, if he has that wherewith to do it. If he has nothing wherewith he can redeem himself, he shall lie in our prison for a year and a day. If after one year and one day he can find sureties for good behaviour he shall go out of our prison, but if he cannot, let him abjure the realm of England.

Stubbs, *Charters,* from
English Society in the Early Middle Ages, D.M. Stenton

WRIT OF HENRY I IN FAVOUR OF THE ABBOT OF WESTMINSTER, JULY 1108-1127

Henry, king of the English, to Richard, bishop of London, greeting. I bid you do full right to the abbot of Westminster concerning the men who forcibly, by night, broke into his church of Wenington. And unless you do it, my barons of the Exchequer will cause it to be done in order that I may hear no further complaint about it for lack of right.

LAWS OF HENRY I

Law varies through the counties as the avarice and the sinister, odious activity of legal experts add more grievous means of injury to established legal process. There is so much perversity, and such affluence of evil that the certain truth of law and the remedy established by settled provision can rarely be found, but to the great confusion of all a new method of impleading is sought out, a new subtlety of injury is found, as if that which was before hurt little, and he is thought of most account who does most harm to most people. To those only we pretend reverence and love whom we cannot do without, and whatever does not agree with our cruelty does not exist for us. We assume the character of tyrants and it is desire of wealth which brings this madness upon us. . . . Legal process is involved in so many and so great anxieties that men avoid these exactions, and the uncertain dice of pleas.

Laws of Henry I, trans. F.M. Stenton,
First Century of English Feudalism

THE CHARTER OF LIBERTIES OF HENRY I, 1101

This important charter was to form the basis of the demands which led to the Magna Carta.

In the year of the incarnation of the Lord, 1101, Henry, son of King William, after the death of his brother William, by the grace of God, king of the English, to all faithful, greeting:

1. Know that by the mercy of God, and by the common counsel of the barons of the whole kingdom of England, I have been crowned king of the same kingdom; and because the kingdom has been oppressed by unjust exactions, I, from regard to God, and from the love which I have toward you, in the first place

make the holy church of God free, so that I will neither sell nor place at rent, nor, when archbishop, or bishop, or abbot is dead, will I take anything from the domain of the church, or from its men, until a successor is installed into it. And all the evil customs by which the realm of England was unjustly oppressed will I take away, which evil customs I partly set down here.

2. If any one of my barons, or earls, or others who hold from me shall have died, his heir shall not redeem his land as he did in the time of my brother, but shall relieve it by a just and legitimate relief. Similarly also the men of my barons shall relieve their lands from their lords by a just and legitimate relief.

3. And if any one of the barons or other men of mine wishes to give his daughter in marriage, or his sister or niece or relation, he must speak with me about it, but I will neither take anything from him for this permission, nor forbid him to give her in marriage, unless he should wish to join her to my enemy. And if when a baron or other man of mine is dead, a daughter remains as his heir, I will give her in marriage according to the judgment of my barons, along with her land. And if when a man is dead his wife remains, and is without children, she shall have her dowry and right of marriage, and I will not give her to a husband except to her will.

4. And if a wife has survived with children, she shall have her dowry and right of marriage, so long as she shall have kept her body legitimately, and I will not give her in marriage, except according to her will. And the guardian of the land and children shall be either the wife or another one of the relatives as shall seem to be most just. And I require that my barons should deal similarly with the sons and daughters or wives of their men.

5. The common tax on money which used to be taken through the cities and counties, which was not taken in the time of King Edward, I now forbid altogether henceforth to be taken. If any one shall have been seized, whether a moneyer or any other, with false money, strict justice shall be done for it.

6. All fines and all debts which were owed to my brother, I remit, except my rightful rents, and except those payments which had been agreed upon for the inheritances of others or for those which more justly affected others. And if any one for his own inheritance has stipulated anything, this I remit, and all reliefs which had been agreed upon for rightful inheritances.

which had been agreed upon for rightful inheritances.

7. And if any one of my barons or men shall become feeble, however he himself shall give or arrange to give his money, I grant that it shall be so given. Moreover, if he himself, prevented by arms, or by weakness, shall not have bestowed his money, or arranged to bestow it, his wife or his children or his parents, and his legitimate men shall divide it for his soul, as to them shall seem best.

8. If any of my barons or men shall have committed an offence he shall not give security to the extent of forfeiture of his money, as he did in the time of my father, or of my brother, but according to the measure of the offence so shall he pay, as he would have paid from the time of my father backward, in the time of my other predecessors; so that if he shall have been convicted of treachery or of crime, he shall pay as is just.

9. All murders moreover before that day in which I was crowned king, I pardon: and those which shall be done henceforth shall be punished justly according to the law of King Edward.

10. The forests, by the common agreement of my barons, I have retained in my own hand, as my father held them.

11. To those knights who hold their land by the cuirass, I yield of my own gift the lands of their demesne ploughs free from all payments and from all labour, so that as they have thus been favoured by such a great alleviation, so they may readily provide themselves with horses and arms for my service and for the defence of my kingdom.

12. A firm peace in my whole kingdom I establish and require to be kept from henceforth.

13. The law of King Edward I give to you again with those changes with which my father changed it by the counsel of his barons.

14. If any one has taken anything from my possessions since the death of King William, my brother, or from the possessions of any one, let the whole be immediately returned without alteration, and if any one shall have retained anything thence, he upon whom it is found will pay it heavily to me. Witnesses Maurice, bishop of London, and Gundulf, bishop, and William, bishop-elect, and Henry, earl, and Simon, earl, and Walter Giffard, and Robert de

Montfort, and Roger Bigod, and Henry de Port, at London, when I was crowned.

Ancient Laws and Institutes of England.
Translations and Reprints

THE 'LAWS OF KING HENRY I' (LEGES HENRICI PRIMI), Early Twelfth Century

VII, 1. According to ancient custom, and as lately established by the beneficent rule of the king [Henry I], the general pleas of the shire court shall be held at the recognized terms and times throughout the different provinces of England. Nor shall anyone be burdened further unless the needs of the king and the convenience of the realm demand that meetings shall be more frequent.

VII, 2. There shall take part in these meetings bishops, earls, sheriffs, representatives, hundred men, aldermen, stewards, reeves, barons, vavassors, town reeves and other lords of land. And these shall diligently labour so that the humble may not suffer their wonted injuries through lack of punishment being meted out to evildoers, or through the crimes of oppressors, or through the subversion of judgments.

VII, 3. The true laws of Christianity ought to be dealt with first; then the pleas of the king; and lastly the needs of individuals which are held to be worthy of consideration. And all disputes which are brought to the notice of the shire court shall be settled thereat, either by amicable arrangement or by the rigour of judgment.

VII, 4. The shire moot and the borough moot ought to meet twice a year; and the hundred moot and the wapentake moot twelve times a year. And seven days notice must be given of the meetings unless the public weal, or those things necessary to the efficiency of the king's government demand greater speed.

VII, 5. And if, owing to lack of judges or by any other chance, a matter which should be dealt with by the hundred court is delayed beyond two or three or more meetings of that court, let it be brought to a just settlement.

VII, 6. And if anyone, by lack of right, or by violence, shall so disturb his plea in the hundred court or in any other properly appointed place that it is brought for hearing into the shire court, let him lose it, or otherwise make such amends as may be just.

VII, 7. Any one of the barons of the king, or any one of the barons of any other man taking part in the shire court according to law shall there be entitled to speak in respect of all the land (and the men upon it) which in that shire he holds in demesne. And it shall be likewise done if his steward shall there properly represent him. If either the baron or his steward be absent from necessity, then the reeve and the priest and four of the better men of the village shall represent all those who shall not have been summoned by name to the plea.

VII, 8. Likewise we have decreed what should be done concerning the time and place and manner of judgment in the hundred court, and concerning the just hearing of the causes of individuals, and concerning the presence either of the lord and his steward, or of the priest and reeve and four good men.

VIII, 1. If, however, there be need of a specially full session of the hundred court, let there be summoned twice a year to the hundred court all the freemen who are 'hearth-fast' and householders so that they may decide, among other things, whether the tithings are complete, and who for any reason has left them, or whether any of them are over-full.

VIII, 1*a*. Let there be in each tithing one man as leader over the other nine; and likewise in each hundred let there be one of the better men who may be called alderman, and let him be zealous to promote with all vigilance the observance of the laws of God and man.

VIII, 2. It is provided for the common welfare that each man, who wishes to be held fully worthy of his were and his wite and his law, shall be in a hundred from the twelfth year of his age, and also in a tithing or frankpledge [system of compulsory collective bail fixed for individuals]. Hired men, mercenaries and wage-earners shall however be in the surety of their lords.

VIII, 3. And let every lord have with him those who are subject to his jurisdiction, so that he may hold them to justice for their crimes, or if necessary plead on their behalf.

VIII, 4. It has been said of those who do not hold land that if they serve in another shire and visit their kindred, then shall their kindred be responsible for them to public justice, and if they incur fines their kindred shall make payment for them.

XIX, 2. Over all the lands which the king has in his demesne he has also the jurisdiction. But out of certain lands the king has given manors and the jurisdiction over them as well. And out of other lands the king has given manors but retained the jurisdiction in his own hand. Nor are the royal rights of jurisdiction inevitably alienated when manors are given: rather it is a matter for individual arrangement.

XXIX. The judges for the king are the barons of the shire who hold freelands therein. Through them are to be judged the causes of individuals by means of alternate pleadings. But villeins and cottars and farthingmen [holders of quarter virgates] and those who are base-born and without property are not to be numbered among the judges of the laws.

XXXI, 3. In the business of the shire court there shall take part bishops, earls and other powers, who shall declare with just consideration the laws of God and man.

XXXI, 4. No man may dispute the judgment of the king's court, but it shall be permitted to men who have knowledge of the plea to appeal against the judgment of other courts.

XXXI, 5. No man may be convicted in a capital plea by evidence alone.

XXXI, 7. Each man is to be judged by his equals and by men of the same province.

XXXII, 2. No man shall sit in judgment on his lord, and in the case of the lord to whom he owes liege homage, he shall not do this even if the king is interested in the plea.

XXXIII, 1. If anyone has a plea to bring forward in his court, or in any place properly appointed for such purpose, let him call together his equals and his neighbours, in order that by the judgment they may thus be compelled to give, he may be able fully to prove the justice of his cause in a manner which cannot be disputed.

XLIII, 6. Whoever holds his lands from several lords shall be chiefly responsible to the lord from whom he holds his chief residence and who is his liege lord.

XLIII, 6*a*. If a man has given homage to several lords, and is seized and impleaded by one of them, then his liege lord, from whom he holds his residence, may be his pledge by right against all the others, nor can the liege lord be denied the 'manbot' [fine paid if the man is killed] of his man. . . .

XLIII, 8. If the lord takes away from his man the land or the fief by reason of which he is that lord's man, or if the lord deserts his man in the man's mortal need, then may the man make the lord suffer forfeiture of his rights over him.

XLIII, 9. None the less, the man must suffer insult and injury from his lord for thirty days in time of war, and for a year and a day in time of peace; but during the interval he may demand justice from his lord by legal process through his equals, his neighbours, his household officials or through strangers.

LV, 1. Every lord is allowed to summon his men, so that he may do justice upon them in his court. If the man be resident in a manor far from the honour from which he holds, he shall none the less go to the plea if the lord summon him. But if his lord holds several fiefs, he cannot legally compel a man of one honour to go to the court of another, unless the plea to which the lord summons him concerns a man of that honour.

LV, 2. If the man holds of several lords and honours, he owes more to him from whom he holds his dwelling, and he shall be judged by that lord to whom he shall owe liege honours.

LV, 3. Every man owes duty to his lord for the lord's life and limbs and earthly honour, and for the keeping of the lord's counsel honestly and with profit saving only his fealty to God and to the prince of his country. Theft and treachery and murder and what is against God and the Catholic faith are not to be condoned or demanded. But faith shall be kept to all lords, except in respect of these things, and chiefly to him who is a man's liege lord. And the permission of the liege lord must be obtained before his man makes any other his lord.

A FULL HEAVY YEAR, 1124

In the same year, after St Andrew's Mass, before Christmas Ralph Basset and the king's thegns held a meeting of the Witan at Hundehoge in Leicestershire, and there hanged so many thieves as never were before, that was, in that little while, altogether four and forty men, and six men were deprived of their eyes. Many truthful men said that there were many unjustly mutilated. A full heavy year it was.

Peterborough Chronicle

HENRY I PUNISHES FALSE MONEY-MAKERS, 1125

In 1087 the word 'sterling' became a new name for the English penny. It meant 'tough' or 'strong', was adopted because such pennies should be of the same weight and of high quality, an example of the high standards of William I's days.

In this year [1125] King Henry sent to England from Normandy before Christmas [of 1124], and ordered that all the moneyers who were in England should be mutilated – *i.e.* that each should lose the right hand and be castrated. That was because the man who had a pound could not get a pennyworth at a market. And Bishop Roger of Salisbury sent over all England and ordered them all to come to Winchester at Christmas [1124]. When they got there, they were taken one by one and each deprived of the right hand and castrated. All this was done before Twelfth Night [6 January 1125], and it was done very justly because they had ruined all the country with their great false-dealing: they all paid for it.

Anglo-Saxon Chronicle

89. The executioner, twelfth century

SURVEY RECORDING THE DUTIES AND PAYMENTS OF MEN IN PYTCHLEY IN NORTHAMPTONSHIRE, 1125

When John, abbot of Peterborough abbey, died in 1125 the property was taken in the hands of the king, entrusted to Walter the archdeacon who made a detailed account to the royal exchequer.

There are there 9 full villeins and 9 half villeins and 5 cottagers. The full villeins work 3 days a week up to the feast of St Peter in August and thence up to Michaelmas every day by custom, and the half villeins in accordance with their tenures; and the cottagers one day a week and two in August. All together they have 8 plough teams. Each full villein ought to plough and harrow one acre at the winter ploughing and one at the spring, and winnow the seed in his lord's grange and sow it. The half villeins do as much as belongs to them. Beyond this they should lend their plough teams 3 times at the winter ploughing and 3 times at the spring ploughing and once for harrowing. And what they plough they reap and cart. And they render 5 shillings at Christmas and 5 shillings at Easter and 32 pence at St Peter's feast.

And Agemund the miller renders 26 shillings for his mill and one for yardland. And all the villeins render 32 pence at St Peter's feast.

And Agemund the miller renders 26 shillings for his mill and for one yardland. And all the villeins render 32 hens at Christmas. The full villeins render 20 eggs and the half villeins 10 eggs and the cottagers 5 eggs at Easter. Viel renders 3 shillings for one yardland and Aze 5; the priest, for the church and 2 yardlands, 5 shillings. Walter the free man pays 2 shillings for a half yardland. Leofric the smith pays 12 pence for one loft. Aegelric of Kettering pays 6 pence for the land he rents and Aegelric of Broughton 12 pence and Lambert 12 pence. And Ralf the sokeman lends his plough 3 times a year. Martin gives a penny and Azo a penny and Ulf and Lambert a penny. On the home farm there are 4 plough teams with 30 oxen and 8 oxherds who each hold a half yardland of the home farm. There are 2 draught horses, 220 sheep, 20 pigs, and 10 old sheep in their second year.

From, *English Society in the Early Middle Ages*,
D.M. Stenton

THE MANOR COURT, Twelfth Century

Walter of the Moor, thou art attached to answer in this court wherefore by night and against the lord's peace thou didst enter the preserve of the lord and didst carry off at thy will divers manner of fish (and didst make largess of it by gift and sale). How wilt thou acquit thyself or make amends? For know this, that were anyone to prosecute thee, thou wouldst be in peril of life and member; so be advised:

Sir, by thy leave I will impart.

Then afterwards he speaks thus: Sir, for God's sake do not take it ill of me if I tell thee the truth, how I went the other evening along the bank of this pond and looked at the fish which were playing in the water, so beautiful and so bright, and for the great desire that I had for a tench I laid me down on the bank and just with my hands, quite simply, and without any other device, I caught that tench and carried it off. And now I will tell you the cause of my covetousness and my desire. My dear wife had lain abed a right full month, as my neighbours who are here know, and she could never eat or drink anything to her liking, and for the great desire that she had to eat a tench I went to the bank of the pond to take just one tench; and that never other fish from the pond did I take, ready am I to do by way of proof whatever thou shalt award me.

Walter, saith the steward, at least thou hast confessed in this court a tench taken and carried away in other wise than it should have been, for thou mightest have come by it in fairer fashion. Therefore we tell thee that thou art in the lord's mercy, and besides this thou must wage us a law six-handed that thou didst not take at that or any other time any other manner fish.

As you honour pleases . . .

From *Court Baron*

SUMMONSES ARE ISSUED IN ORDER THAT THE EXCHEQUER MAY BE HELD

After a writ of summons, sealed with the image of royal authority, has been dispatched, those whose attendance is necessary are convoked to the place named. For they are not obliged to come unless the summons has first been sent. Some, moreover, attend to sit as judges, others to pay and be judged. The barons, whom we mentioned above, sit and act as judges either by virtue of their office or by mandate of the king. But the sheriffs and many others in the kingdom discharge their accounts and are judged accordingly. Of these, some are liable for voluntary payments, others for compulsory ones. Concerning the latter we shall speak more fully below in treating of the sheriff. Now, as there are a great number of such persons in all the counties, it should be specifically stated in each case in the summons how much is due to be paid at the forthcoming term, and the cause thereof added, as if it were said: "Thou shalt have from so-and-so such-and-such a sum for such-and-such a reason." But if anything should be demanded from the sheriff, when he is sitting to render account, in respect of any debtor in his county, of whom, however, no mention was made in the summons, he will not be held liable for it, but will rather be excused, because the summons has not preceded the demand. Summonses are issued, therefore, in order that the king's 'farm' and the dues demanded for a variety of reasons may flow into the Treasury. There are indeed some revenues which must necessarily be transmitted through the hand of the sheriff, even though no summons be issued concerning them, but these are casual [e.g. treasure trove, chattels of felons and fugitives] rather than fixed or definite payments, as will appear from what follows.

Dialogus de Scaccario

FROM THE EARLY WELSH LAWS c.1150

. . . A freeman's wife may give away her tunic and her mantle and her kerchief and her shoes, and her flour and cheese and butter and milk without her husband's permission, and may lend all the household utensils. The wife of a villein may not give away anything without her husband's permission except her headdress; and she cannot lend anything except her sieve and riddle, and that only as far as her cry may be heard when her foot is on her threshold . . .

. . . An adult woman who elopes with a man and is taken by him to a wood or a thicket or a house, and is violated and let go again, if she complains to her family and in the courts, as proof of her chastity a bull of three winters is to be taken and its tail is to be shaved and smeared with fat, and then the tail is to be thrust through a hurdle. And then the woman shall go into the house and put her foot on the threshold and take the tail in her hands. And a man shall come on either side of the bull with a goad in the hand of each, to stir up the bull. And if she can hold the bull she may take it for her insult-fine and as recompense for her chastity; and if she cannot she may take as much of the fat as sticks to her hands.

A woman who gives herself up to a man in wood or thicket, and is abandoned by the man to woo another, and comes to complain to her family and to the courts, if the man denies it let him swear on oath on a bell without a clapper; but if he offers to make compensation, let him pay her with a penny as broad as her behind . . .

From *A Celtic Miscellany*,
translated by Kenneth Hurlstone Jackson

Famous People

RANULPH FLAMBARD

The rapacity of his [William II's] disposition was seconded by Ranulph, the inciter of his covetousness; a clergyman of the poorest origin, but raised to eminence by his wit and subtlety. If at any time a royal edict was issued that England should pay a certain tribute it was doubled by this plunderer of the rich, this exterminator of the poor, this confiscator of other men's inheritance. He was an invincible pleader, as unrestrained in his words as in his actions; and equally furious against the meek or the turbulent. Wherefore the king used to laugh and say that he was the only man who knew how to employ his talents in this way, and cared for no one's hatred, so that he could please his master. At Flambard's suggestion, the sacred honours of the church, as the pastors died, were exposed to sale; for whenever the death of any bishop or abbot was announced, directly one of the king's clerks was admitted who made an inventory of everything, and carried all future rents into the royal exchequer. In the meantime some person was sought out fit to supply the place of the deceased; not from proof of morals, but of money; and, eventually, if I may so say, the empty honour was conferred, and even that purchased at great price. These things appeared the more disgraceful, because in his [William II] father's time, after the decease of a bishop or abbot, all rents were reserved entire, to be given up to the succeeding pastor; and persons truly meritorious, on account of their religion, were elected. But in the lapse of a very few years everything was changed.

William of Malmesbury, *Gesta Regum Anglorum*
translated by J.A. Giles

King William was in Normandy at Christmas [1099], and came to this country at Easter, and at Whitsuntide held his court for the first time in his new building at Westminster, and there gave the bishopric of Durham to his chaplain, Ranulf, who had managed his councils over all England, and superintended them.

Anglo-Saxon Chronicle,
English Historical Documents Vol.II

At this time a certain clerk called Ranulph gained the confidence of William Rufus, and acquired pre-eminence over all the king's officers by his subtlety in prosecutions and his skill in flattery. This man was of an acute intellect and handsome person, a fluent speaker, fond of the pleasures of the table, and addicted to wine and lust, he was, at the same time, cruel and ambitious, prodigal to his own adherents, but most rapacious in his exactions from strangers. Sprung from poor and low parents, and rising to a level far beyond that to which his birth entitled him, his arrogance was swelled by the losses he inflicted on others. He was the son of one Thurstan, an obscure priest of the diocese of Bayeux, and, having been brought up from his earliest years among the vile parasites of the court, was better skilled in crafty intrigues and verbal subtleties than in sound learning. Inflated with ambition to raise himself above the eminent men who adorned the court of the great king William, he undertook many things without orders, and of which that prince was ignorant, making important and vexatious accusations in the king's court, and arrogantly overawing his superiors as if he was supported by the royal authority. In consequence Robert, the king's steward, gave him the surname of Flambard, which, indeed, prophetically suited his genuis and conduct; for, like a devouring flame, he tormented the people and turned the daily chants of the church into lamentations, by the new practices he introduced into the country . . . he shamefully oppressed the king's faithful and humble subjects, impoverishing them by the loss of their property, and reducing them from affluence to great indigence.

Ordericus Vitalis,
translated by T. Forester, Vol.II

EARL GODWIN

When God's rod of justice had swept away by the oppression of the Danes what had displeased Him among the people, and the kingdom as a result of the vicissitudes of war, had passed to Cnut, among the new nobles of the conquered kingdom attached to the king's side that Godwin, whom we have just mentioned, was judged by the king himself the most cautious in counsel and the most active in war. He was, too, because of his equable temperament, most acceptable both to the people and to the king himself; he was incomparable in his tireless application to work, and with pleasing and ready courtesy polite to all. When, however, some fitting business of the kingdom called Cnut to his own people – for in his absence some unbridled men, putting off his authority from their necks, had prepared to rebel – Godwin was

90. Hugo, the illuminator, makes this sketch of himself in the margin of Jerome's *Commentary on Isaiah* about 1100. He has the tonsure and habit of a monk. He dips the quill pen in an inkhorn, holding a knife in his other hand to sharpen it.

his inseparable companion on the whole journey. Here the king tested more closely his wisdom, here his perseverance, here his courage in war, and here the strength of this nobleman. He also found out how profound he was in eloquence, and what advantage it would be to him in his newly acquired kingdom if he were to bind him more closely to him by means of some fitting reward. Consequently he admitted the man, whom he tested in this was for so long, to his council and gave him his sister as wife. And when Godwin returned home, having performed all things well, he was appointed by him earl and office-bearer of almost all the kingdom. Having obtained this pre-eminent honour, Godwin did not carry himself high, but showed himself to all good men as much as he could like a father; and he did not discard the gentleness he had learned from boyhood, but, as something implanted in him by nature, took infinite trouble to cultivate it in all his dealings with inferiors and among equals. Whatever wrongs appeared, right and law were promptly restored there. Hence he was regarded not as a master but was revered by all the country's sons as a father. There were born anon sons and daughters not unworthy of such a sire, but rather distinguished by their parents' good qualities; and in their education attention was paid specially to those arts which would prepare them to be a strength and help to future rulers. And since our purpose centres on this point, that the virtues of these children, with the duteous aid of our description, should not be hidden from posterity, we should reserve these things to be told in their proper places, and those which are not to be omitted at the beginning we shall tell plainly and briefly in their right order.

In the reign of this King Cnut, Godwin flourished in the royal palace, having the first place among the highest nobles of the kingdom; and, as was just, what he wrote all decreed should be written, and what he erased, erased.

The Life of King Edward the Confessor,
edited by Frank Barlow

ROBERT OF JUMIEGÈS

When King Edward of holy memory returned from Francia, quite a number of men of that nation, and they not base-born, accompanied him. And these, since he was master of the whole kingdom, he kept with him, enriched them with many honours, and made them his privy counsellors and administrators of the royal palace. Among them had come a certain abbot named Robert, who overseas had ruled the monastery of Jumièges, and who, they say, always the most powerful confidential adviser of the king. By his counsel many things both good and bad were done in the kingdom, with varying result, as is the way of the world. Moreover, on the death of the bishop of London he succeeded by royal favour to the see of his pontifical cathedral, and with the authority derived from this promotion intruded himself more than was necessary in directing the course of the royal councils and acts; so much so, indeed, that, according to the saying, 'Evil communications corrupt good manners', through his assiduous communication with him the King began to neglect more useful advice. Hence, as generally happens, he offended quite a number of the nobles of his kingdom by means of another's fault. And for such reasons his realm gradually became disturbed, because, when the holders of dignities died, one set of men wanted the vacant sees for their own friends, and others were alienating them to strangers.

The Life of King Edward the Confessor,
edited by Frank Barlow

THURSTAN, A NORMAN ABBOT, 1083

1083. In this year arose the discord at Glastonbury between the abbot Thurstan [once a monk of Caen] and his monks. In the first instance, it came of the abbot's lack of wisdom in misgoverning the monks in many matters, and the monks complained of it to him in a kindly way and asked him to rule them justly and to love them, and they would be loyal and obedient to him. But the abbot would do nothing of the sort [the dispute was on the chanting and the celebration of Saints' Days], but gave them bad treatment and threatened them with worse. One day the abbot went into the chapter and spoke against them and wanted to ill-treat them, and then sent for some laymen [household knights], and they came into the chapter, and fell upon the monks fully armed. And then the monks were very much afraid of them, and did not know what they had better do. But they scattered; some ran into the church and locked the doors on themselves – and they went after them into the monastery and meant to drag them out when they dared not go out. But a grievous thing happened that day – the Frenchmen [knights mentioned above] broke into the choir and threw missiles towards the altar where the monks were, and some of the retainers went up to the upper story and shot arrows down towards the shrine, so that many arrows stuck in the cross that stood above the altar; and the wretched monks were lying round about the altar, and some crept under it, and cried to God zealously, asking for his mercy when they could get no mercy from men. What can we say, except that they shot fiercely, and the others broke down the doors there, and went in and killed some of the monks and wounded many there in the church, so that the blood came from the altar on to the steps, and from the steps on to the floor. Three were killed there and eighteen wounded.

Anglo-Saxon Chronicle,
English Historical Documents Vol.II

THURSTAN, ARCHBISHOP OF YORK, Twelfth Century

On the morrow of the Assumption of the most holy Virgin, the king's chaplain, Thurstan, canon of St Paul's, London, took upon him our church, a learned clerk, prudent and diligent in worldly affairs, energetic and courteously efficient in providing, preparing, and acting in domestic and military matters, and in necessary payments abroad. For these reasons he was a favourite member of the household of William II, and a trusted servant of King Henry, with whom he had great influence. The king, having full confidence in him, whether present in England or absent in Normandy, used him to make arrangements and payments, and do business of all kinds. His prudence and free-handedness in this made him known and beloved by gentle and simple in and around the Court. In welcoming and doing honour to foreigners and strangers, religious and secular, he was lavish and cheerful, serving them kindly and becomingly. This too added to his honour and advantage in many places and at the right time.

Hugh the Chantor,
translated by C. Johnson

91. Geoffrey Plantagenet, Count of Anjou, enamel at Le Mans, *c*.1151. He married Maud, the daughter of Henry I, after the death of her first husband, Emperor Henry V. Their son became the renowned king, Henry II.

Upon this marriage in 1127, Geoffrey Plantagenet was knighted by Henry I, a shield painted with golden lions on a blue field, was hung about his neck. Such a shield is shown in the portrait above.

ROGER, ARCHBISHOP OF YORK

In the same year [1181] also died Roger, archbishop of York, a learned and eloquent man, and in worldly affairs prudent almost to singularity. In his episcopal office indeed, that is, in the cure of souls, he was less conscientious; but he was zealous to good purpose in the preservation and advancement of those things which God had not joined to his office but which the world had added to it for God's sake. Certainly, in temporal goods he so raised the archbishopric of York that he left to his successors hardly any anxieties in respect either of the increase of their revenues or the grandeur of their buildings. Further, he used his opportunities for the aggrandisement of his finances to such an extent, and so excelled in his management of them that he rarely overlooked or neglected a chance to improve them. Instead of ecclesiastics of eminence, with whom the church of York was formerly studded as with jewels, he preferred to benefices beardless youths or even boys, still under the master's rod and more suited by their age

'to build toy houses, to yoke mice to a little cart,
to play at odd and even, and to ride a hobby-horse'

than to sustain the character of church dignitaries. And this he did with the intent that until they became of age he might undertake the care of their persons and appropriate the entire revenues of their benefices. Christian philosophers, that is to say, men of the religious Orders, he abhorred to such a degree that he is reported to have said that Thurstan [the hero of the battle of the Standard, 1138] of happy memory, the former archbishop of York, had never committed a more grievous sin than when he built the abbey of Fountains, that shining mirror of Christian philosophy. Perceiving that some of those present were shocked at this remark, he added, 'You are laymen and cannot comprehend the meaning of the term.' He was wont also to say that an ecclesiastical benefice ought rather to be conferred on a dissolute priest than on a monk. This rule he openly and scrupulously kept all his days, and in nearly everything he made the lot of the monks worse than that of the secular clergy.

William of Newburgh, *Historia Rerum Anglicarum*, 1154-1170, *English Historical Documents*, Vol.II

GODRIC THE MERCHANT, Twelfth Century

This holy man's father was named Ailward, and his mother Edwenna; both of slender rank and wealth, but abundant in righteousness and virtue. They were born in Norfolk, and had long lived in the township called Walpole. . . . Aspiring to the merchant's trade, he began to follow the chapman's way of life, first learning how to gain in small bargains and things of insignificant price; and thence, while yet a youth, his mind advanced little by little to buy and sell and gain from things of greater expense. For, in his beginnings, he was wont to wander with small wares around the villages and farmsteads of his own neighbourhood; but in process of time, he gradually associated himself by compact with city merchants. Hence, within a brief space of time, the youth who had trudged for many weary hours from village to village, from farm to farm, did so profit by his increase of age and wisdom as to travel with associates of his own age through towns and boroughs, fortresses and cities, to fairs and to all the various booths of the market-place, in pursuit of his public chaffer. . . . At first, he lived as a chapman for four years in Lincolnshire, going on foot and carrying the smallest wares; then he travelled abroad, first to St. Andrews in Scotland and then for the first time to Rome. On his return, having formed a familiar friendship with certain young men who were eager for merchandise, he began to launch upon bolder courses, and to coast frequently by sea to the foreign lands that lay around him. Thus, sailing often to and fro . . . he traded in many divers wares and, amid these occupations, learned much worldly wisdom. . . . For he laboured not only as a merchant but also as a shipman . . . to Denmark and Flanders and Scotland; in all which he found certain rare, and therefore more precious, wares . . . for he sold dear in one place the wares which he had bought elsewhere at a small price.

Then he purchased the half of a merchant-ship with certain of his partners in the trade; and again by his prudence he bought the fourth part of another ship. At length, by his skill in navigation, wherein he excelled all his fellows, he earned promotion to the post of steersman. . . .

For he was vigorous and strenuous in mind, whole of limb and strong in body. He was of middle stature, broad-shouldered and deep-chested, with a long face, grey eyes most clear and piercing, bushy brows, a broad forehead, long and open nostrils, a nose of comely curve, and a pointed chin. His beard was thick, and longer than the ordinary, his mouth well-shaped, with lips of moderate thickness; in youth his hair was black, in age as white as snow; his neck was short and thick, knotted with veins and sinews; his legs were somewhat slender, his instep high, his knees hardened and horny with frequent kneeling; his whole skin rough beyond the ordinary, until all this roughness was softened by old age. . . . In labour he was strenuous, assiduous above all men; and, when by chance his bodily strength proved insufficient, he compassed his ends with great ease by the skill which his daily labours had given, and by a prudence born of long experience. . . . He knew, from the aspect of sea and stars, how to foretell fair or foul weather. In his various voyages he visited many saints' shrines, to whose protection he was wont most devoutly to commend himself; more especially the church of St. Andrew in Scotland, where he most frequently made and paid his vows. On the way thither, he oftentimes touched at the island of Lindisfarne, wherein St. Cuthbert had been bishop, and at the isle of Farne, where the Saint had lived as an anchoret, and where St. Godric (as he himself would tell afterwards) would meditate on the Saint's life with abundant tears. Thence he began to yearn for solitude, and to hold his merchandise in less esteem than heretofore. . . .

Reginald, monk of Durham, *Life of St Godric,*
translated by G.G. Coulton

92. Henry of Blois was Abbot of Glastonbury 1126-1171, and Bishop of Winchester 1129-1171. He gained accession to the throne for his brother, Stephen of Blois in 1135. Henry known as the warrior monk, consecrated Becket as archbishop.

AILRED OF RIEVAULX, CISTERCIAN ABBOT, c.1140

Our father was in boyhood remarkable, and even when of tender years had the makings of a fine man . . . The king was so fond of him that he made him great in his house and glorious in his palace. He was put in charge of many things and was as a second lord and prince over a host of officials and all the men of the court. . . . In any case, he was steward of the royal household. Nothing, inside or out, was done without him. He was respected by all in all things and never failed; and no wonder, for God had taught him patience and had enriched his active spirit with no little prudence, so that in the largeness of his pure heart he was without hatred or rancour, nourished no discord, no bitterness, and, though in a position to harm many, was serviceable to all. . . .

He rises quickly nor sits long in the same place, but hastens to some labour of his hands. See how he set about this, to the grace of the brethren and his own well-being. . . . And with it all he displayed such deftness that even the slack and negligent, when they saw him, were stirred to endure the sweat of honest toil. Weak though he was in body, his splendid spirit carried him through the labours of stronger and strenuous men. He did not spare the soft skin of his hands, but manfully wielded with his slender fingers the rough tools of his field-tasks to the admiration of all. . . . He was ready and easy in speech, said what he wished to say and said it well. But enough of this. His writings preserved for posterity by the labour of my own hand, show quite well enough how he was wont to express himself. . . .

He turned the house of Rievaulx into a stronghold for the sustaining of the weak, the nourishment of the strong and whole; it was the home of piety and peace, the abode of perfect love of God and neighbour. Who was there, however despised and rejected, who did not find in it a place of rest? . . . and that is the singular and supreme glory of the house of Rievaulx that above all else it teaches tolerance of the infirm and compassion with others in their necessities. . . .

. . . I must not omit to mention the extent to which this holy mansion, the house of Rievaulx grew under the hand of the venerable father. He doubled all things in it – monks, conversi, laymen, farms, lands and every kind of equipment; indeed he trebled the intensity of the monastic life and its charity. On feast days you might see the church crowded with the brethren like bees in a hive, unable to move forward because of the multitude, clustered together, rather, and compacted into one angelical body. Hence it was that the father left behind him at Rievaulx, when he returned to Christ, one hundred and forty monks and five hundred conversi and laymen. His material legacy was great enough, under prudent management, to feed and clothe a still greater number and to leave something over for their successors.

Walter Daniel, edited, *Life of Ailred*,
F.M. Powicke

HAROLD AND TOSTIG

And since the occasion offers, we wish, to the best of our small powers, to inform posterity about life, habits, and deeds of these two brothers. And we do not think our wish to do this unreasonable, both on account of the plan of the work, and also so that their posterity shall have models for imitation. Both had the advantage of distinctly handsome and graceful persons, similar in strength, as we gather; and both were equally brave. But the elder, Harold, was the taller, well practised in endless fatigues and doing without sleep and food, and endowed with mildness and temper and a more ready understanding. He could bear contradiction well, not readily revealing or retaliating—never, I think, on a fellow citizen or compatriot. With anyone he thought loyal he would sometimes share the plan of his project, sometimes defer this so long, some would judge—if one ought to say this—as to be hardly to his advantage. Indeed, the fault of rashness or levity is not one that anybody could charge against him, or Tostig, or any son born of Godwin, or anyone brought up under his rule or instruction. And Eark Tostig himself was endowed with very great and prudent restraint—although occasionally he was a little over-zealous in attacking evil—and with bold and inflexible constancy of mind. He would first ponder much and by himself the plans in his mind, and when he had ascertained by appreciation of the matter the final issue, he would set them in order; and these he would not readily share with anyone. Also sometimes he was so cautiously active that his action seemed to come before his planning; and this often enough was advantageous to him in the theatre of the world. When he gave, he was lavish with liberal bounty, and, urged by his religious wife, it was done more frequently in honour of Christ than for any fickle favour of men. In his word, deed, or promise he was distinguished by adamantine steadfastness. He renounced desire for all women except his wife of royal stock, and chastely, with restraint, and wisely he governed the use of his body and tongue. Both persevered with what they had begun; but Tostig vigorously, Harold prudently; the one in action aimed at success, the other also at happiness. Both at times so cleverly disguised their intentions that one who did not know them was in doubt what to think. And to sum up their characters for our readers, no age and no province has reared two mortals of such worth at the same time. The king appreciated this, and with them thus stationed in his kingdom, he lived all his life free from care of either flank, for the one drove back the foe from the south and the other scared them off from the north.

The Life of King Edward the Confessor, edited by F. Barlow

WILLIAM OF ST CALAIS, BISHOP OF DURHAM

In the year of our Lord 1080, Walcher, bishop of Durham, was killed by the men of his diocese, and after six months and ten days he was succeeded by William, who was elected bishop of Durham on 9 November, and ordained on 5 January at Gloucester by Thomas, archbishop of York, in the presence of William the king [William I] and of all the bishops of England. This William who was made bishop of Durham had been one of the clergy of Bayeux; he became a monk in the monastery of St Calais; he was then successively prior of the cloister, major prior, and abbot of the monastery of St Vincent; and finally he was translated to the bishopric of Durham by King William, who had found him assiduous in the conduct of difficult business. He was a man of acute mind, being supple in counsel and of great eloquence and wisdom. Moreover, he had read in the *Ecclesiastical History of the English People* [by Bede] and in the *Life of St Cuthbert* [also by Bede] that, before the time of St Cuthbert and for many years afterwards, a convent of monks had served God in the church of Durham, but that subsequently, together with nearly all other churches and monasteries, it had been destroyed by the pagans. He therefore determined to restore the ancient monastic practice in the capital church of his diocese. Wherefore he went to Rome at the bidding of King William, and faithfully reported to Pope Gregory VII the ancient and present state of the church at Durham. Coming back with the apostolic command and authority, he restored the monastic life around the body of St Cuthbert at Pentecost on 28 May in the third year of his episcopate and in the seventeenth year of King William's reign.

Concerning the unjust persecution of William, Bishop of Durham, *English Historical Documents*, Vol. II

93. A portrait of Eadwine, monk and scribe of Christchurch, Canterbury

ROGER OF SALISBURY, d.1139

In the reign of William the younger [William II] he [Roger] was an indigent priest, living by his office, as it is said, in the suburbs of Caen. At the time when Henry the younger was engaged in war against the king his brother [William II], during a journey he accidentally turned with his companions into the church where Roger was officiating, and entreated him to say mass for him. The priest granting the request, was as ready to begin as he was quick in getting through the service; in both of which he so pleased the soldiers that they declared such a suitable chaplain for knights was nowhere else to be found. And when the royal youth said 'Follow me,' he stuck as closely to him as Peter formerly did to the Lord of Heaven when he uttered the like command. For, as Peter left his boat and followed the King of kings, so this man quitted his church and followed the noble youth, and, being a blind leader of the blind; and though he was almost illiterate, yet he was so subtle by nature, that in a short time he became dear to his lord, and managed his most private concerns. Afterwards, when his master became king, he advanced him to the bishopric of Salisbury, as having deserved well of him, both before and during his reign; and, moreover, as to a person approved in many things, faithful and industrious, he entrusted him with the management of public affairs, that he might be not only distinguished in the church, but even the second person in the kingdom.

William of Newburgh, *Historia Rerum Anglicarum*,
translated by J. Stevenson

Henry had among his counsellors, Roger, bishop of Salisbury, on whose advice he principally relied. For, before his accession, he had made him regulator of his household, and on becoming king, having had proof of his abilities, appointed him first chancellor and then a bishop. The able discharge of his episcopal functions led to a hope that he might be deserving of a higher office. He therefore committed to his care the administration of the whole kingdom, whether he might himself be resident in England or absent in Normandy. The bishop refused to embroil himself in cares of such magnitude until the three archbishops of Canterbury, Anselm, Ralph, William, and lastly the pope, enjoined on him the duty of obedience. Henry was extremely eager to effect this, aware that Roger would faithfully perform everything for his advantage. Nor did he deceive the royal expectation, but conducted himself with so much integrity and diligence, that not a spark of envy was kindled against him. Moreover, the king was frequently detained in Normandy, sometimes for three, sometimes four years, and sometimes for a longer period; and on his return to his kingdom, he gave credit to the chancellor's discretion for finding little or nothing to distress him. Amid all these affairs, he did not neglect his ecclesiastical duties, but daily diligently transacted them in the morning, that he might be more ready and undisturbed for other business. He was a prelate of great mind, and spared no expense towards completing his designs, especially in buildings, which may be seen in other places, but more particularly at Salisbury and at Malmesbury. For there he erected extensive edifices, at vast cost, and with surpassing beauty; the courses of stone being so correctly laid that the joint deceives the eye, and leads it to imagine that the whole wall is composed of a single block. He built anew the church of Salisbury, and beautified it in such a manner that it yields to none in England, but surpasses many, so that he had just cause to say 'Lord, I have loved the glory of thy house'.

William of Malmesbury, *Gesta Regum Anglorum*,
translated by J.A. Giles

In the meantime there arose a man of prudence, far-sighted in counsel, eloquent in discourse, and by the grace of God, remarkably qualified to deal with great affairs. It may be said that in him was fulfilled what is written, 'the grace of the Holy Spirit knows no belated efforts'. Being summoned to court by this same king, unknown yet not ignoble, he taught by his example, 'how extreme poverty can be most fruitful of heroes!' This man, therefore, increasing in favour with the king, the clergy and people, was made bishop of Salisbury; he enjoyed the highest offices and honours in the kingdom, and acquired a most profound knowledge of the Exchequer; so much so that, as without doubt the rolls themselves made manifest, it flourished mightily under him. From his legacy, indeed, I have received by direct inheritance the little knowledge which I possess. Upon this point I refrain from saying much at present, since as became the nature of his rank, he left to posterity a memory which gives proof of a most noble mind. Subsequently on the king's orders he came to the Exchequer.

'Dialogue of the Exchequer',
English Historical Documents, Vol.II

GEOFFREY DE MANDEVILLE, d.1144

At this time, King Stephen, attending more to what was expedient than what was strictly honourable, seized Geoffrey de Mandeville, in his court at St. Albans, not quite fairly, indeed, and consistently with the law of nations, but according to his deserts and his own fear. For he was a most desperate character and possessed of equal power and artifice. He was master of the celebrated Tower of London, together with two other considerable fortresses, and he aimed at great things by his consummate craft. As, therefore, from these circumstances, he was an object of terror to the king, Stephen cautiously dissembled the injury he had received from him, and eagerly watched a seasonable opportunity for revenge. The injury this abandoned man had done to the king was this: Stephen, some years before, as I have before said, had seized on the treasures of the bishop of Salisbury, and transmitted a vast sum of the money to Louis, king of France, to whose sister, Constantia, he had affianced his son Eustace; purposing, by an affinity with so great a prince, to strengthen his succession against the count of Anjou and his sons. Constantia was at that time in London with the queen her mother-in-law; but when the queen was desirous of removing with her daughter-in-law to another place, Geoffrey de Mandeville, who at that time commanded the Tower, opposed her and took the daughter from the protection of the mother; and though she resisted with all her might, yet he detained her, and suffered the queen to depart with ignominy. Afterwards, indeed, he reluctantly yielded up his noble prisoner to the king her father-in-law, who claimed her; and Stephen dissembled for a while his just indignation. This outrage had appeared to have long since been consigned to oblivion; but, behold, on a meeting of the nobility being summoned by the king's command at St Albans, this freebooter made his appearance among the rest, and the king, seizing this opportunity for exercising his just indignation, threw him into confinement, and deprived him of the Tower of London, with the two other fortresses he possessed. Despoiled of his strongholds, but set at liberty, this restless man – vast in design, and subtle beyond comparison, as well as wise beyond measure, for the perpetration of evil – collecting a band of desperadoes, seized the monastery at Ramsey, and without the least compunction at having expelled the monks and made so celebrated and holy a place a den of thieves, and converted the sanctuary of God into the habitation of the devil, he infested the neighbourhood with perpetual attacks and incursions. Then, gaining confidence from his success, he proceeded further, and harassed and alarmed King Stephen with the most daring aggressions; and, while he was thus continuing his mad career, God seemed to sleep, and to be regardless both of the affairs of men and His own; that is to say, ecclesiastical affairs. . . . At length . . . the wretch himself, amidst the thickest of his troops, attacking a fortress of the enemy, was struck on the head with an arrow, by a common foot-soldier. Although this ferocious man at first disregarded his wound as trifling, yet he died in consequence of it a few days afterwards, and carried with him to hell the indissoluble bond of an ecclesiastical anathema.

William of Newburgh, *Historia Rerum Anglicarum*
translated by J. Stevenson

94. Seal of Gilbert de Clare, Earl of Pembroke, 1141-1146, of the great house of Clare (and an uncle of Waleran, Earl of Worcester). It shows him on horseback, bearing a shield charged with chevrons, six in number, red on gold. Arms of the later Clares were three in number.

ODO, 1035-1097, BISHOP OF BAYEUX

Half-brother (through his mother) of Duke William and brother of Robert of Mortain

Odo's friends persuaded the dying William I to release Odo from prison. Ordericus Vitalis expresses what must have been in William's mind on this occasion.

The king[William I] was exhausted by the numerous solicitations from so many quarters for the release of the bishop of Bayeux; but at length he said: 'I wonder that your penetration has not discovered the character of the man for whom you supplicate me. Are you not making petitions for a prelate who has long held religion in contempt, and who is the subtle promoter of fatal division? Have I not already incarcerated for four years this bishop, who, when he ought to have proved himself exemplary in the just government of England, became a most cruel oppressor of the people and destroyer of the convents of monks? In desiring the liberation of this seditious man you are ill-advised and are bringing on yourself a serious calamity. It is clear that my brother, Odo, is an untrustworthy man, ambitious, given to fleshly desires, and of enormous cruelty; and that he will never be converted from his whoredoms and ruinous follies. I satisfied myself of this on several occasions, and therefore I imprisoned, not the bishop, but the tyrannical earl. There is no doubt that if he is released, he will disturb the whole country and be the ruin of thousands. I say this not from hatred, as if I were his enemy, but as the father of my country, watching over the welfare of a Christian people. It would indeed give me inexpressible and heart-felt joy to think that he would conduct himself with chastity and moderation, as becomes a priest and minister of God.' [This alludes to the war of 1088]

Ordericus Vitalis, *Historia Ecclesiastica*, 1123-1141
English Historical Documents, Vol.II

ROBERT OF BELLÊME c.1057-c.1131, EARL OF SHREWSBURY

He was a man intolerable from the barbarity of his manners, and pitiless to the faults of others; remarkable besides for his cruelty; and, among other instances, on account of some trifling fault of its father, he blinded his godchild, who was his hostage, tearing out the little wretch's eyes with his accursed nails. This civil and cunning hypocrite used to deceive the unwary by his serene face and charm of speech.

William of Malmesbury, *Gesta Regum Anglorum*
translated by J.A. Giles

LANFRANC, ARCHBISHOP OF CANTERBURY, 1070-1089

There was a certain man of Italian birth named Lanfranc, who was universally acclaimed with the love and respect due to him as supreme master of the Latin tongue, the knowledge of which he had restored to its former state. Even Greece too, the mistress of the nations in the liberal arts, gratefully acknowledged his pupils and marvelled at their prowess. This man left his native land and came to Normandy, where he attracted a band of scholars of high renown. Deeming it, however, a vain thing to secure the favour of mortal men, and recognizing that all things come to naught save God who is eternal and those who wait upon him, the learned man steadfastly applied his mind to win his love. So he followed the plan of doing God's will, which he found to be the more perfect in his studies; forsaking everything and renouncing even his liberty in order to follow him who said: 'If any man will come after me, let him deny himself, and take up his cross and follow me'. And because he now desired to become as lowly as once he had been great, he thought to find a place where there were no men of letters to hold him in honour and esteem. Accordingly he came to Bec, which was considered to be the poorest and most despised of all monasteries. It chanced that at the moment he arrived, the abbot [Herluin, founder of Le Bec and first abbot] was occupied in building an oven, working at it with his own hands. His lowly demeanour and dignity of speech gained Lanfranc's respect, and there he was made a monk.

Then might have been witnessed a godly rivalry between the two men. The abbot who had grown old as a layman before being made a clerk, regarded with awe the eminence of such a teacher now placed under his governance. Lanfranc, however, displayed no arrogance over his learning, but was humbly obedient in everything, observing, admiring and commending the grace which God had granted the abbot in understanding the Scriptures. The abbot, on his part, showed him fitting reverence, while Lanfranc endeavoured to give him his entire obedience. Both had to live together as members of a family, the one engaged in active pursuits, the other in the life of contemplation. The abbot was skilful in settling disputes of a wordly character and far-sighted in matters pertaining to the abbey's external affairs: no one could have been more prudent or efficient in constructing buildings and procuring the necessities of life, saving his obligations towards holy religion. . . .

But the other, the great teacher, gave all his time to silence and solitude in the cloister, cultivating the fallow fields of his heart with the seed of God's word by constant reading and often watering them with the fragrant tears of repentance. So for three years he dwelt in solitude, unvisited by men, rejoicing in his anonymity, unknown to all save the very few with whom he occasionally conversed. But once his identity was discovered, the rumour spread far and wide, and the fame of the distinguished scholar soon published the name of Bec and Abbot Herluim abroad throughout the world. Clerks, the scions of noble houses and the foremost masters of the Latin schools flocked thither [including the future Pope Alexander II, Anslem, Theobald, Ivo, bishop of Chartres, Gilbert Crispin, abbot of Westminster], while lay magnates and many men of high lineage bestowed numerous lands upon the church of Bec out of love for Lanfranc. Forthwith the abbey was enriched with furniture, possessions and the persons of noble and honourable men. Within the abbey religion and learning increased apace; without, the supply of all necessities began to flow in abundance. . .

In the meantime William, duke of the Normans, taking possession of his hereditary kingdom of England, subjugated the rebel forces to his authority by force of arms. After this he turned his attention to the improvement of the condition of the churches there. Having sought the advice of Pope Alexander II, a man of upright life and great experience, and having also obtained the willing assent of all the magnates of the realm, both English and Norman, King William adopted the plan which he alone had first conceived, and appointed Lanfranc to this task. Overcome by a variety of arguments the latter was translated to England and undertook the office of archbishop of Canterbury which carried with it the primacy of the island across the seas . . . the monastic order which had wholly lapsed into worldly corruption, was reformed in accordance with the discipline of the most approved houses; clerks were compelled to live under canonical rule; the idle vanities of barbarian customs were forbidden to the laity, and they were instructed in the true faith and the right way of life.

Gilbert Crispin, *English Historical Documents,* Vol.II

On the death of King William, his son William succeeded him in the realm of England. Endeavouring to forestall his brother, Robert [eldest son of the Conqueror, succeeded to the duchy of Normandy on his father's death], in gaining possession of the

95. Dunstan copying the Rule of St.Benedict, drawn 1150-1180

crown, he found that Lanfranc, without whose consent he could by no means ascend the throne, was not altogether willing to satisfy his desire in the matter. Fearing, therefore, lest any delay in his coronation might entail the loss of the coveted title, he made the following promises on oath to Lanfranc, both for himself and on behalf of all whom he could muster; namely first, to maintain justice, mercy and equity in all his dealings throughout the realm, if he should become king; secondly, to defend the peace, freedom and security of the Church against all men; and thirdly, to obey the orders and accept the advice of the archbishop in everything. But once he had become established in the kingdom, he forsook his promises and lapsed into evil ways. Whereupon, being humbly reproved by Lanfranc and charged with breach of faith towards him, the king flared up into a passion and said, 'Who among men can fulfil all his promises?' From this time forth he was unable to look the archbishop straight in the eyes, although in some matters to which his self-will inclined him, he preserved moderation out of respect for the archbishop during his life-time. For this same Lanfranc was a man highly-skilled in laws both human and divine, and the government of the whole kingdom waited upon his word.

Eadmer, *Historia Novorum*,
English Historical Documents, Vol.II

ORDERICUS VITALIS, 1075-1143, TELLS OF HIS EARLY LIFE

He was the son of Odeler, a French priest, who came to England as confessor to Roger, earl of Shrewsbury. 'Odeler not only persuaded the earl to build a monastery at Shrewsbury, but entered it himself with half his property. Though Orderic was sent in early life to the abbey of Ouche or St-Evroul in Normandy, he never lost his affection for England.'

The aforesaid Odeler, my father [when the monastery at Shrewsbury had been finished], fulfilled to the letter all that he had promised: for he gave two hundred pounds of silver, and his son Benedict to be a monk; after earl Roger's death, he himself took the cowl there. In that house he served God seven years according to the Rule of St Benedict; and on Friday in Whitsun week, after very many labours borne for God's sake, he covered his sins by uncovering them with confession and bitter tears, and died anointed and fortified with the holy Eucharist. . . .

Lo! here is a digression, be it of what account it may, about the building of the monastery on my father's land, which is now inhabited by the family of Christ, and where my father himself, as I remember, an old man of sixty, willingly bore to the end the yoke of Christ.

Forgive me, good reader, and let it not be an offence to thee if I commit to record something about my father, whom I have never seen since the time when, as if I had been a hated step-child, he sent me forth for the love of his Maker into exile. It is now forty-two years ago; and in those years many changes have been, far and wide, in the world. While I often think of these things, and commit some of them to my paper, carefully resisting idleness, I thus exercise myself in inditing them. Now I return to my work, and speak to those younger than myself – a stranger, to those of the country – about their own affairs, things they know not; and in this way, by God's help, I do them useful service.

Ordericus Vitalis, *Historia Ecclesiastica,*
translated by Dean Church in his *St Anselm*

ANSELM, ARCHBISHOP OF CANTERBURY, 1093-1109

In the meantime certain good men advised the king to release the mother-church of the kingdom from her recent widowhood by the appointment of a new shepherd. He willingly acquiesced and admitted that he had made up his mind to do so. Accordingly they began to seek for a man worthy of the honour. Everything, however, waited on the king's nod and he himself proclaimed Anselm to be the man most worthy of the office; with one voice all welcomed his decision. Aghast at this nomination, Anselm grew pale; and while he was being hurried along to the royal presence to receive investiture of the archbishopric by ring and staff at the king's hands, he resisted with all his might, alleging that many obstacles prevented his acceptance. Then the bishops came forward to meet him and, leading him apart from the multitude, addressed him as follows: 'What art thou about? What meanest thou by this? Why does thou strive against God? Thou seest that religion has well nigh perished in England, that everything has fallen into confusion and wickedness is rampart, and we, the bishops, the appointed rulers of God's Church, stand in peril of eternal death through this man's tyranny; and yet, when thou couldst bring succour, thou scornedst to do so. What art thou dreaming of thou paragon of men? Whither have thy wits strayed? The church of Canterbury, in whose oppression we all are oppressed and destroyed, summons thee to deliver her from bondage and us from anxiety; yet thou wouldst prefer thine own ease and quiet to undertaking her liberation and the relief of our distress, thou wouldst refuse to share in the labours of they brethren'.

To the remonstrances he answered, 'Bear with me, I pray you, bear with me, and give me your attention. I admit that what you have said is true; many are your tribulations and great is your need. But consider I beg you. I am already an old man and unable to sustain earthly cares. I can scarcely perform my own duties; how can I undertake the administration of the whole Church of England? For that matter ever since I became a monk, as my conscience bears witness, I have shunned all worldly business, nor could I ever direct my mind thereto by reason of my profession as a monk, for there is naught therein in which I could ever take pleasure or love. Wherefore, give me leave to remain in peace and do not entangle me in public business which I have never loved and for which I am not fitted'. They reply, 'Only do thou accept the primacy of the Church without hesitation, and go before us in the path of God, informing and commanding us how to act, and

96. Seal of William FitzEmpress who died 1163, the younger brother of Henry II. It shows a single lion rampart on his shield and on the horse-trapper.

we will give our firm support to thee, for we shall not be found wanting in obeying and executing thy commands. Do thou pray to God for us and we will take charge of thy secular business for thee'. 'What you ask', he replied, 'is impossible. I am abbot of a monastery in another land, with an archbishop to whom I owe obedience, a temporal prince to whom I am subject, and monks for whom I must provide counsel and help. Thus I am strictly bound by all these ties; I cannot desert my monks without their consent, nor remove myself from my prince's dominion without his permission; nor can I withdraw obedience from my archbishop without peril to my soul unless absolved by him'. 'All these matters', they complain, 'are of small account and may easily be arranged'. To this he answered, 'It is no use, what you purpose shall not be accomplished'.

At this they seized him by force and brought him to the bedside of the sick king, to whom they openly declared his obstinacy. Almost weeping with sorrow the king spake unto him, 'O Anselm, what art thou about? Why dost thou deliver me to everlasting torment? . . . ' At these words some of the bystanders were moved with compassion and began to upbraid Anselm for making excuses and showing reluctance to shoulder so heavy a burden at this juncture, importuning him angrily and in some confusion. . . . Then the king, feeling that all their labour was being expended in vain, made them all fall at Anselm's feet, whether perchance they might thereby constrain him to give consent. But lo! as they prostrated themselves, he in turn fell on his knee before them and would not budge from his first refusal. At length, incensed against him and vexed at themselves for their irresolution in allowing his objections to defeat their purpose for so long, they raised the cry, 'Bring hither the pastoral staff! the pastoral staff!' And seizing his right arm, some of them dragged him forward while others pushed him from behind, and so they forced him struggling to the king's bedside. But when the king held out the staff to him, he closed his fist against it, and would not receive it. The bishops then tried to wrench open his fingers, which he kept firmly fixed in the palm of his hand, in order to place the staff therein. But after some moments spent in vain endeavour, while Anselm cried out with the pain he was suffering, the index finger which they had succeeded in raising being once more immediately closed by him, finally the staff was placed against his clenched fist and held there by the hands of the bishops. While the crowd shouted, 'Long live the bishop!' and the other bishops together with the clergy, began to chant in a loud voice the *Te Deum Laudamus*, the elected prelate was carried rather than led into the church nearby, still resisting with all his might and crying out, 'It is naught that you are doing; it is naught that you are doing'. The formalities of the church customary on such an occasion having been complied with, Anselm returned to the king, and thus addressed him, 'I tell thee, my lord king, that thou wilt not die of this sickness, and therefore I wish thee to know how easily thou mayst alter what has been done with me; for I have neither acknowledged, nor do I acknowledge its validity'. Having thus said, he withdrew from the royal chamber and retraced his steps, the bishops together with the lay magnates escorting him. Turning on them he upbraided them in these words, 'Do you realize what you have done? You have yoked together in the plough the untamed bull and the old feeble sheep, and what good will come of it? . . . In England this plough is managed and drawn by two oxen which excel all others, namely the king and the archbishop of Canterbury. . . . One of these twain, Archbishop Lanfranc is dead, and the other, possessed of the ferocity of an untameable bull, already as a young man was pre-destined to the plough; and now in the place of the dead ox you would join me, an old feeble sheep, to the untamed bull. . . .' At these words his tears began to flow and, unable to conceal his sorrow of heart, he dismissed the assembly and returned to his lodging. All this took place on the First Sunday in Lent, 6 March, in the year of our Lord 1093.

Eadmer, *Historia Novorum*,
English Historical Documents, Vol.II

1093. In this year King William [II] was taken so seriously ill in the spring that everywhere he was declared to be dead: and in his affliction he made many vows to God to lead his own justly, and to protect and secure God's churches, and never move again to sell them for money, and to have all just laws among his people. And the archbishopric of Canterbury which had remained in his own control he committed to Anselm [in 1093] who had been abbot at Bec: and to Robert [Bloet, 1094], his chancellor, the bishopric of Lincoln: and he granted land to many monasteries, but he soon took it away when he had recovered, and dispensed with all the good laws he had promised us.

Anglo-Saxon Chronicle, English Historical Documents, Vol.II

97. William Longespée, Earl of Salisbury, died 1226. Effigy in Salisbury cathedral. He was the natural son of Henry II, and bore the arms of his grandfather, Geoffrey Plantagenet

THE ABBOT HENRY OF POITOU, INFAMOUS SELF-SEEKER, 1127

In the course of this same year, 1127, King Henry gave the abbacy of Peterborough to an abbot called Henry of Poitou [son of William VII, duke of Aquitaine], who had possession of his abbacy of St Jean d'Angely, and all the archbishops and bishops said that it was uncanonical and that he could not have possession of two abbacies. But this same Henry gave the king to understand that he had left his abbacy because of the great disturbance that there was in the country, and that he did it by the advice and permission of Rome and of the abbot of Cluny, and because he was legate in respect of Peter's Pence: but it was none the more like that for all his words – but, on the contrary, he wished to have possession of both: and he had them like that, as long as it was God's will. While a secular clerk, he was bishop of Soissons; then he became a monk at Cluny, then prior in this same monastery, and then he became prior at Savigny; after that, because he was a relative of the King of England and the count of Poitou, the count gave him the abbacy of the monastery of St Jean d'Angely.

Afterwards, by means of his greater stratagems, he then obtained the archbishopric of Besançon and had possession of it for *three days,* and he justly lost it because he had unjustly obtained it. Then he afterwards obtained the bishopric of Saintes which was five miles from where he was abbot; he had possession of that *very nearly a week.* Then the abbot of Cluny took him out of that as he had done earlier out of Besançon.

Then he bethought himself that if he could get himself rooted in England, he could have everything he wished. He asked the king, and told him that he was an old and broken-down man, and he could not put up with the great injustices and the great disturbances that there were in their country. Then personally and through all his friends he especially desired the abbacy of Peterborough; and the king granted it to him because he was his relative and because he was a principal man in swearing the oath and bearing witness when the son of the count of Normandy and the daughter of the count of Anjou were separated for being within the prohibited degrees of relationship.

Thus miserably was the abbacy given, between Christmas and Candlemas, at London, and so he went with the king to Winchester and from there he came to Peterborough, and there he stayed exactly as drones do in a hive. All that the bees carry in, the drones eat and carry out, and so did he: all that he could take inside and outside from clerics and laymen he thus sent overseas and did nothing good there and left nothing good there.

Let it not be thought remarkable, when we tell the truth, because it was fully known over all the country, that as soon as he came there (that was on the Sunday when *Exsurge quare obdormis Domine* is sung), then soon afterwards many people saw and heard many hunters hunting. The hunters were black and big and loathsome, and their hounds were black and wide-eyed and loathsome, and they rode on black horses and black bucks. This was seen in the very deer-park in the town of Peterborough, and in all the woods that there were between this town and Stamford, and the monks heard the horns blow that they were blowing at night. Trustworthy people noticed them at night, and said that it seemed to them there might well be about twenty or thirty hornblowers.

This was seen and heard from the time he came there all Lent up to Easter. This was his coming in — of his going out we can say nothing yet. May God provide!

Anglo-Saxon Chronicle, English Historical Documents, Vol.II

THE TREACHERY OF HENRY OF POITOU AT LAST DISCOVERED

1131. In the course of this same year, before Easter, Abbot Henry went overseas to Normandy and there spoke with the king and told him that the abbot of Cluny had ordered him to come to him and hand over to him the abbacy of Angely: and then with his permission he would come home — and so he went home to his own monastery, and stayed there right up to Midsummer Day. And the next day after St John's Day, the monks elected an abbot from among themselves and brought him into the church with a procession, sung *Te Deum Laudamus,* rang the bells, set him on the abbot's throne and did all such obedience to him as they ought to do to their abbot.

And the earl and all the chief men and the monks of the monastery chased the other abbot, Henry, out of the monastery: they had to, of necessity — in five and twenty years they never experienced one good day!

Now all his great trickery failed him: now he was forced to creep into his big wallet, into every corner of it, to see whether there was at least one poor trick left so that he could deceive Christ and all Christ's people yet once more.

Then he went to Cluny and there was kept, so that he could go neither east nor west — the abbot of Cluny said that they had lost St John's monastery through him and his great folly. Then he knew of no better remedy for himself than to promise them, and to swear oaths on the relics,that if he might visit England,he would get possession of the monastery of Peterborough for them so that he should appoint a prior from Cluny to it, and the sacristan and treasurer and keeper of the wardrobe, and all things that were in the monastery, and outside it, he would commit to them. Then he went to France, and stayed there all the year. Christ take counsel for the wretched monks of Peterborough and for the wretched place: now they need Christ's help and that of all Christian people.

1132. This year King Henry came to this country. Then Abbot Henry came and accused the monks of Peterborough to the king, because he wished to put the monastery under the rule of Cluny, with the result that the king was *nearly* deceived, and sent for the monks. And by the mercy of God and by means of the bishop of Salisbury, the bishop of Lincoln and the other powerful men who were there, the king perceived that he was dealing with treachery.

When he could do no more, he wished that his nephew should be abbot in Peterborough, but Christ did not wish it. It was not long after that, that the king sent for him, and made him give up the abbacy of Peterborough, and go into the country. And the king gave the abbacy to a prior of St Neot's called Martin. He came into the monastery on St Peter's day with great dignity.

Anglo-Saxon Chronicle, English Historical Documents, Vol.II

THE ABBOT SAMSON, 1135-1211

Samson was Abbot of St Edmund's at Bury

Abbot Samson was below the average height, almost bald; his face was neither round nor oblong; his nose was prominent and his lips thick; his eyes were clear and his glance penetrating; his hearing was excellent; his eyebrows arched, and frequently shaved; and a little cold soon made him hoarse. On the day of his election he was forty-seven, and had been a monk for seventeen years. In his ruddy beard there were a few grey hairs, and still fewer in his black and curling hair. But in the course of the first fourteen years after his election all his hair became white as snow.

He was an exceedingly temperate man; he possessed great energy and a strong constitution, and was fond both of riding and walking, until old age prevailed upon him and moderated his ardour in these respects. When he heard the news of the capture of the cross and the fall of Jerusalem, he began to wear under garments made of horse-hair, and a horse-hair shirt, and gave up the use of flesh and meat. None the less, he willed that flesh should be placed before him as he sat at table, that the alms might be increased. He ate sweet milk, honey, and similar sweet things, far more readily than any other food. He hated liars, drunkards, and talkative persons; for virtue ever loves itself and spurns that which is contrary to it. He blamed those who grumbled about their meat and drink, and especially monks who so grumbled, and personally kept to the same manners which he had observed when he was a cloistered monk. Moreover, he had this virtue in himself that he never desired to change the dish which was placed before him. When I was a novice, I wished to prove whether this was really true, and as I happened to serve in the refectory, I thought to place before him food which would have offended any other man, in a very dirty and broken dish. But when he saw this, he was as it were blind to it. Then, as there was some delay, I repented of what I had done and straightway seized the dish, changed the food and dish for better, and carried it to him. He, however, was angry at the change, and disturbed. He was an eloquent man, speaking both French and Latin, but rather careful of the good sense of that which he had to say then the style of his words. He could read books written in English very well, and was wont to preach to the people in English, but in the dialect of Norfolk where he was born and bred. It was for this reason that he ordered a pulpit to be placed in the church, for the sake of those who heard him and for purposes of ornament.

The abbot further appeared to prefer the active to the contemplative life, and praised good officials more than good monks. He rarely commended anyone solely on account of his knowledge of letters, unless the man happened to have knowledge of secular affairs, and if he chanced to hear of any prelate who had given up his pastoral work and become a hermit, he did not praise him for this. He would not praise men who were too kindly, saying, "He who strives to please all men, deserves to please none." . . .

He had also a characteristic which I have never seen in any other man, namely, that he had a strong affection for many to whom he never or seldom showed a loving face, which the common saying declares to be usual, when it says, "Where love is, there the glance follows." And there was another note-worthy thing, that he wittingly suffered loss from his servants in temporal matters, and allowed that he suffered it; but, as I believe, the reason for this was that he waited for a fit season when the matter might be conveniently remedied, or that by concealing his knowledge he might avoid greater loss.

Jocelin of Brakelond, *Chronicle*
translated by L. Cecil Janes

ABBOT SAMSON OF ST EDMUND'S, AN ECCLESIASTICAL LANDLORD

He was no sluggard and began before all else to build barns and byres: and he was more especially eager to cultivate his lands with profit, and was also vigilant in looking after his woods, concerning the granting and diminishing of which he confessed himself most avaricious. One sole manor, that of Thorp, he confirmed by charter to a certain Englishman, an adscript to the soil [he was a villein, not a freeman] in whose faithfulness he had all the greater confidence, because he was a good farmer and could speak no French.

Jocelin of Brakelond, *Chronicle*,
edited by M.E. Butler

ADRIAN IV (NICHOLAS BREAKSPEAR) *d.* 1159

He was elected Pope on the fourth of December, 1154; and was the only English Pope ever elected.

The death of our lord, Pope Adrian, which has dismayed all Christian peoples and nations, has brought especially bitter grief to our country of England, whereof he was a native. He is to be lamented by all good men, but by no one more than myself, whom, though he had a mother and a brother living, he loved with a more intimate affection than he bestowed on them. Alike in public and in private he made no secret of the fact that no one was so dear to him as I; and he had come to think so much of me that he never missed an opportunity of opening his inner thought to me. While he was Pope, he took pleasure in inviting me to his table and in making me, against my will, eat from his plate and drink from his cup. It was at my request that he granted to the illustrious King of the English, Henry II, the hereditary possession of Ireland, as his letter bears witness to the present day; for all the islands are reputed to belong by a long-established right to the Church of Rome by the Donation of Constantine, who instituted and endowed it. Moreover, he sent to the King through me a golden ring, adorned with a fine emerald, in token of his investiture with the government of Ireland; and this ring is still by the King's command preserved in the public treasury. Were I to enumerate all the virtues of the late Pope, this topic alone would fill a large volume.

John of Salisbury

Historic Events

THE DEATH OF THE WITCH OF BERKELEY IN 1065

At the same time something similar occurred in England, not by divine miracle, but by infernal craft; which when I shall have related, the credit of the narrative will not be shaken, though the minds of the hearers should be incredulous; for I have heard it from a man of such character, who swore he had seen it, that I should blush to disbelieve.

There resided at Berkeley a woman addicted to witch-craft, as it afterwards appeared and skilled in ancient augury. On a certain day, as she was regaling, a jackdaw, which was a very great favourite, chattered a little more loudly than usual. On hearing which the woman's knife fell from her hand, her countenance grew pale, and deeply groaning, 'This day,' said she, 'my plough has completed its last furrow; to-day I shall hear of, and suffer, some dreadful calamity.' While yet speaking, the messenger of her misfortunes arrived; and being asked, 'why he approached with so distressed an air', 'I bring news,' said he, 'from that village,' naming the place, 'of the death of your son, and of the whole family, by a sudden accident.' At this intelligence, the woman, sorely afflicted, immediately took to her bed, and perceiving the disorder rapidly approaching the vitals, she summoned her surviving children a monk, and a nun, by hasty letters; and, when they arrived, with faltering voice, addressed them thus: 'Formerly, my children, I constantly administered to my wretched circumstances by demoniacal arts: I have been the sink of every vice, the teacher of every allurement: yet, while practising these crimes, I was accustomed to soothe my hapless soul with the hope of your piety. Despairing of myself, I rested my expectations on you; I advanced you as my defenders against evil spirits, my safeguards against my strongest foes. Now, since I have approached the end of my life, and shall have those eager to punish, who lured me to sin, I entreat you by your mother's breasts, if you have any regard, any affection, at least to alleviate my torments; and, although you cannot revoke the sentence already passed upon my soul, yet you may perhaps rescue my body, by these means: sew up my corpse in the skin of a stag; lay it on its back in a stone coffin; fasten down the lid with lead and iron; on this lay a stone, bound round with three iron chains of enormous weight. let there be psalms sung for fifty nights, and masses said for an equal number of days, to allay the ferocious attacks of my adversaries. If I lie thus secure for three nights, on the fourth day bury your mother in the ground; although I fear, lest the earth, which has been so often burdened with my crimes, should refuse to receive and cherish me in her bosom.' They did their utmost to comply with her injunctions: but alas! vain were pious tears, vows, or entreaties; so great was the woman's guilt, so great the devil's violence. For on the first two nights, while the choir of priests was singing psalms

98. Duke William of Normandy has come to Bayeux where Harold is shown swearing allegiance to him. Harold is touching two shrines as he takes his oath. The one on the left, nearest the Duke seated on his throne, William took with him on his journeys. The other shrine is said to hold relics of two British saints, who suffered martyrdom in France.

around the body, the devils, one by one, with the utmost ease bursting open the door of the church, though closed with an immense bolt, broke asunder the two outer chains; the middle one being more laboriously wrought, remained entire. On the third night, about cock-crow, the whole monastery seemed to be overthrown from its very foundation, by the clamour of the approaching enemy. One devil, more terrible in appearance than the rest, and of loftier stature, broke the gates to shivers by the violence of his attack. The priests grew motionless with fear, their hair stood on end, and they became speechless. He proceeded, as it appeared, with haughty step towards the coffin, and calling on the woman by name, commanded her to rise. She replying that she could not on account of the chains: 'You shall be loosed,' said he, 'and to your cost' and directly he broke the chain, which had mocked the ferocity of the others, with as little exertion as though it had been made of flax. He also beat down the cover of the coffin with his foot, and taking her by the hand, before them all, he dragged her out of the church. At the doors appeared a black horse, proudly neighing, with iron hooks projecting over his whole back; on which the wretched creature was placed, and, immediately, with the whole party, vanished from the eyes of the beholders; her pitiable cries, however, for assistance were heard for nearly the space of four miles. No person will deem this incredible, who has read St. Gregory's Dialogues. . . .

William of Malmesbury, *Gesta Regum Anglorum*,
translated by J.A. Giles

SUCCESSION TO THE ENGLISH THRONE, 1066

i. Edward, king of the English, being, according to the dispensation of God, without an heir, sent Robert [abbot of Jumièges, bishop of London, 1044, archibishop of Canterbury, 1051], archbishop of Canterbury, to the duke, with a message appointing the duke as heir to the kingdom which God had entrusted to him. He also at a later time sent to the duke, Harold, the greatest of all the counts in his kingdom alike in riches and honour and power. This he did in order that Harold might guarantee the crown to the duke by his fealty and confirm the same with an oath according to Christian usage.

William of Jumièges, *English Historical Documents,* Vol.II

99. Here the Bayeux Tapestry shows Harold seated on the throne in Westminster Abbey soon after his coronation. Beside him stands Archbishop Stigand, clearly marked with the tonsure, wearing a chasuble, an alb and a stole, with a maniple in his left hand. Harold holds the traditional orb and sceptre.

ii. About the same time [1063], Edward, king of the English, who loved William as a brother or a son, established him as his heir with a stronger pledge than ever before. The king, who in his holy life showed his desire for a celestial kingdom, felt the hour of his death approaching, and wished to anticipate its inevitable consequences. He, therefore, dispatched Harold to William in order that he might confirm this promise by an oath. This Harold was of all the king's subjects the richest and the most exalted in honour and power, and his brother and his cousins had previously been offered as hostages in respect of the same succession. The king, indeed, here acted with great prudence in choosing Harold for this task, in the hope that the riches and the authority of this magnate might check disturbance throughout England if the people with their accustomed perfidy should be disposed to overturn what had been determined. . . .

iii. Harold in that place swore fealty to the duke employing the sacred ritual recognized among Christian men. And as is testified by the most truthful and most honourable men who were there present, he took an oath of his own free will in the following terms: firstly that he would be the representative [*vicarius*] of Duke William at the court of his lord, King Edward, as long as the king lived; secondly that he would employ all his influence and wealth to ensure that after the death of King Edward the kingdom of England should be confirmed in the possession of the duke; thirdly that he would place a garrison of the duke's knights in the castle of Dover and maintain these at his own care and cost; fourthly that in other parts of England at the pleasure of the duke he would maintain garrisons in other castles and make complete provision for their sustenance.

William of Poitiers, *English Historical Documents*, Vol.II

After his [Edward's] burial the under-king, Harold, son of Earl Godwin, whom the king had nominated as his successor, was chosen king by the chief magnates of all England; and on the same day Harold was crowned with great ceremony by Aldred, archbishop of York.

Florence of Worcester, *English Historical Documents*, Vol.II

100. These people are marvelling at the tailed comet or 'hairy star' which appeared at the time of Harold's coronation in April, 'a portent pregnant it was felt, with dangers and disasters soon to come', and now identified as Halley's Comet. William was preparing his invasion fleet.

HALLEY'S COMET

At that time [24 April 1066] throughout all England, a portent such as men had never seen before was seen in the heavens. Some declared that the star was a comet, which some called the 'long-haired star'.

Anglo-Saxon Chronicle, English Historical Documents, Vol.II

ROYAL CONFISCATION OF SAXON LAND

I, William the king, give friendly greeting to Aethelmaer the bishop and Ralph the earl and to all my thegns in Suffolk and in Norfolk. I give you to know that I will that Abbot Baldwin hand to me all the land which those men held who belonged to St Edmund's soke and who stood in battle against me and there were slain. And I will that those men be now the abbot's men, who were previously held by his predecessor, even as their predecessors were. And I will not allow anyone to take from him anything that I have given him.

Regusta Regum I, English Historical Documents, Vol.II

A STOWAWAY FROM GRIMSBY, 1074

Obtaining by money a mitigation of his imprisonment, he at great risk privily made his escape to the Norwegians, who were then loading a merchant vessel at Grimsby for Norway. In this vessel also certain ambassadors, whom king William was sending to Norway, had procured a passage; and now when the ship in full sail was out of sight of land, lo! the king's run-away hostage emerging from the hold of the vessel in which the Norwegians had concealed him, astounded the ambassadors and their companions. For when a diligent search had been everywhere made, the king's inspectors had examined this very vessel, but the cunning of the concealers baffled the observation of the searchers. The ambassadors then insisted that they should lower the sails, and should somehow or other take back the ship with the king's fugitive to England. This the Norwegians sharply resisted, as a voyage so well begun would carry the vessel forward prosperously. Such a quarrel of the parties ensued that they betook themselves to arms on both sides; but since the force of numbers was with the Norwegians, the insolence of the ambassadors was soon repressed, and the nearer they approached the land the more submissive did they become. When they arrived there, the young refugee by his modest and discreet behaviour rendered himself agreeable to the nobles and the gentry.

Simeon of Durham, translated by Rev. J. Stevenson in *The Church Historians of England*

101. This section of the Bayeux Tapestry shows the Normans carrying to their ships arms, suits of chain mail, barrels of wine. There is no sign of food.

DOMESDAY SURVEY, 1085

1085. Then at Christmas, the king was at Gloucester with his council, and held his court there for five days, and then the archbishop and clerics had a synod for three days. There Maurice was elected bishop of London, and William for Norfolk and Robert for Cheshire – they were all the king's clerics.

After this, the king had much thought and very deep discussion with his council about this country – how it was occupied or with what sort of people. Then he sent his men [the inquiry which resulted in Domesday Book] over all England into every shire and had them find out how many hundred hides there were in the shire, or what land and cattle the king himself had in the country, or what dues he ought to have in twelve months from the shire.

Also he had a record made of how much land his archbishops had, and his bishops and his abbots and his earls – and though I relate it at too great length – what or how much everybody had who was occupying land in England, in land or cattle, and how much money it was worth. So very narrowly did he have it investigated, that there was no single hide nor a yard of land, nor indeed (it is a shame to relate but it seemed no shame to him to do) one ox nor one cow nor one pig was there left out, and not put down in his record: and all these records were brought to him afterwards.

Anglo-Saxon Chronicle, English Historical Documents, Vol.II

In the twentieth year of his reign by order of William, king of the English, there was made a survey of the whole of England, that is to say, of the lands of the several provinces of England, and of the possessions of each and all of the magnates. This was done in respect of ploughland and habitations, and of men both bond and free, both of those who dwelt in cottages, and those who had their homes and their share in the fields; and in respect of ploughs and horses and other animals; and in respect of the services and payments due from all men in the whole land. Other investigators followed the first; and men were sent into provinces which they did not know, and where they were themselves unknown, in order that they might be given the opportunity of checking the first survey and, if necessary, of denouncing its authors as guilty to the king. And the land was vexed with much violence arising from the collection of the royal taxes.

Roberta Losinga, bishop of Hereford, 1079-1095,
added this note to the chronicle of Marianus Scotus

Here is written down the inquest of lands, in what manner the king's barons have made inquisition, namely, by oath of the sheriff of the shire and of all the barons and of their Frenchmen and of the whole hundred, of the priest, the reeve and six villeins of each vill. Next the name of the manor, who held it in the time of King Edward, who holds it now; the number of hides; the number of ploughs on the demesne, the number of those of the men; the number of villeins; the number of cottars; the number of serfs; the number of freemen; the number of sokemen; the amount of forest; the amount of meadow; the number of pastures; the number of mills; the number of fishponds; how much it has been increased or diminished; how much it was all worth then; and how much now; how much each freeman and sokeman held and holds there. All this three times over, namely, in the time of King Edward, and when King William gave it, and as it now is, and if more can be had than is had.

Prologue to the Ely Inquest, *English Historical Documents,* Vol.II

Here are noted those holding lands in Huntingdonshire

1. King William
2. The bishop of Lincoln
3. The bishop of Coutances
4. The abbey of Ely
5. The abbey of Crowland
6. The abbey of Ramsey
7. The abbey of Thorney
8. The abbey of Peterborough
9. Count Eustace
10. The count of Eu
11. Earl Hugh
12. Walter Giffard
13. William of Warenne
14. Hugh of Bolbec
15. Eudo, son of Hubert
16. Sweyn of Essex
17. Roger of Ivry
18. Arnulf of Hesdins
19. Eustace the sheriff
20. The Countess Judith
21. Gilbert of Ghent
22. Aubrey 'de Vere'
23. William, son of Ansculf
24. Rannulf, the brother of Ilger
25. Robert Fafiton
26. William 'Ingania'
27. Ralph, son of Osmund
28. Rohais, the wife of Richard
29. The king's thegns

1. The land of the king

Hurstingstone hundred

A manor. In Hartford King Edward has 15 hides assessed to the geld. There is land for 17 ploughs. Rannulf the brother of Ilger keeps it now. There are 4 ploughs now on the demesne; and 30 villeins and 3 bordars have 8 ploughs. There is a priest; 2 churches; 2 mills rendering 4 pounds; and 40 acres of meadow. Woodland for pannage; 1 league in length and half a league in breadth. T.R.E. it was worth 24 pounds; now 15 pounds.

Normancross hundred

A manor. In Bottlebridge King Edward had 5 hides assessed to the geld. There is land for 8 ploughs. The king has 1 plough now on the demesne; and 15 villeins have 5 ploughs. There is a priest and a church; 60 acres of meadow and 12 acres of woodland for pannage in Northamptonshire. T.R.E. it was worth 100 shillings; now 8 pounds. Rannulf keeps it.

In this manor belonging to the king, and in other manors, the enclosure of the abbot of Thorney is doing harm to 300 acres of meadow.

In Stilton the king's sokemen of Normancross have 3 virgates of land assessed to the geld. There is land for 2 ploughs, and there are 5 ploughing oxen.

In Orton the king has soke over 3½ hides of land in the land of the abbot of Peterborough which was Godwin's.

Domesday Book, Volume I,
English Historical Documents, Vol.II

102. Here the Norman ships are coming to Pevensey, where knights and horses disembark.

DOMESDAY BOOK

When that renowned conqueror of England, King William – a near kinsman to this same prelate – had subjugated the farthest limits of the island and thoroughly tamed the minds of the rebels by the terror of his vengeance, lest a further opportunity of wrongdoing should again be accorded them, he ordained that the people subject to him should submit to written laws and customs. Accordingly, the laws of the English having been set before him in their triple form, that is, Mercian law, Danish law and the law of the West Saxons, some he rejected while others he approved, adding to them also those laws of Neustria overseas, which seemed most efficacious for preserving the peace of the realm. At length, lest aught should be lacking to the full sum of his foresight, after taking counsel he dispatched the most prudent men in his court on circuit throughout the kingdom. In this manner, and by these agents, a careful survey was made of the whole country, of its woods, pastures and meadows, as well as of its arable land. All this was set down in common language and compiled in a book, in order that each man, being content with his own rights, should not with impunity usurp the rights of another. The survey was made by counties, hundreds and hides, the king's name being written at the head of the list, followed in turn by the names of other magnates set down according to the dignity of their rank, that is, the names of the tenants-in-chief of the king. Further, after the individual names have been arranged in order, numbers are placed against them, by means of which, in the course of the book below, the matters which concern them may more easily be found. This book is called by the English "Doomsday", that is, by metaphor, the day of judgment. For just as the sentence of that strict and terrible Last Judgment cannot be evaded by any art or subterfuge, so, when a dispute arises in this realm concerning facts which are there written down, and an appeal is made to the book itself, the evidence it gives cannot be set at naught or evaded with impunity. For this cause we have called this same book "Doomsday", not because it passes judgment on any doubtful points raised, but because it is not permissible to contradict its decisions, any more than it will be those of the Last Judgment.

Dialogus de Scaccario

A DOMESDAY MANOR: HECHAM, ESSEX, A.D.1086

Peter de Valence holds in domain Hecham, which Haldane a freeman held in the time of King Edward, as a manor, and as 5 hides. There have always been 2 ploughs in the demesne, 4 ploughs of the men. At that time there were 8 villeins, now 10; then there were 2 bordars [villein of the lowest rank] , now 3; at both times 4 *servi*, woods for 300 swine, 18 acres of meadow.

Then there were 2 fish ponds and a half, now there are none. At that time there was 1 ox, now there are 15 cattle and 1 small horse and 18 swine and 2 hives of bees. At that time it was worth 60s., now £4.10s. When he received this manor he found only 1 ox and 1 planted acre. Of those 5 hides spoken of above, one was held in the time of King Edward by 2 freemen, and was added to this manor in the time of King William. It was worth in the time of King Edward 10s., now 22s., and William holds this from Peter de Valence.

THE DEATH OF WILLIAM RUFUS, 1100

The day before the king died, he dreamed he was let blood by a surgeon, and that the stream reaching to heaven clouded the light and obscured the day. Calling upon St Mary for protection, he suddenly awoke, and told his attendants they were not to leave him. Thus they watched with him for several hours even unto daybreak. Shortly afterwards, just as the day began to dawn, a certain foreign monk came to Robert, son of Haimo, one of the chief magnates at the court and told him that he had that night dreamed a strange and fearful dream about the king. 'The king', he said, 'came into a certain church with threats and boasting as is his custom. He looked contemptuously on those present, and then seizing the crucifix he gnawed the arms and almost tore away the legs. The image endured this for a while, but at last struck the king with its foot so that he fell backwards, and from his mouth as he lay on the ground came out such a flame that the smoke touched the very stars.' Robert, thinking this dream ought not to be neglected, ventured to tell it to the king, with whom he was very intimate. William burst into long laughter, and said, 'He is a monk and dreams for money. Give him a hundred shillings.' Nonetheless he was not unmoved, and hesitated a long time whether he would go out hunting as he had planned, and his friends urged him not to take the risk of testing these omens. He therefore did not hunt before dinner, but attended to serious business instead, hoping by occupation to dispel his uneasiness. And they say that he soothed his cares with more food and wine than usual. After dinner he went into the forest with a very small number of attendants. Among these the most intimate with the king was Walter, surnamed Tirel, who had come from France attracted by the liberality of the king. This man alone remained with him, while the others were widely scattered in the chase. The sun was now setting, and the king drawing his bow let fly an arrow which slightly wounded a stag which passed before him. He ran in pursuit, keeping his gaze rigidly fixed on the quarry, and holding up his hand to shield his eyes from the sun's rays. At this instant Walter, forming in his mind a project which seemed fine to him, tried to transfix another stag which by chance came near him while the king's attention was otherwise occupied. And thus it was that unknowingly, and without power to prevent it (oh, gracious God!), he pierced the king's breast with a fatal arrow. When the king received the arrow he said not a word, but breaking off the shaft of the arrow where it stuck out of his body, he fell upon the ground and thus made more speedy his own death. Walter immediately ran up, but finding the king senseless and speechless, he leapt quickly on his horse and escaped at full gallop. Indeed, there was none to pursue him. Some connived at his flight. Others pitied him. And all were intent on other matters. Some began to fortify their dwellings, others to plunder, and the rest went to look for a new king. A few countrymen recovered the body and took it on a cart to the cathedral at Winchester, the blood dripping from it all the way. Here it was committed to the ground within the tower, attended by many of the magnates, but mourned by few. Next year the tower fell [in 1077 in fact], but I forbear to mention the different opinions about this lest I should seem too readily to assent to unsupported trifles, the more especially as the building might have fallen through imperfect construction even if he had not been buried there. He died in the year of the Incarnation of our Lord 1100 on 2 August, aged above forty years. He formed mighty plans which he would have brought to effect, could he have spun out the tissue of fate, or broken through the violence of fortune. Such was the energy of his mind that he was bold enough to promise himself any kingdom whatsoever. Indeed the day before his death, when asked where he would keep Christmas he said, 'in Poitou'. For the count of Poitou [William VII, count of Poitou] who wished to go to Jerusalem was said to be anxious to pawn his territory to the king of England.

Thus not content with that he had inherited, he was lured on by his hope of greater glory, and grasped at honours which were not his by right. He was a man much to be pitied by the clergy for throwing away a soul which they could not save. He earned the love of hired soldiers for he was lavish in his gifts to them. But by the common people he is not to be mourned because he allowed them to be plundered. I remember no council being held in his time wherein the health of the church might be strengthened by the correction of abuses. He delayed long in appointing to ecclesiastical offices, either for the sake of the money he gained thereby, or because he wished to consider the merits of those who might be advanced. Thus on the day he died he held in his own hands three vacant bishoprics, and twelve vacant abbeys.

William of Malmesbury, *Gesta Regum Anglorum*,
English Historical Documents, Vol.II

103. This scene of the Bayeux Tapestry depicts the Normans feasting at Hastings before the battle. On the left, servants are assembling food on shields laid on trestles forming a make-shift table. One servant blows his horn to announce the meal. Roasted birds on spits are brought from the kitchen. Bishop Odo, in the centre, with a fish before him, gives the blessing. Duke William is on his right.

CORONATION OF HENRY I, 1100

On the Thursday [2 August 1100] he [William II] was killed, and buried next morning: and when he was buried the councillors who were near at hand chose his brother Henry as king, and he forthwith gave the bishopric of Winchester to William Giffard [he was not consecrated till 1107], and then went to London, and on the Sunday after that, before the altar at Westminster he vowed to God and all the people to put down all the injustices that there were in his brother's time, and to maintain the best laws that stood in any king's day before him. And after that Maurice, the bishop of London, consecrated him king [5 August], and all in this country submitted to him and swore oaths and became his men.

Anglo-Saxon Chronicle,
English Historical Documents, Vol. II

CORONATION CHARTER OF HENRY I, 5 August 1100

Henry, king of the English, to Samson the bishop, and Urse of Abbetot, and to all his barons and faithful vassals, both French and English, in Worcestershire, greeting.

1. Know that by the mercy of God and by the common counsel of the barons of the whole kingdom of England I have been crowned king of his realm. And because the kingdom has been oppressed by unjust exactions, I now, being moved by reverence towards God and by the love I bear you all, make free the church of God; so that I will neither sell nor lease its property; nor on the death of an archbishop or a bishop or an abbot will I take anything from the demesne of the church or from its vassals during the period which elapses before a successor is installed. I abolish all the evil customs by which the kingdom of England has been unjustly oppressed. Some of those evil customs are here set forth.

2. If any of my barons or of my earls or of any other of my tenants shall die his heir shall not redeem his land as he wont to do in the time of my brother, but he shall henceforward redeem it by means of a just and lawful 'relief'. Similarly the men of barons shall redeem their lands from their lords by means of a just and lawful 'relief'.

3. If any of my barons or of my tenants shall wish to give in

marriage his daughter or his sister or his niece or his cousin, he shall consult me about the matter; but I will neither seek payment for my consent, nor will I refuse my permission, unless he wishes to give her in marriage to one of my enemies. And if, on the death of one of my barons or of one of my tenants, a daughter should be his heir, I will dispose of her in marriage and of her lands according to the counsel given me by my barons. And, if the wife of one of my tenants shall survive her husband and be without children, she shall have her dower and marriage portion, and I will not give her in marriage unless she herself consents.

4. If a widow survives with children under age, she shall have her dower and her marriage portion, so long as she keeps her body chaste; and I will not give her in marriage except with her consent. And the guardian of the land, and of the children, shall be either the widow or another of their relations, as may seem more proper. And I order my barons shall likewise act towards the sons and daughters of their men.

5. I utterly forbid that the common mintage [forced levy to prevent loss to the king from depreciation of the coinage], which has been taken from the towns and shires, shall henceforth be levied, since it was not so levied in the time of King Edward. If any moneyer or other person be taken with false money in his possession, let true justice be visited upon him.

6. I forgive all pleas and debts which were owing to my brother except my own proper dues, and except those things which were agreed to belong to the inheritance of others, or to concern the property which justly belongs to others. And if anyone had promised anything for his heritage, I remit it, and I also remit all 'reliefs' which were promised for direct inheritance.

7. If any of my barons or of my men, being ill, shall give away or bequeath his movable property, I will that it shall be bestowed according to his desires. But if, prevented either by violence or through sickness, he shall die intestate as far as concerns his movable property, his widow or his children or his relatives or one of his true men shall make such division for the sake of his soul, as may seem best to them.

8. If any of my barons or of my men shall incur a forfeit, he shall not be compelled to pledge his movable property to an unlimited amount, as was done in the time of my father and my

brother; but he shall only make payment according to the extent of his legal forfeiture, as was done before the time of my father and in the time of my earlier predecessors. Nevertheless, if he be convicted of breach of faith or of crime, he shall suffer such penalty as is just.

9. I remit all murder-fines which were incurred before the day on which I was crowned king, and such murder-fines as shall now be incurred shall be paid justly according to the law of King Edward.

10. By the common counsel of my barons I have retained the forests in my own hands as my father did before me.

11. The knights, who in return for their estates perform military service equipped with a hauberk of mail, shall hold their demesne lands quit of all gelds and all work; I make this concession as my own free gift in order that, being thus relieved of so great a burden, they may furnish themselves so well with horses and arms that they may be properly equipped and prepared to discharge my service and to defend my kingdom.

12. I establish a firm peace in all my kingdom and I order that this peace shall henceforth be kept.

13. I restore you to the law of King Edward together with such emendations to it as my father made with the counsel of his barons.

14. If since the death of my brother, King William, anyone shall have seized any of my property, or the property of any other man, let him speedily return the whole of it. If he does no penalty will be exacted, but if he retains any part of it he shall when discovered, pay a heavy penalty to me.

Witness: Maurice, bishop of London; William [Giffard], bishop-elect of Winchester; Gerard, bishop of Hereford; Henry, the earl [of Warwick]; Simon, the earl [of Huntingdon]; Walter Giffard; Robert of Montfort-sur-Risle; Roger Bigot; Eduo the Steward; Robert, son of Haimo; and Robert Malet.

At London when I was crowned. Farewell.

English Historical Documents, Vol.II

104. TINTAGEL, Twelfth Century
We are looking to the west. Moving along the white path in the foreground we pass the upper ward on the left, and the lower ward on the right. These form part of the castle on the headland. A broad path leads on to the 'island'. Here is the inner ward of the castle, built in the twelfth century. There are clear indications of a hall once over the strong walls. A zig-zag path to the left from the inner ward leads to a large site, centred on the twelfth-century chapel. Round it stand the walls of a Celtic monastery. Near the medieval chapel is a tomb-shrine for housing relics of saints and founders. There was probably an oratory, a sacristy and a guest-house for pilgrims. The white rectangle showing clearly above is the medieval walled garden. Beyond this, towards the sea, lie three buildings enclosing a small court. One building divided by slabs on edge provided stalls for cattle. Another was in part a drying-kiln. These agricultural activities formed part of a Celtic monastery.

On the eastern cliff, just outside the inner ward of the castle are two buildings – their arrangement suggests the library and scriptorium. Smaller sctructures might be there as writing rooms. Beyond them, up the slope, stand buildings which would be dwelling quarters. Near by, a spring ran down a narrow channel providing the water supply. Further on is another group of buildings – the main dwelling quarters of the monks.

The weathered stone wall on the extreme right is known as the Iton Gate.

THE WRECK OF THE WHITE SHIP, 1120

And on that journey were drowned [the wreck occurred between 25 and 26 November] the king's two sons William and Richard, and Richard, earl of Chester, and Ottuel, his brother, and many of the king's court – stewards and chamberlains and cupbearers and people of various offices and a very immense number of excellent people with them.

Anglo-Saxon Chronicle, English Historical Documents, Vol.II

On 25 November the king gave orders for his return to England, and set sail from Barfleur just before twilight on the evening of

that day. But the young man who was just over seventeen and himself a king in all but name, commanded that another vessel should be prepared for himself, and almost all the young nobility, being his boon companions, gathered round him. The sailors, too, who had drunk overmuch, cried out with true seamen's hilarity that they must overtake the ship that had already set out since their own ship was of the best construction and newly equipped. Wherefore these rash youths, who were flown with wine, launched their vessel from the shore although it was now dark. She flew swifter than an arrow, sweeping the rippling surface of the deep, but the carelessness of her drunken crew drove her on to a rock which rose above the waves not far from the shore. All in consternation rushed on deck and with loud cries got ready their boat-hooks in an endeavour to force the vessel off, but fate was against them and brought to naught their efforts. The oars, too, lashing ineffectively, crashed against the rock, and the battered prow remained fixed. Then the waves washed some of the crew overboard and the water entering the vessel through chinks in its side drowned others. A boat was, however, at last launched and the young prince was taken into it. He might easily have reached the shore in safety had not his bastard sister, the countess of Perche, now struggling with death in the larger vessel, implored his assistance. She cried out that her brother should not abandon her so heartlessly. Whereupon, touched with pity, he ordered his boat to return to the ship that he might rescue his sister, and it was thus that the unhappy youth met his death; for the boat overcharged by the multitude that leapt into her capsized and sank and buried all indiscriminately in the deep. One rustic alone, floating all night upon a mast, survived until the morning to describe the dismal catastrophe. No ship ever brought so much misery to England; none was ever so notorious in the history of the world.

William of Malmesbury, *Gesta Regum Anglorum*
translated by D.C. Douglas, *English Historical Documents,* Vol.II

EVILS OF THE REIGN OF HENRY I

i. It is not easy to describe the miseries this country was suffering at this time [1104], because of various and different injustices and taxes that never ceased and failed, and always wherever the king went there was complete ravaging of his wretched people caused by his court, and in the course of it often there were burnings and killings.

ii. 1124. In the course of this same year after St Andrew's Day before Christmas, Ralph Basset, and the king's thegns held a council at Hundcot in Leicestershire, and hanged there more thieves than ever had been hanged before; that was in all forty-four men in that little time: and six men were blinded and castrated. A large number of trustworthy men said that many were destroyed very unjustly there, but our Lord God Almighty that sees and knows all secrets – He sees the wretched people are treated with complete injustice — first they are robbed of their property and then they are killed. It was a very troublesome year: the man who had any property was deprived of it by severe taxes and severe courts: the man who had none died of hunger.

Anglo-Saxon Chronicle, English Historical Documents, Vol.II

105. The Tower of London was begun by William the Conqueror to overawe Saxon London. The White Tower is one of the oldest and largest surviving Keeps in western Europe. It has served as a fortress, a royal residence, a prison, an arsenal and a barracks, and has housed the Royal Mint, Public Records, the Crown Jewels and the Royal Menagerie. It is a show-place of much of British history.

THE OATH TO ATHELIC [MAUD], 1127

1127. This year King Henry held his court at Christmas at Windsor, and David, king of Scots was there, and all the chief men, both clerics and laymen, that there were in England. And there he [King Henry] caused archbishops and bishops and abbots and earls and all the thegns that were there to give England and Normandy after his death into the hand of his daughter Athelic [Maud], who had been wife of the emperor of Saxony [Henry V]; and then he sent her to Normandy . . . and had her married to the son of the count of Anjou, called Geoffrey Martel. All the same, it displeased all the French and English: but the king did it to have peace with the count of Anjou, and to have help against his nephew, William [William 'Clito', son of Robert].

Anglo-Saxon Chronicle, English Historical Documents, Vol.II

106. The foundation of Warwick Castle is attributed to Ethelfleda, daughter of King Alfred, famous for the castles she built to resist the Danes. At the Conquest it was held by Turchil, the Saxon, as lieutenant of the King of Mercia, who enlarged its fortifications under the orders of William I. It stands on a rock beside the River Avon, one of the most splendid castles in the Midlands.

CHARTER OF THE CITY OF LONDON FROM HENRY I

Henry, by the grace of God, King of England, to the archbishop of Canterbury, and to the bishops and abbots, earls and barons, justices and sheriffs, and to all his faithful subjects of England, French and English, greeting.

Know ye that I have granted to my citizens of London, to hold Middlesex to farm for three hundred pounds, upon accompt to them and their heirs; so that the said citizens shall place as sheriff whom they will of themselves; and shall place whomsoever, or such a one as they will of themselves, for keeping of the pleas of the crown, and of the pleadings of the same, and none other shall be justice over the same men of London; and the citizens of London shall not plead without the walls of London for any plea.

And be they free from scot and lot and danegeld, and of all murder; and none of them shall wage battle. And if any one of the citizens shall be impleaded concerning the pleas of the crown, the man of London shall discharge himself by his oath, which shall be adjudged within the city; and none shall lodge within the walls, neither of my household, nor any other, nor lodging delivered by force.

And all the men of London shall be quit and free, and all their goods, throughout England, and the ports of the sea, of and from all toll and passage and lestage, and all other customs; and the churches and barons and citizens shall and may peaceably and quietly have and hold their sokes [district under a particular jurisdiction]; so that the strangers that shall be lodged in the sokes shall give custom to none but to him to whom the soke appertains, or to his officer.

And a man of London shall not be adjudged in amerciaments [fines] of money but of one hundred shillings (I speak of the pleas which appertain to money): And further there shall be no miskenning in the hustings, nor in the folk-mote, nor in other pleas within the city; and the hustings may sit once in a week, that is to say, on Monday: And I will cause my citizens to have their lands, promises, bonds, and debts, within the city and without; and I will do them right by the law of the city, of the lands of which they shall complain to me:

And if any shall take toll or custom of any citizen of London, the citizens of London in the city shall take of the borough or town, where toll or custom was so taken, as much as the man of London gave for toll, and as he received damage thereby: And all debtors, which do owe debts to the citizens of London, shall pay them in London, or else discharge themselves in London, that they owe none; but if they will not pay the same, neither come to clear themselves that they owe none, the citizens of London, to whom the debts shall be due, may take their goods in the city of London, of the borough or town, or of the country wherein he remains who shall owe the debt: And all citizens of London may have their chances to hunt, as well and fully as their ancestors have had, that is to say, in Chiltre, and in Middlesex and Surrey.

Witness the bishop of Winchester, and Robert son of Richier, and Hugh Bygot, and Alured of Toteneys, and William of Albaspina and Hubert the king's Chamberlain, and William de Montficket, and Hangulf de Taney, and John Bellet, and Robert son of Siward. At Westminster.

The Historical Charters and Constitutional Documents of the City of London

TROUVÈRE WACE DESCRIBES THE NORMAN PEASANTS' REVOLT UNDER THE RULE OF RICHARD LE BON, Eleventh Century

The peasants and the villeins, the men of the forest and of the plain, I know not by what enticement nor under whose first leadership, held councils by twenties, by thirties, by hundreds . . . and have sworn together, that never by their own freewill shall they have lord or bailiff. The lords [they said] do them nought but harm; they can have no reason with them, nor no gain from their own work. Daily the peasants go with great grief, in pain and in toil; last year was ill, this year is worse; daily their cattle are taken for taxes or for services; there are so many pleas [in the manor-court] and quarrels, so many customs, old and new, that they cannot have an hour's peace. . . . They can have no warranty against their lord or his servant, who keep no covenant with the peasant; "son of a whore," they say. Wherefore then do we let them harm us; let us shake ourselves free from their domination! We, too, are men as they; limbs we have like theirs, and our bodies are as big and we can endure as much; all that we need is only a heart. Let us bind ourselves together by oath to defend ourselves and our goods; let us hold together, and then, if they will war against us, we have one or two score peasants, able to fight, against every knight of theirs.

107. Berkhamsted, showing clearly the outline of a Norman motte-and-bailey castle. The motte or mound on the right is the essential part of the fortification and had a wooden tower on its summit; the bailey is the outer enclosure bounded by a wooden palisade and a deep ditch or moat. Domesday Book mentions forty-nine castles as existing in 1086, this is certainly not a full list.

ON THE ACCESSION OF STEPHEN, 1135

. . . So on the death of the great King Henry I the verdict of the people was freely expressed concerning him, as is usually the case after the death of a notable personage. Some said that he was eminently distinguished for three splendid qualities: great wisdom, for he was most deep in counsel, keen foresight and outstanding eloquence; success in war, besides other fine achievements he had overcome the king of France [Louis VI]; and riches, for he was more wealthy than any of his predecessors. Others, however, taking a different view, attributed to him three vices: gross avarice through which, though himself wealthy like all his ancestors, he devoured the poor by tolls and exactions, entangling them in the toils of his informers; cruelty in that he put out the eyes of his kinsman, the count of Mortain [Henry I's half-brother, William], during his captivity, about which nothing could be known until death revealed the king's secrets, and other examples of greed were also cited which I forbear to mention; and also incontinence, for like Solomon he was perpetually enslaved by the rule of women. Such diverse opinions were freely expressed by the common people. But in the terrible times which followed later through the insensate treachery of the Normans, whatsoever King Henry had done, whether in the manner of a tyrant or of a true king, appeared most excellent in comparison with their evil deeds. For without delay came Stephen, younger brother of Theobald, count of Blois, a man of great resolution and audacity, who, although he had sworn an oath of fealty for the realm of England to the daughter of King Henry [Maud], trusting in his strength, shamelessly tempted God and seized the crown of the kingdom. William, archbishop of Canterbury, who had been the first to swear allegiance to the king's daughter, alas! crowned Stephen king, wherefore God visited him with the same judgment which he had inflicted on him who had stricken Jeremiah, the great priest; namely, that he should not live out the year. Roger, the great bishop of Salisbury, who had been the second to take the aforesaid oath and had ordered all the others to do likewise, contributed everything in his power to secure for him the crown. He, too, by the just judgment of God was afterwards taken captive by him whom he had made king and in dire torments came to a wretched end. But why tarry? All those who had sworn fealty, whether prelates, earls or magnates, offered to accept Stephen and paid homage to him. This indeed was an evil sign, that the whole of England should so suddenly and without delay or struggle, and as it were, in the twinkling of an eye, submit to Stephen. So, after his coronation at Christmastide, he held his court at London.

Meanwhile the body of King Henry lay still unburied in Normandy, for he died on 1 December. . . . At last the royal remains were transported to England and buried within twelve days of Christmas in the abbey of Reading which King Henry had founded and endowed with great possessions. Thither came King Stephen, after holding his court in London that same Christmastide, to meet the body of his uncle, and William, archbishop of Canterbury, with many prelates and lay magnates. There they buried King Henry with the honour due to so great a man. From thence King Stephen proceeded to Oxford where were recorded and confirmed the covenants which he had granted to God and the people and to holy Church on theday of his coronation. . . .

Henry of Huntingdon, *Historia Anglorum*

THE ANARCHY OF STEPHEN'S REIGN

1137. This year King Stephen went overseas to Normandy and was received there because they expected that he would be just as his uncle had been, and because he still had his treasure; but he distributed it and squandered it like a fool. King Henry had gathered a great amount – gold and silver – and no good to his soul was done with it.

When King Stephen came to England he held his council at Oxford, and there he took Roger, bishop of Salisbury, and Alexander, bishop of Lincoln, and the chancellor Roger, his nephews [nephews of Roger, bishop of Salisbury], and put them all in prison till they surrendered their castles.

108. Carlisle Castle, Cumberland, originally a wooden structure built in 1092 by William II to control the western part of the Scottish border, was changed to stone walls and keep from 1157. Its position was of considerable strategic importance.

When the traitors understood that he was a mild man, and gentle and good, and did not exact the full penalties of the law, they perpetrated every enormity. They had done him homage, and sworn oaths, but they kept no pledge; all of them were perjured and their pledges nullified, for every powerful man built his castles and held them against him and they filled the country full of castles. They oppressed the wretched people of the country severely with castle building. When the castles were built, they filled them with devils and wicked men. Then, both by night and day they took those people that they thought had any goods – men and women – and put them in prison and tortured them with indescribable torture to extort gold and silver – for no martyrs were ever so tortured as they were. They were hung by the thumbs or by the head, and corselets were hung on their feet. Knotted ropes were put round their heads and twisted till they penetrated to the brain. They put them in prisons where there were adders and snakes and toads, and killed them like that. Some they put in a 'torture chamber', that is in a chest that was short, narrow and shallow, and they put sharp stones in it and pressed the man in it so that he had all his limbs broken. In many of the castles was a 'noose-and-trap'–consisting of chains of such a kind that two or three men had enough to do to carry one. It was so made that it was fastened to a beam, and they used to put a sharp iron around the man's throat and his neck, so that he could not in any direction either sit or lie or sleep, but had to carry all that iron. Many thousands they killed by starvation.

I have neither the ability nor the power to tell all the horrors nor all the torments they inflicted upon wretched people in this country: and that lasted the nineteen years while Stephen was king, and it was always going from bad to worse.

They levied taxes on the village every so often, and called it 'protection money'. When the wretched people had no more to give, they robbed and burned all the villages, so that you could easily go a whole day's journey and never find anyone occupying a village, nor land tilled. Then corn was dear, and meat and butter and cheese, because there was none other in the country. Wretched people died of starvation; some lived by begging for alms, who had once been rich men; some fled the country.

There had never been till then greater misery in the country, nor had heathens ever done worse than they did. For contrary to custom, they respected neither church nor churchyard, but took all the property that was inside, and then burnt the church and everything together. Neither did they respect bishops' land nor abbots' nor priests', but robbed monks and clerics, and everyone robbed somebody else if he had the greater power. If two or three men came riding to a village, all the villagers fled, because they expected they would be robbers. The bishops and learned men were always excommunicating them, but they thought nothing of it, because they were all utterly accursed and perjured and doomed to perdition.

Wherever cultivation was done, the ground produced no corn, because the land was all ruined by such doings, and they said openly that Christ and his saints were asleep. Such things, too much for us to describe, we suffered nineteen years for our sins.

Anglo-Saxon Chronicle,
English Historical Documents Vol. II

THE STATE OF ENGLAND UNDER STEPHEN, A.D.1141

AT this period England was in a very disturbed state. On the one hand, the king and those who took his part grievously oppressed the people, on the other, frequent turmoils were raised by the Earl

109. The existing Pembroke Castle was begun in 1093, when Arnulph de Montgomery fortified the site against the Welsh. Gerald de Windesor repulsed the attacks of Cadwgan ap Bleddyn, a soldier who later captured Gerald's wife, Nest, at Cilgerran Castle. The boy, later to become Henry VII, was born at Pembroke Castle in 1457.

of Gloucester. What with the tyranny of the one, and the turbulence of the other, there was universal turmoil and desolation. Some for whom their country had lost its charm, chose rather to make their abode in foreign lands; others drew to the churches for protection, and constructing mean hovels in their precincts, passed their days in fear and trouble.

Food being scarce, for there was a dreadful famine throughout England, some of the people disgustingly devoured the flesh of dogs and horses; others appeased their insatiable hunger with the garbage of uncooked herbs and roots; many, in all parts, sunk under the severity of the famine and died in heaps; others with their whole families went sorrowfully into voluntary banishment and disappeared.

There were seen famous cities deserted and depopulated by the death of their inhabitants of every age and sex, and fields white for the harvest, for it was near the season of autumn, but none to gather it, all having been struck down by the famine. Thus the whole aspect of England presented a scene of calamity and sorrow, misery and oppression. It tended to increase the evil that a crowd of fierce strangers who had flocked to England in bands to take service in the war, and who were devoid of all bowels of mercy and feelings of humanity, were scattered among the people thus suffering. In all the castles their sole business was to contrive the most flagitious outrages; and the employment on which all the powers of their malicious minds were bent, was to watch every opportunity of plundering the weak, to foment troubles, and to cause bloodshed in every direction. And as the barons who had assembled them from the remotest districts were neither able to discharge their pay out of their own revenues, nor satisfy their insatiable thirst for plunder and renumerate themselves by pillage as they had done before, because there was nothing left anywhere whole and undamaged, they had recourse to the possession of the monasteries, or the neighbouring municipalities or any others which they could send forth troops enough to infest.

At one time they loaded their victims with false accusations and virulent abuse; at another they ground them down with vexatious claims and extortions; some they stripped of their property, either by open robbery or secret contrivance, and others they reduced to complete subjection in the most shameless manner.

110. The great tower-keep of Rochester Castle built about 1127 by the Archbishop of Canterbury. Earlier, on the site, William the Conqueror had built a 'motte and bailey' castle to control the position where Watling Street crosses the Medway. In 1089 this was replaced by a stone castle designed by Gundulf, Bishop of Rochester.

If any of the reverend monks, or of the secular clergy, came to complain of the exactions laid on church property, he was met with abuse, and abruptly silenced with outrageous threats. The servants who attended him on his journey were often severely scourged before his face, and he himself, whatever his rank and order might be, was shamefully stripped of his effects, and even his garments, and driven away, or left helpless, from the severe beating to which he was subjected.

Acts of King Stephen, II, translated by T. Forester

THE TREATY OF WINCHESTER, 1153

And the count of Anjou died [7 September 1151], and his son Henry succeeded to the dominions: and the queen [of France, Eleanor, wife of Louis VII] separated from the [French] king and came to young Count Henry and he took her as his wife, and all

111. Chepstow, Monmouth, was the earliest and the most important castle from which the Normans conquered South Wales. It stands on a rocky spur, with the cliffs above the Wye on one side and a ravine between the Upper and Middle Baileys. It dates from the mid-eleventh century.

Poitou with her. Then he went with a big army into England [January 1153], and won castles, and the king went against him with a much bigger army, and all the same they did not fight, but the archbishop and the wise men went between them and made an agreement that the king should be liege lord and king as long as he lived and after his day Henry should be king: they should be as father and son: and there should always be peace and concord between them and in all England [The Treaty of Winchester was made on 6 November 1153]. This, and all the other conditions that they made, the king and the count and the bishops and the earls and powerful men all swore to keep. Then the count was received at Winchester and in London with great honour, and all did him homage, and swore to keep the peace: and it soon became a good peace, such as there never was before. Then the king was stronger than he had been till then, and the count went overseas and everybody loved him because he exacted strict justice and made peace.

Anglo-Saxon Chronicle, English Historical Documents, Vol.II

Warfare

THE BATTLE OF STAMFORD BRIDGE, 25 September 1066
Fought on foot, in the manner of Vikings and the Teutons, sword against sword, axe to axe.

Meanwhile Earl Tostig came into the Humber with sixty ships, and Earl Edwin came with land levies and drove him out, and the ship men deserted him. He sailed to Scotland with twelve small vessels, where he was met by King Harold from Norway with three hundred ships, to whom Tostig gave allegiance and became his man. Together they sailed into the Humber until they came to York, where Earl Edwin and Earl Morcar, his brother, fought against them, but the Norwegians had the victory. Then King Harold was informed how the fight had gone – it took place on the vigil of St Matthew's day [20 September]. Then Harold our king came unexpectedly upon the Norwegians, and met them beyond York at Stamford Bridge with a great host of Englishmen, and that day a very stubborn battle was fought by both sides. There were slain Harold Hardrada and Earl Tostig, and the remaining Norwegians were put to flight, while the English fiercely assailed their rear until some of them reached their ships: some were drowned, others burnt to death, and thus perished in various ways so that there were few survivors, and the English had possession of the place of slaughter. The king then gave quarter to Olaf, the son of the king of the Norwegians, to their bishop, to the earl of Orkneys, and to all those who were left aboard the ships. They then went inland to our king, and swore oaths that they would ever maintain peace and friendship with this land; and the king let them sail home with twenty-four ships. These two pitched battles were fought within five days.

Anglo-Saxon Chronicle, English Historical Documents, Vol.II

THE NORMAN CONQUEST

1066. In this year the minster of Westminster was consecrated on Holy Innocents' Day, and King Edward died on the eve of Epiphany and was buried on the Feast of the Epiphany in the newly consecrated church at Westminster. And Earl Harold succeeded to the realm of England, just as the king had granted it to him, and as he had been chosen to the position. And he was consecrated king on the Feast of the Epiphany. And the same year that he became king he went out with a naval force against William and meanwhile Earl Tostig came into the Humber with sixty ships and Earl Edwin came with a land force and drove him out and the sailors deserted him, and he went to Scotland with twelve small vessels and Harold, king of Norway, met him with three hundred ships, and Tostig submitted to him; and they both went up the Humber until they reached York. And Earl Morcar and Earl Edwin fought against them, and the king of Norway had the victory. And King Harold was informed as to what had been done, and what had happened, and he came with a very great force of Englishmen and met him at Stamford Bridge, and killed him and Earl Tostig and valiantly overcame all the invaders. Meanwhile Count William landed at Hastings on Michaelmas Day, and Harold came from the north and fought with him before all the army had come, and there he fell and his two brothers Gurth and Leofwine; and William conquered this country, and came to Westminster, and Archbishop Aldred consecrated him king, and people paid taxes to him, and gave him hostages and afterwards bought their lands.

Anglo-Saxon Chronicle, English Historical Documents, Vol.II

THE DEEDS OF WILLIAM, DUKE OF THE NORMANS AND KING OF THE ENGLISH

... About the same time [1063] Edward, king of the English, who loved William as a brother or a son, established him as his heir with a stronger pledge than ever before. The king, who in his holy life showed his desire for a celestial kingdom, felt the hour of his death approaching, and wished to anticipate its inevitable consequences. He therefore dispatched Harold to William in order that he might confirm his promise by an oath. This Harold was of all the king's subjects the richest and the most exalted in honour and power, and his brother and cousins had previously been offered as hostages in respect of the same succession. The king, indeed, here acted with great prudence in choosing Harold for this task, in the hope that the riches and the authority of this magnate might check disturbances throughout England if the people with their accustomed perfidy should be disposed to overturn what had been determined. Whilst travelling upon this errand Harold only escaped the perils of the sea by making a forced landing on the coast of Ponthieu where he fell into the hands of Count Guy, who threw him and his companions into prison. He might well have thought this a greater misfortune even than shipwreck, since among many peoples of the Gauls there was an abominable custom utterly contrary to Christian charity, whereby, when the powerful and rich were captured, they were thrown ignominiously into prison, and there maltreated and tortured even to the point of death, and afterwards sold as slaves to some magnate. When Duke William heard what had happened he sent messengers at speed, and by prayers and threats he brought about Harold's honourable release. As a result Guy in person conducted his prisoner to the castle of Eu, although he could at his pleasure have tortured or killed him, or sold him into slavery. Since, moreover, he did this very honourably without the compulsion of force or bribes, William in gratitude bestowed upon him rich gifts of land and money, and then took Harold with proper honour to Rouen. This was the chief city of the Norman duchy, and there William sumptuously refreshed Harold with splendid hospitality after all the hardships of his journey. For the duke rejoiced to have so illustrious a guest in a man who had been sent him by the nearest and dearest of his friends: one, moreover, who was in England second only to the king, and who might prove a faithful mediator between him and the English. When they had come together in conference at Bonneville, Harold in that place swore fealty to the duke employing the sacred ritual recognized among Christian men. And as is testified by the most truthful and most honourable men who were there present, he took an oath of his own free will in the following terms: firstly that he would be the representative of Duke William at the court of his lord, King Edward, as long as the king lived; secondly that he would employ all his influence and wealth to ensure that after the death of King Edward the kingdom of England should be confirmed in the possession of the duke; thirdly that he would place a garrison of the duke's knights in the castle of Dover and maintain these at his own care and cost; fourthly that in other parts of England at the pleasure of the duke he would maintain garrisons in other castles and make complete provision for their sustenance. The duke on his part who before the oath was taken had received ceremonial homage from him, confirmed to him at his request all his lands and dignities. For Edward in his illness could not be expected to live much longer. . . . After this there came the unwelcome report that the land of England had lost its king, and that Harold had been crowned in his stead. This insensate Englishman did not wait for the public choice, but breaking his oath, and with the support of a few ill-disposed partisans, he seized the throne of the best of kings on the very day of his funeral, and when all the people were bewailing their loss. He was ordained king by the unhallowed consecration of Stigand who had justly been deprived of his priesthood by the zeal and anathema of the apostolic see. Duke William therefore having taken counsel with his men resolved to avenge the insult by force of arms, and to regain his inheritance by war.

William of Poitiers,
Gesta Willelmi ducis Normannorum et regis Anglorum

DESCRIPTION OF THE INVASION OF ENGLAND BY WILLIAM, DUKE OF NORMANDY

In due course King Edward completed the term of his happy life, and departed from this world in the year of the Incarnation of our Lord 1065. Then Harold immediately seized the kingdom, thus violating the oath which he had sworn to the duke. Therefore, the duke at once sent messengers to Harold urging him to desist from this mad policy, and to keep the faith which he had pledged with his oath. Harold, however, not only disdained to listen to this message, but seduced all the English people away from obedience to the duke. In these days a star with three long rays appeared. It lit up the greater part of the southern sky for the space of a fortnight, and many thought that this portended a great change in some kingdom.

Prince William was thus compelled to watch the strength of Harold increasing daily at a time when it was the duke who should have been crowned with a royal diadem. He therefore hastily built a fleet of three thousand ships. At length he brought this fleet to anchor at St. Valery in Ponthieu where he filled it with mighty horses and most valiant men, with hauberks and helmets. Then when a favourable wind began to blow, he set sail, and crossing the sea he landed at Pevensey where he immediately built a castle with a strong rampart. He left this in charge of some troops, and with others he hurried to Hastings where he erected another similar fortress. Harold, rejecting caution, advanced against this, and, after riding all night, he appeared on the field of battle early in the morning.

But the duke had taken precautions against night-attacks by the enemy, and as the darkness approached he had ordered his men to stand by until dawn. At first light, having disposed his troops in three lines of battle, he advanced undaunted against the terrible enemy. The battle began at the third hour of the day, and continued amid a weltage of carnage and slaughter until nightfall. Harold himself, fighting amid the front rank of his army, fell covered with deadly wounds. And the English, seeing their king dead, lost confidence in their own safety, and as night was approaching they turned and fled.

William of Jumièges, *Gesta Normannorum Ducum*

112. The sword-dance, or combat with swords and bucklers, regulated by music, was performed by Saxon gleemen. These combats, in some ways, resembled those performed by Roman gladiators. For this reason the jugglers were sometimes called Gladiators by early historians.

THE BATTLE OF HASTINGS, 14 October 1066

'Events were to show that William had won one of the battles which at rare intervals have decided the fate of nations.'

F.M. Stenton

Duke William and the whole army committed themselves to God's protection, with prayers, and offerings, and vows, and accompanied a procession from the church, carrying the relics of St. Valeri, confessor of Christ, to obtain a favourable wind. At last when by God's grace it suddenly came round to the quarter which was the object of so many prayers, the duke, full of ardour, lost no time in embarking the troops, and giving the signal for hastening the departure of the fleet. The Norman expedition, therefore, crossed the sea on the night of the third of the calends of October [29th September], which the Catholic Church observes as the feast of St. Michael the archangel, and meeting with no resistance, and landing safely on the coast of England, took possession of Pevensey and Hastings, the defence of which was entrusted to a chosen body of soldiers, to cover a retreat and guard the fleet.

Meanwhile the English usurper, after having put to the sword his brother Tostig, and his royal enemy, and slaughtered their immense army, returned in triumph to London. As however wordly prosperity soon vanishes like smoke before the wind, Harold's rejoicings for his bloody victory were soon darkened by the threatening clouds of a still heavier storm. Nor was he suffered long to enjoy the security procured by his brother's death; for a hasty messenger brought him the intelligence that the Normans had embarked. Learning soon afterwards that they had actually landed, he made preparations for a fresh conflict. For his intrepidity was dauntless, and his conduct of affairs admirable, while his personal strength was great, his presence commanding, and he had the arts of a persuasive eloquence, and of a courtesy which endeared him to his supporters. Still his mother Githa, who was much afflicted by the death of her son Tostig, and his other faithful friends, dissuaded him from engaging in battle with the Normans; his brother, Earl Gurth, thus addressing him: "It is best, dearest brother and lord, that your courage should be tempered by discretion. You are worn by the conflict with the Norwegians from which you are only just come, and you are in eager haste to give battle to the Normans. Allow youself, I pray you, some time for rest. Reflect also, in your wisdom, on the oath you have taken to the duke of Normandy. Beware of incurring the guilt of perjury, lest by so great a crime you draw ruin on yourself and the forces of this nation, and stain forever the honour of our own race. For myself, I am bound by no oaths, I am under no obligations to Count William. I am therefore in a position to fight with him undauntedly in defence of our native soil. But do you, my brother, rest awhile in peace, and wait the issue of the contest, so that the liberty which is the glory of England, may not be ruined by your fall."

Harold was very indignant at this speech. Holding in contempt the wholesome advice of his friends, he loaded his brother with reproaches for his faithful counsel, and even forgot himself so far as to kick his mother when she hung about him in her too great anxiety to detain him with her. For six days Harold sent forth the summons to call the people to arms from all quarters, and having assembled vast numbers of the English, he led them by forced marches against the enemy. It was his design to take them unawares, and crush them at once by a night attack, or, at least, by a sudden onset, and, that they might not escape by sea, he caused a fleet of seventy ships, full of soldiers, to guard the coast. Duke William, having intelligence of Harold's approach, ordered his troops to take to their arms on the morning of Saturday. He then heard mass, strengthening both body and soul by partaking of the consecrated host; he also reverently suspended from his neck the holy relics on which Harold had sworn. Many of the clergy who followed the Norman army, among who were two bishops, Odo, of Bayeux, and Geoffrey, of Coutances, with attendant clerks and monks, whose duty it was to aid the war with their prayers and counsels. The battle commenced at the third hour of the Ides [14th] of October, and was fought desperately the whole day, with the loss of many thousand men on both sides. The Norman duke drew up his light troops, consisting of archers and men armed with cross-bows, in the first line; the infantry in armour formed the second rank; and in the third were placed the cavalry, in the centre of which the duke stationed himself with the flower of his troops, so as to be able to issue his commands, and give support to every part of the army.

On the other side, the English troops, assembled from all parts of the neighbourhood, took post at a place which was anciently called Senlac, many of them personally devoted to the cause of Harold, and all to that of their country, which they were resolved to defend against the foreigners. Dismounting from their horses, on which it was determined not to rely, they formed a solid column of infantry, and thus stood firm in the position they had taken.

Turstin, son of Rollo, bore the standard of Normandy. The sound of the trumpets in both armies was the terrible signal for beginning the battle. The Normans made the first attack with ardour and gallantry, their infantry rushing forward to provoke the English, and spreading wounds and death through their ranks by showers of arrows and bolts. The English, on their side, made a stout resistance, each man straining his powers to the utmost. The battle raged for some time with the utmost violence between both parties. At length the indomitable bravery of the English threw the Bretons, both horse and foot, and the other auxiliary troops composing the left wing, into confusion, and, in their rout, they drew with them almost all the rest of the duke's army, who, in their panic, believed that he was slain. The duke, perceiving that large bodies from the enemy had broken their ranks in pursuit of his flying troops, rode up to the fugitives and checked their retreat, loudly threatening them, and striking with his lance. Taking off his helmet, and exposing his naked head, he shouted: 'See, I am here; I am still living, and, by God's help, shall yet have the victory." Suddenly the courage of the fugitives was restored by these bold words of the duke; and, intercepting some thousands of their pursuers, they cut them down in a moment. In this manner, the Normans, twice again pretending to retreat, and when they were followed by the English, suddenly wheeling their horses, cut their pursuers off from the main body, surrounded and slew them. The ranks of the English were much thinned by these dangerous feints, through which they fell separated from each other; so that, when thousands were thus slaughtered, the Normans attacked the survivors with still greater vigour. They were charged home by the troops of Maine, France, Brittany, and Aquitaine, and great numbers of them miserably perished.

Among those present at this battle, were Eustace, Count de

Boulogne, William, son of Richard, Count d'Exreux, Geoffrey, son of Robert, Count de Mortagne, William Fitz-Osborn, Robert, son of Robert de Beaumont, a novice in arms, Aimer, Viscount de Thouars, Earl Hugh, the constable, Walter Giffard, and Ralph Toni, Hugh de Grantmesnil, and William de Warrenne, with many other knights illustrious for their military achievements, and whose names merit a record in the annals of history amongst the most famous warriors. Duke William surpassed them all in courage and conduct; for he nobly performed the duties of a general, staying the flight of his troops, re-animating their courage, their comrade in the greatest dangers, and more frequently calling on them to follow where he led, than commanding them to advance before him. He had three horses killed under him in the battle; thrice he remounted, and did not suffer his steeds to be long unavenged. Shields, helmets, and coats of mail were shivered by the furious and impatient thrust of his sword; some he dashed to the earth with his shield, and was at all times as ready to cover and protect his friends, as to deal death among his foes.

Although the battle was fought with the greatest fury from nine o'clock in the morning, King Harold was slain in the first onset, and his brother Earl Leofwin fell some time afterwards, with many thousands of the royal army. Towards evening, the English finding that their king and the chief nobles of the realm, with a great part of their army, had fallen, while the Normans still showed a bold front, and made desperate attacks on all who made any resistance, they had reçourse to flight as expeditiously as they could. Various were the fortunes which attended their retreat; some recovering their horses, some on foot, attempted to escape by the highways; more sought to save themselves by striking across the country. The Normans, finding the English completely routed, pursued them vigorously all Sunday night, but not without suffering a great loss; for, galloping onward in hot pursuit, they fell unawares, horses and armour, into an ancient trench, overgrown and concealed by rank grass, and men in their armour and horses rolling over each other, were crushed and smothered. This accident restored confidence to the routed English, for, perceiving the advantage given them by the mouldering rampart and a succession of ditches, they rallied in a body, and, making a sudden stand, caused the Normans severe loss. At this place Eugenulf, lord of Laigle, and many others fell, the number of Normans who perished being, as reported by some who were present, nearly fifteen thousand. Thus did Almighty God, on the eve of the Ides of October, punish in various ways the innumerable sinners in both armies. For, on this Saturday, the Normans butchered with remorseless cruelty thousands of the English, who long before had murdered the innocent prince Alfred and his attendants; and on the Saturday before the present battle, had massacred without pity King Harold and Earl Tostig, with multitudes of Norwegians. The righteous Judge avenged the English on Sunday night, when the furious Normans were precipitated into the concealed trench; for they had broken the divine law by their boundless covetousness; and, as the Psalmist says: "Their feet were swift to shed blood," whereupon, "sorrow and unhappiness was in their ways."

Duke William, perceiving that the English troops suddenly rallied, did not halt; and when he found Count Eustace with fifty men-at-arms retreating, and the count wished him to have the signal sounded for recalling the pursuers, he commanded him with a loud voice to stand firm. The count, however, familiarly approaching the duke, whispered in his ear that it would be safer to retreat, predicting his sudden death if he persisted in the pursuit. While he was saying this, Eustace received a blow between the shoulders, so violent that the noise of the stroke was plainly heard, and it caused blood to flow from his mouth and nostrils, and he was borne off by his comrades in a dying state.

113. This is a quintain from a boat with a square piece of board used instead of a shield. The young man will try to break his lance against it and retain his balance. If he fails to break his lance, the board or shield, on a pivot, will throw him in the water.

The victory being secured, the duke returned to the field of battle, where he viewed the dreadful carnage, which could not be seen without commiseration. There the flower of the youth and nobility of England covered the ground far and near stained with blood. Harold could not be discovered by his features, but was recognized by other tokens, and his corpse, being borne to the duke's camp, was, by order of the conqueror, delivered to William Mallet for interment near the sea-shore, which had long been guarded by his arms.

Ordericus Vitalis, *Historia Ecclesiastica*, translated by T. Forester

Then Duke William sailed from Normandy into Pevensey, on the eve of Michaelmas [28 September]. As soon as his men were fit for service, they constructed a castle at Hastings. When King Harold was informed of this, he gathered together a great host, and came to oppose him at the grey-apple tree, and William came upon him unexpectedly before his army was set in order. Nevertheless the king fought against him most resolutely with those men who wished to stand by him, and there was great slaughter on both sides. King Harold was slain, and Leofwine his brother, and Earl Gurth his brother, and many good men. The French had possession of the place of slaughter, as God granted them because of the nation's sins. Archbishop Ealdred and the citizens of London wished to have Prince Edgar for king, as was indeed his right by birth, and Edwin and Morcar promised that they would fight for him, but always when some initiative should have been shown there was delay from day to day until matters went from bad to worse, as everything did in the end. This battle took place on the day of Pope Calixtus [14 October]. Duke William returned to Hastings, and waited there to see if there would be any surrender; but when he realized that none were willing to come to him, he marched inland with what was left of his host, together with reinforcements lately come from overseas, and harried that part of the country through which he advanced until he came to Berkhamsted. There he was met by Bishop Ealdred, Prince Edgar, Earl Edwin, Earl Morcar, and all the best men from London, who submitted from force of circumstances, but only when the depredation was complete. . . . Then on Christmas Day Archbishop Ealdred consecrated him king in Westminster; but before he would accept the crown he gave a pledge on the Gospels, and swore an oath besides that he would govern this nation according to the best practice of his predecessors if they were loyal to him. Nevertheless he imposed a very heavy tax on the country and went overseas to Normandy in the spring. . . . Bishop Odo and Earl William were left behind here, and they built castles far and wide throughout the land, oppressing the unhappy people, and things went ever from bad to worse. When God wills may the end be good.

Anglo-Saxon Chronicle, English Historical Documents, Vol.II

AFTER THE BATTLE OF HASTINGS

It would have been just if wolves and vultures had devoured the flesh of these English who had rightly incurred their doom and if the fields had received their unburied bones. But such a fate seemed cruel to the duke, and he allowed all who wished to do so to collect the bodies for burial . Then, having arranged for the honourable interment of his own men, he left Hastings in charge of a brave commander, and proceeded to Romney, where he punished at his pleasure those who had previously killed some of his men after a struggle.

Then he marched to Dover, which had been reported impregnable and held by a large force. The English, stricken with fear at his approach, had confidence neither in their ramparts nor in the natural strength of the site, nor in the number of their troops. This castle is situated on a rock adjoining the sea, and it is raised up by nature and so strongly fortified that it stands like a straight wall as high as an arrow's flight. Its side is washed by the sea. While the inhabitants were preparing to surrender unconditionally, our men, greedy for booty, set fire to the castle, and the greater part of it was soon enveloped in flames. The duke, unwilling that those who had offered to surrender should suffer loss, gave them a recompense in money for the damage of the castle and their property; and he would have severely punished those who had started the fire if their numbers and base condition had not prevented their detection. Having taken possession of the castle the duke spent eight days adding new fortifications to it.

Owing to the foul water and bad food his knights were there stricken with severe dysentery, and many were brought by weakness almost to the point of death. But this adversity did not daunt the duke.

William of Poitiers, 'The Deeds of William, Duke of the Normans and King of the English', translated by D.C. Douglas, G.W. Greenaway, *English Historical Documents*, Vol.II

THE COMING OF FEUDALISM, 1066

Normandy is the classic example of the creation of the feudal state.

At the beginning of his abbacy [Abbot Athelhelm] deemed it necessary never to go about without an armed retinue, for in the midst of the conspiracies which broke out almost daily against the king and the kingdom, he felt compelled to take measures for his own protection. Then castles were built at Wallingford and Oxford and Windsor and other places for the safety of the realm, and the king ordered this abbey [Abingdon] to provide guards in Windsor. For this purpose soldiers who had come to England from overseas were considered to be the most suitable. In the midst of such upheavals the lord abbot, Athelhelm, securely protected the place committed to his charge with an armed force of knights. For this purpose he first used stipendiary knights. But after the disturbances had died down, it was noted in the annals by the king's command what knights should be demanded from bishoprics and abbacies for the defence of the realm when the need arose. Abbot Athelhelm, therefore, having retained the lands which had aforetime been given to the church, afterwards allotted the manors of those who would hold them from the church, and in each case he declared what would be the obligations involved in its tenure. These estates had previously been held by men called thegns who had been killed in the battle of Hastings.

Abingdon Chronicle, English Historical Documents, Vol.II

MALCOLM, KING OF THE SCOTS, IN REVENGE, MASSACRES THE ENGLISH, 1070

. . . scarcely able to contain himself for fury, he ordered his troops no longer to spare any of the English nation, but either to smite all to the earth, or to carry them off captives under the yoke of perpetual slavery. Having received this licence, it was misery even to witness their deeds against the English. Some aged men and women were beheaded with the sword; others were thrust through with pikes, like swine destined for food; infants snatched from their mother's breasts were thrown high into the air, and in their fall were received on the points of lances and pikes thickly placed in the ground. The Scots, more savage than wild beasts, delighted in this cruelty, as an amusing spectacle. These children of the age of innocence, suspended between heaven and earth, gave up their souls to heaven. Young men also and maidens, and whoever seemed fit to toil and labour, were bound and driven before the face of their enemies, to be reduced in perpetual exile to slaves and bondmaids. Some of these females, worn out by running in front of their drivers further than their strength would bear, falling to the earth, perished even where they fell.

Seeing these things, Malcolm was not yet moved to pity by tears, nor groans of the unhappy wretches; but, on the contrary, gave orders that they should be still further pressed onward in the march. Scotland was, therefore, filled with slaves and handmaids of the English race; so that even to this day, I do not say no little village, but even no cottage, can be found without one of them.

Simeon of Durham, translated by Rev. J. Stevenson in
The Church Historians of England

THE SACK OF PETERBOROUGH, 2 June 1070

The same year king Sweyn came from Denmark into the Humber, and the people of those parts came to meet him and made an alliance with him, for they believed that he would conquer the land. Then the Danish bishop Christien, and Earl Osbern, and their Danish retainers, came into Ely, and all the people of the fens joined them, for they believed that they should conquer the whole country. Now the monks of Peterborough were told that some of their own men, namely, Hereward and his train,would pillage the monastery, because they had heard that the king had given the abbacy to a French abbot called Turold, and that he was a very stern man, and that he was come into Stamford with all his French followers. There was, at that time, a churchwarden named Ywar: who took all that he could by night, gospels, mass-robes, cassocks, and other garments, and such other small things as he could carry

114. The sling used in hunting and in warfare is here shown with both ends held in the hand; with one end released and the stone discharged; attached to a staff, or truncheon, wielded with both hands.

away, and he came before day to the abbot Turold, and told him that he sought his protection, and told how the outlaws were coming to Peterborough, and he said that he had done this at the desire of the monks. Then early in the morning all the outlaws came with many ships, and they endeavoured to enter the monastery, but the monks withstood them, so that they were not able to get in. Then they set fire to it, and burned all the monks' houses, and all those in the town, save one: and they broke in through the fire at Bolhithe-gate [Bulldyke gate], and the monks came before them and desired peace. However they gave no heed to them, but went into the monastery, and climbed up to the holy crucifix, took the crown from our Lord's head, which was all of the purest gold, and the footstool of red gold from under his feet. And they climbed up to the steeple, and brought down the table [crozier or cope?] which was hidden there; it was all of gold and silver. They also seized two gilt shrines, and nine of silver, and they carried off fifteen great crosses of gold and silver. And they took so much gold and silver, and so much treasure in money, robes, and books, that no man can compute the amount; saying they did this because of their allegiance to the monastery: and afterwards they betook themselves to their ships and went to Ely, where they secured their treasures. The Danes believed that they should overcome the Frenchmen, and they drove away all the monks, leaving only one named Leofwin the Long, and he lay sick in the hospital. Then came the abbot Turold, and eight score Frenchmen with him, all well armed; and when he arrived he found all burnt both within and without, excepting the church itself; and all the outlaws were then embarked, knowing that he would come thither. This happened on the fourth day before the Nones of June [2 June]. Then the two kings, William and Sweyn, made peace with each other, on which the Danes departed from Ely, carrying with them all the aforesaid treasure. When they were come into the midst of the sea, there arose a great storm, which dispersed all the ships in which the treasures were: some were driven to Norway, some to Ireland, and others to Denmark, and all the spoils that reached the latter country, being the table [crozier or cope?] and some of the shrines and crosses, and many of the other treasures, they brought to one of the king's towns called . . . , and laid it all up in the church. But one night – through their carelessness and drunkenness the church was burned and all that was in it. Thus was the monastery of Peterborough burned and pillaged. May Almighty God have pity on it in his great mercy: and thus the abbot Turold came to Peterborough, and the monks returned thither and performed Christian worship in the church, which had stood a full week without service of any kind. When Bishop Egelric heard this, he excommunicated all the men who had done this evil.

Anglo-Saxon Chronicle,
English Historical Documents Vol. II

THE NEW FOREST, 1087

This is the place which William [the Conqueror] . . . . desolating the towns and destroying the churches for more than thirty miles, had appropriated for the nurture and refuge of wild beasts; a dreadful spectacle, indeed, that where before had existed human intercourse and the worship of God, there deer, and goats, and other animals of that kind, should now range unrestrained, and these not subjected to the general service of mankind. Hence it is truly asserted that, in this very forest, William [Rufus] his son, and his grandson Richard, son of Robert, Earl of Normandy, by the severe judgment of God, met their deaths, one by a wound in the breast by an arrow, the other by a wound in the neck, or as some say, from being suspended by the jaws on the branch of a tree, as his horse passed beneath it.

William of Malmesbury, Gesta Regum Anglorum,
translated by J. A. Giles

THE ARMING OF A KNIGHT, Twelfth Century

He caused a Limoges rug to be spread before him on the ground. The other ran to get the arms . . . And he brought them on the rug. Erec sat opposite on a Leopard design which was portrayed on the rug. He prepares to arm himself. First he caused to be laced on his *chauces* of white steel. Afterwards he dons a *hauberc* so valuable that one could not cut a single link. For it was made completely of silver of fine woven links . . . When they had armed him with the *hauberc* a boy laced upon his head a helmet reinforced with a gold band more shiny than a mirror.

Erec et Enide

SLINGING OF STONES

As military weapons stones are easily found, and the slings are not cumbersome to the bearers; skill in slinging stones should be acquired by all soldiers.

Use eek the cast of stone, with slynge or honde:
It falleth ofte, yf other shot there none is,
Men harneysed in steel may not withstonde,
The multitude and myghty cast of stonys;
And stonys in effecte, are every where,
And slynges are not noyous for to beare.

From *Of Knyghthode and Batayle*
Ms. Cotton, Titus A xxiii

HOW TO USE THE HEAVY LANCE

This is described by Usamah, a Moslem warrior, who fought against the Franks in many a Crusade.

He who is on the point of striking with his heavy lance should hold it as tightly as possible with his hand and under his arm, close to his side, and should let the horse run and effect the required thrust; for if he should move his hand while holding the lance or stretch out his arm with the lance, then his thrust would have no effect whatsoever and would result in no aim.

EFFECTS OF THE CRUSADING SPIRIT EXPRESSED IN GLOWING TERMS, 1096

The appeal of Pope Urban II at Clermont in 1095 led to the First Crusade.

This ardent love not only inspired the continental provinces, but even all who had heard the name of Christ, whether in the most distant islands, or savage countries. The Welshman left his hunting; the Scot his fellowship with vermin; the Dane his drinking party; the Norwegian his raw fish. Lands were deserted of their husbandmen; houses of their inhabitants, even whole cities migrated. There was no regard to relationship, affection to their country was held in little esteem; God alone was placed before their eyes.

Whatever was stored in granaries or hoarded in chamber, to answer to the hopes of the avaricious husbandman, or the covetousness of the miser, all, all was deserted; they hungered and thirsted after Jerusalem alone. Joy attended such as proceeded; while grief oppressed those who remained. But why do I say remained? You might see the husband departing with his wife, indeed, with all his family, you would smile to see the whole household laden on a carriage, about to proceed on their journey. The road was too narrow for the passengers, the path too confined for the travellers, so thickly were they thronged with endless multitudes. The number surpassed all human imagination.

William of Malmesbury, *Gesta Regum Anglorum*, IV, ii,
translated by J.A. Giles

BATTLE OF TINCHEBRAI, 1106, DESCRIBED BY A PRIEST OF FÉCAMP

Henry I defeated his brother Robert at Tinchebrai, Orne, Normandy, deprived him of the dukedom of Normandy, which he annexed to the English kingdom.

To his lord, the priest of Sêez, the priest of Fécamp, sends greeting and prayers. I bring you good news, my lord, inasmuch as I realize you are eager for tidings in this matter.

Our lord king fought with his brother at Tinchebrai on 28 September at the third hour. Thus was the battle disposed. In the first line were the men of the Bessin, the Avranchin and the Cotentin, and these were all on foot. In the second line was the king with his very numerous barons and these likewise were on foot. Seven hundred mounted knights were placed with each line; and besides these the count of Maine, and Alan Fergaunt, count of Brittany, flanked the army with about a thousand mounted knights. The whole army of the king may be reckoned as having consisted of about forty thousand men.

When the battle had lasted only an hour, Robert of Bellême turned and fled, and all his men were dispersed. The count himself was captured, and the count of Mortain with his barons, and my friend, Robert of Estoneville. The rest all disappeared in flight. Wherefore the land became subject to the king.

Nor must I fail to tell you about this marvel: that the king in the battle lost only two men; and only one was wounded, namely Robert of Bonnebose. When I came to the king, he received me very graciously at Caen, and he willingly granted all those things which he had exacted from our land. And now, thank God, peace is restored in the land. Let us pray that it may continue, and that God may grant us good health in mind and body. Farewell.

English Historical Documents, Vol.II

STEPHEN OVERCOMES EXETER CASTLE, 1136

Exeter is a large city, ranking, they say, the fourth in England. It is surrounded by ancient Roman walls, and is famous for its sea fisheries, for abundance of meat, and for its trade and commerce. Its castle stands on a lofty mound protected by impregnable walls, and towers of hewn stone.

Baldwin had thrown into it a strong garrison chosen from the flower of the youth of England, who were bound by oaths to resist the king to the last extremity. Baldwin himself, with his wife and sons, shut himself up in the citadel, prepared for the worst; and the garrison, manning the battlements and towers with glittering arms, taunted the king and his followers as they approached the walls. Sometimes they made unexpected sallies and fell furiously on the royal army; at others they shot arrows and launched missiles against them from above, using all the means in their power to molest the enemy.

Meanwhile the king, with his barons, who had accompanied him, and who afterwards gathered their forces and joined his army, made every exertion to press the garrison from the outer wall, which was built on a high mound to defend the citadel, and retained possession of it. He also succeeded in breaking down the inner bridge which gave access to the city from the castle, and with surprising address raised lofty wooden towers, from which the defenders of the castle were assailed.

Day and night he perseveringly pushed the siege, at one time mounting the hill with his troops, on horseback, and challenging the besieged to fight; at another causing his slingers to annoy them by hurling stones. He also employed miners to sap the fortifications, and had all manner of machines constructed, some of great height, to overlook what was passing within the garrison, and others on a level with the foundation of the walls which they were intended to batter down. The besieged on their side lost no time in destroying the machines, and all the ingenuity employed in their construction was wasted. Thus the contest was maintained with great vigour and ability on both parts. [The garrison eventually surrendered as the water supply failed.]

Acts of King Stephen, I, translated by T. Forester

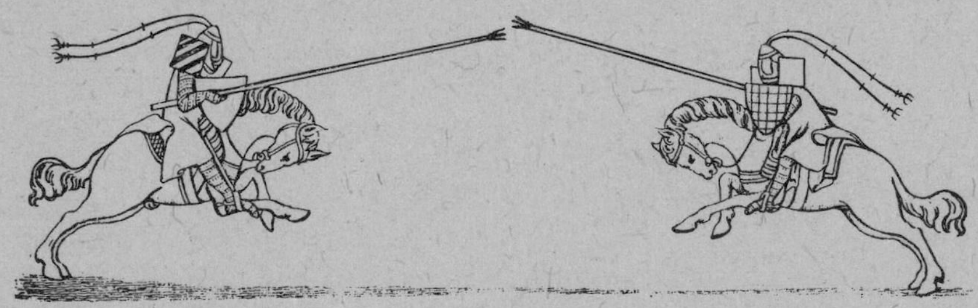

115. In this presentation of a joust, two knights tilt at each other with blunted spears aimed at the opponent's helmet to lift him from his horse or break the spear. This was before the introduction of the barrier, a boarded railing, about four feet high. The combatants rode on separate sides, preventing their horses from running upon each other.

HOW STEPHEN DEALT WITH HIS REBELLIOUS BARONS, 1136

The king raised an army from all parts of England to lay siege to Bedford. Aware of his approach Milo swept off all the provisions he could lay his hands on, making violent seizures both from the townsmen and the inhabitants of the neighbourhood with whom before he had been on good terms, as belonging to his lordship. These supplies he stored in the castle, and securely closing the gates, he for this time excluded the king's people without any loss on his own side.

This king, however, after carefully reconnoitring the fortifications, placed under cover bands of archers, at convenient posts, with directions to maintain such a constant discharge of arrows against those who manned the battlements and towers as should prevent their keeping a good look-out and hold them always in a state of confusion.

Meanwhile, he exerted all his energies to have engines constructed for filling the trenches and battering the walls. All skill and ingenuity, labour and expense could compass, was effected. Night watches were posted at all the castle gates to prevent any communication by the besieged to their friends without, or provisions or necessaries being introduced within the fortress. By day, every effort that skill could devise was made to distress and annoy the enemy. But the castle stood on a very high mound, and was surrounded by a solid and lofty wall, and it had a strong and impregnable keep, and contained a numerous garrison of stout and resolute men, so that the expectation of soon taking it proved abortive, and the king having other affairs on his hands which required immediate attention, withdrew, leaving the greatest part of his army to carry on the siege.

His orders were, that if the engines could not effect the reduction of the place, a blockade should be maintained, till want and hunger compelled its surrender. After the king's departure the besieging army continued their hostilities, till, their provisions being exhausted and their strength failing, the garrison confessed that they could hold the place no longer. They therefore surrendered it to the king, according to the laws of war.

Acts of King Stephen, I, translated by T. Forester

THE BATTLE OF THE STANDARD, 1138

In Scotland, which borders on England, with a river fixing the boundary between the two kingdoms, there was a king of gentle heart, born of religious parents and equal to them in his just way of living. . . . At last King Henry's daughter sent him a letter, stating that she had been disinherited and deprived of the kingdom promised to her on oath . . . and therefore she humbly and mournfully besought him to aid her as a relation. . . . So King David, for that was his name, sent out a decree through Scotland and summoned all to arms, and giving them free licence he commanded them to commit against the English without pity, the most savage and cruel deeds they could invent.

Scotland, which is also called Albany, is a land hemmed in by marshy places, well supplied with productive forests, milk and herds, encircled by safe harbours and rich islands, but it has inhabitants that are barbarous and filthy, neither overcome by excess of cold nor enfeebled by severe hunger, putting their trust in swiftness of foot and light equipment; in their own country they care nothing for the awful moment of the bitterness of death; among foreigners they surpass all in cruelty. From this people then and from the nearer parts of Scotland the king collected a mass of rebels into an incredible army and led it towards England, and after crossing the boundary between the two kingdoms into the region of Northumbria, which was wide and populous and filled with supplies of all things needful, he there encamped.

The Deeds of Stephen, translated by K.R. Potter

. . . Their archbishop Thurstan, a man of great firmness and worth, animated them [the Northern barons] by his counsel and exhortations . . . he promised them also that the priests of his diocese, bearing crosses, should march with them to battle together with their flocks . . . and although he was himself so greatly reduced by age and infirmity, that he had to be carried on a litter where need was, yet, in order to animate their courage, he would readily have accompanied them to the field of battle. But they compelled him to stay behind . . . and they proceeded to Thirsk, from whence they dispatched Robert 'de Bruce' and Bernard 'de Baliol' to the king of the Scots. . . . They very humbly and courteously besought him that he would at least desist from his acts of ferocity. . . . But he, together with his followers, with a hardened heart, spurned their request, and disdainfully taunted them. They therefore returned to their associates; Robert abjured the homage he had rendered to the Scottish king, and Bernard the fealty he had sworn to him on one occasion, when he had been taken prisoner. . . .

While thus awaiting the approach of the Scots, the scouts whom they had sent forward to reconnoitre, returned, bringing the information that the king with his army had already passed the river Tees and was ravaging their province in his wonted manner. They hastened to resist them; and, passing the village of Northallerton, they arrived early in the morning at a plain distant from it by about two miles. Some of them soon erected, in the centre of a frame which they brought, the mast of a ship, to which they gave the name of the Standard; whence those lines of Hugh 'Sotevagina', archdeacon of York:

> Soldiers, to-day shall fight or fall
>   Strong in the Standard's right
> Its holy Sign, confessed by all,
>   Shall fortify our might.

On the top of this pole they hung a silver pyx containing the Host, and the banner of St. Peter the apostle, and John of Beverley and Wilfrid of Ripon, confessors and bishops. In doing this, their hope was that our Lord Jesus Christ, by the efficacy of his Body, might be their leader in the contest. They also provided for their men a certain and conspicuous rallying-point, by which they might rejoin their comrades in the event of their being cut off.

Scarcely had they put themselves in battle array when tidings were brought that the king of Scots was close at hand with his whole force, ready and eager for the onset. The greater part of the knights, then dismounting, became foot-soldiers, a chosen body of whom, interspersed with archers, were arranged in the front rank. The others, with the exception of those who were to dispose and rally the forces, mustered with the barons in the centre, near and around the Standard, and they were guarded by the rest of the host, who closed in on all sides. The troop of cavalry, lest they should take fright at the shouting and uproar of the Scots. In like manner, on the enemy's side, the king and almost all his followers were on foot, their horses being kept at a distance. In front of the battle were the Picts; in the centre, the king with his knights and English; and the rest of the barbarian host poured roaring around them.

As they advanced in this order of battle, the Standard with its banners became visible at no great distance; and at once the hearts of the king and his followers were overpowered by extreme terror and consternation; yet they persisted in their wickedness, they pressed on to accomplish their evil ends. On the Octave of the Assumption of St. Mary, being Monday, 22 August, between the first and third hours, the struggle of this battle was begun and finished. For numberless Picts being slain immediately on the first attack, the rest, throwing down their arms, disgracefully fled. The plain was strewed with corpses; very many were taken prisoner; the king and all the others took to flight; and at length of that immense army all were either slain, captured, or scattered as sheep without a shepherd. They fled like persons bereft of reason, away from their own country instead of towards it, thus entering the land of their enemies. But wherever they were discovered, they were put to death like sheep for the slaughter; and so, by the righteous judgment of God, those who had cruelly massacred multitudes, and left them unburied, giving them neither their country's nor a foreign rite of burial (leaving them a prey to dogs, birds, and wild beasts), were themselves either dismembered and torn to pieces or left to decay and rot in the open air. The king also . . . fled dishonoured and meanly attended, and barely escaped with his life. . . . Of that army which came out of Scotland alone, more than ten thousand were missing; and in various localities of the Deirans, Bernicians, Northumbrians, and Cumbrians, many more perished in the flight than fell in the battle. The army of the English thus, by God's help, with a small loss, easily obtained the victory, and took possession of the spoil, which was found in great abundance.

Richard of Hexham, *English Historical Documents*, Vol.II

THE KILLING OF HYWEL AB OWEIN

'This elegy on Hywel, a prince of North Wales, was composed by his foster-brother Peryf, one of the seven sons of Cedifor, on the occasion of his killing by the army of his stepmother Cristin and her sons Dafydd and Rhodri, at the battle of Pentraeth in south-east Anglesey in 1170.' K.H. Jackson

While we were seven, thrice seven dared not
attack us, nor made us retreat while we
lived; alas, there are now but three of the
seven, men unflinching in fight.

Seven men were we who were faultless,
undaunted, irresistible in attack, seven
mighty men from whom flight gave no protection,
seven who would brook no wrong till now.

Since Hywel is gone, who bore battle gladly, by
whom we used to stand, we are all avowedly
lost, and the host of Heaven is the fairer.

The sons of Cedifor, an ample band of offspring,
in the dale above Pentraeth they were fierce
and full of bold purpose, and they were
cut down alongside their foster-brother.

Because of the treason hatched by Cristin
and her sons – un-Christian Britons! – may
no man of the bald freckled descendants of
Brochfael be left alive in Anglesey.

Come what may of wealth from land domain,
yet this world is a deceptive dwelling-place;
with a spear (woe to false Dafydd!) Hywell
the Tall, the hawk of war, was pierced.

Welsh; Peryf ap Cedifor; 1170

From *A Celtic Miscellany*,
translated by Kenneth Hurlstone Jackson

THE IDEALS AND REALITIES OF KNIGHTHOOD IN THE TWELFTH CENTURY

But what is the function of orderly knighthood? To protect the church, to fight against treachery, to reverence the priesthood, to fend off injustice from the poor, to make peace in our own province, to shed your blood for your brethren, and, if needs must, lay down your life.

John of Salisbury, *Policraticus*

116. In the twelfth century the mounted cavalryman still crouched behind a kite-shaped shield and attacked with the couched lance.

I cannot bear the vaunting and vainglory of the knights your nephews . . . The Order of Knighthood, in these days of ours, is mere disorder. For he whose mouth is defiled with the foulest words, whose oaths are most detestable, who least fears God who vilifies God's ministers, who feareth not the church – that man nowadays is reputed bravest and most renowned of the knightly band . . . The knights of old were wont to bind themselves by an oath to maintain the state, never to flee in battle, and to set the common weal before their own life. Nay, even nowadays aspirants receive their swords from the altar in order that they may profess themselves sons of the church, acknowledging themselves to have received their weapons for the honour of the priesthood, the defence of the poor, the avenging of wrongs and the freedom of their country.

Yet in practice they do the contrary . . . These men, who should have used their strength against the enemies of the cross of Christ, contend in wassail and drunkenness; they stagnate in sluggardy and rot in riotous living; dragging through their degenerate lives in uncleanness, they dishonour the name and order of knighthood . . . If these knights of ours are sometimes constrained to take the field, then their sumpter-beasts are laden not with steel but with wine, not with spears but with cheeses, not with swords but with wine-skins, not with javelins but with spits.

You would think they were on their way to feast, and not to fight. They bear shields bright with beaten gold, as who should hope rather for prey than for hard fighting; and in truth these same shields (if I may so say) come back intact in their virginity. Nevertheless they embroider their saddles and blazon their shields with scenes of battle and tourney, delighting in a certain imagination of those wars which, in very deed, they dare not mingle in or behold.

Peter of Blois, Archdeacon of Bath, *Epistolae*

SCORCHED EARTH IN 1149

Stephen plundered the district round Salisbury after he had tried to seize Henry Plantagenet, who had been knighted by the Scottish King.

Not long after this the king was much concerned with suppressing the hostilities that were on the increase round York; sometimes he destroyed castles belonging to the enemy or his own adherents that were burdensome to the city, sometimes he built others in more suitable and advantageous places. After acquiring much treasure in those regions he went back with great glory to London, and there, when some days had passed, he deliberated on the most effective means of shattering his opponents and the easiest way of checking the continual disorder that they fomented in the kingdom. Different people gave advice of different sorts, but at last it seemed to him sound and judicious to attack the enemy everywhere, plunder and destroy all that was in their possession, set fire to the crops and every other means of supporting human life and let nothing remain anywhere, that under this duress, reduced to the extremity of want, they might at last be compelled to yield and surrender. It was indeed evil, he thought, to take away the sustenance of human life that God had vouchsafed, yet far worse for the kingdom to be constantly disturbed by the enemy's raiding and impoverished by daily pillage; it was more endurable to put up for a time with whatever troubles cruel fate might offer than bear so much continually from each one of the enemy. And no wonder, either, if he must rage with such cruelty against the enemy, as many opponents cannot be wiped out without much slaughter. So gathering together a large body of finely equipped knights, his son too with his men and some of the barons massed on the opposite flank, he sets himself to lay waste that fair and delightful district, so full of all good things, round Salisbury; they took and plundered everything they came upon, set fire to houses and churches, and what was a cruel and brutal sight, consumed and brought to nothing everything edible they found. They raged with this bestial cruelty especially round Marlborough; they showed it also very terribly round Devizes, and they had in mind to do the same to their adversaries all over England.

The Deeds of Stephen, translated by K.R. Potter

A DESCRIPTION OF A NORMAN CASTLE AND ITS UPKEEP, Late Twelfth Century

If a castle is to be decently built, it should be girded by a double moat. Nature must provide the proper site as the mote or mound should be set upon native rock. Where Nature fails, the benefit of skill must take over, and a heavy massive wall made from stone and cement, has to grow, or rise as an arduous task. Outside this a fearsome stockade with squared pales and prickly briars should be well erected. The foundation of the stone wall must be deep in the earth. The wall should be supported with pilasters inside and out. Small towers must flank the mainkeep, or donjon, which is set on the summit of the mound . . .

One needs a spring that flows continuously. There should be small posterns, portcullises, also crossbows, catapults, slings, shields, lances . . . There should be palfreys or riding horses, and pacing war horses more suitable for the use of knights. In order that the knights going out may be better cheered, there should sound together trumpets, pipes, flutes and horns. The divisions and echelons of the fighting men shall be ranged in order by the constables, even when they go forth to a tourney. There should be poorer horses, with jolting gait, for the riff-raff.

The castle should have also prudent men, without whose advice nothing should be done in time of hostility, a power which constitutes the greatest strength and highest council of a kingdom – men by whose intercession tortures are applied more mildly, by whose sternness digressors, lawbreakers, violators of ordinances, horse thieves, and murderers may be whipped, punished or condemned to death.

The group of knights can consist of three kinds – knights answering the feudal summons, those brought together casually [mercenaries], and the knights of the Church – whom the trumpet of the lord or leader urges on in the midst of missiles, and who choose the hazards of war.

In the castle will also be dungeons where prisoners are kept in hand shackles, the more dangerous wearing leg shackles as well.

U.T. Holmes, Jr., *Daily Living in the Twelfth Century based on the Observations of Alexander Neckam*

England and the Sea

THE NORMAN FLEET

The fleet of the Conqueror, when he came over into England, consisted of 896 ships, though the author of *Roman de Rou,* cited by Mr Lancelot, confines the number to 696. But either of these was a vast fleet for that time. Yet we must observe, that these were not strong, well-built ships, but rather slight vessels, knocked up quickly, for the transportation of his army only; and this must have been the case, for William had only from the first of January till the latter end of August for his artificers to complete the whole of his navy.

John Speed, *Historie of Great Britaine,* 1611

AFTER A CHANNEL CROSSING A TRAVELLER DESCRIBES HOW TO FIT OUT A SHIP, Late Twelfth Century

If anyone wishes to fit out a ship let him have an asbestos stone, in order that the benefit of fire may not be lacking. If such a stone is once lit it is unquenchable. He should have a needle placed on a pivot; the needle will rotate and revolve until the point looks towards the east, and thus sailors understand where they should steer when the Little Bear constellation is hidden in the storm, although this constellation never sets because of the brevity of its circle.

It is necessary also to be supplied with grain and wine, also with arms and with an axe by which the mast can be cut down when a storm comes up, which is the greatest of evils, and so that the traps of pirates can be avoided. Side planking should be fastened with cords and nails, and, when fitted together, let them be daubed with pitch mixed with wax on the inside, or with paint, and let them be smoothed on the outside, sparing the use of too much paint. Cross-weaving and wattling are required, in order that the swift and frequent jarrings may not unfasten or loosen the joints. It is needful to join the boards proportionately, with forecastle and aftercastle separated.

Let the mast be raised in a socket on the flooring . . . then let the sail be fastened to the mast, and have the cordage extend from side to side; . . . the lowest part of the sail is fastened to a spar carried crosswise. The swelling of the sail is its belly. Yard braces are needed; may these be placed almost 'before the water', of which the upper ends are called horns. The sail yard is called *cheruca*, which means also 'weather cock', which in French is named *cochet*. Let there be also openings through which oars can run, if rowing is required when a wind is lacking . . . Let stays be extended, that is very large ropes. Likewise let there be shrouds supporting the mast . . . The oar has a blade and an arm; the end is called the blade . . . Let the skipper have a transverse seat or thwart . . . near this let there be a windlass that the lines may be bound more firmly and that the sail may be raised according to the shift of wind . . . And anchor is needed. Have a mallet – and note that the mallet is called *malleus* – by which the sailor gives signals to his comrades.

U.T. Holmes, Jr., *Daily Living in the Twelfth Century based on the Observations of Alexander Neckam*

A BUSY HARBOUR, Late Twelfth Century

There were the ships brought and the crews assembled. You would see many a ship made ready, ships touching each other, anchoring, drying out, and being floated, ships being repaired with pegs and nails, ropes being hauled, masts set up, gang planks being thrust over the side, and ships loading. Lances were being straigthened up and horses were pulling. Knights and men-at-arms were going on board, and the one would call to the other, some remaining and some leaving.

Wace of Jersey, *Roman de Brut*

PROVISIONING A VESSEL, Late Twelfth Century

. . . the casks were piled on one another; salt meat, bread, wine, and grain . . . and chests aplenty, and fine arms and handsome shields were there . . . The banners they had fastened to the castles fore and aft . . . Eight full days passed before the fleet moved from there; the air was balmy and soft, so the ship could not move. At midnight the wind rose, strong and powerful, which struck the sails. Bauches cried, 'Now, let's get to the ship quickly!'

Anseÿs de Mes

SHIPS GETTING UNDER WAY, Late Twelfth Century

When they were all manned they had tide and a good wind. Then you would see the anchors raised, the pulling taut of stays, the tightening of shrouds, sailors climbing over the vessels to break out the sails and canvas. Some work at the windlass; others are at the luff [side of fore-and-aft sail next mast or stay] and the halyards. The pilots are aft – the master steersman, the finest – and each does his best at the steering oar. 'Hard on the helm', and she goes to the left; 'Up on the helm', and she goes to the right. In order to gather the wind into the sails they make the outer edges taut and fasten the boltropes [round sail-edge to prevent tearing]. Some pull on the ratlines, and some shorten sail, in order to get the ship to proceed more slowly. They fasten clew lines and sheets, and make the ropes fast; they slacken the runners and lower the sails. They pull on bowlines . . . they make fast the brails [small ropes on sail-edges for trussing sails] to the mast, that the wind may not escape underneath.

Wace of Jersey, *Roman de Brut*

SELECT BIBLIOGRAPHY

Armitage, E.S., *Norman Castles of the British Isles* (London)

Barrow, G.W.S., *Feudal Britain* (London)
Beeler, J., *Warfare in England, 1066-1189* (New York)
Bonser, W., *The Medical Background to Anglo-Saxon England* (London)
Brooke, C.N.L., *Saxon and Norman Kings* (London)
Brooke, Z.N., *The English Church and the Papacy* (Cambridge)
Brown, R.A., *English Medieval Castles* (London)

Coulton, G.G., *Medieval Panorama* (Cambridge)
Coulton, G.G., *The Medieval Village* (Cambridge)

Douglas, D.C., and Greenaway, G.W., *English Historical Documents*, volume ii, 1042-1189 (London)

Edwards, J.G., 'The Normans and the Welsh March'. (Proceedings of the British Academy xlii 1956)

Freeman, E.A., *History of the Norman Conquest* (Oxford)

Galbraith, V.H., *The Making of Domesday Book* (Oxford)
Garmonsway, G.N., *The Anglo-Saxon Chronicle* (London)

Haskins, C.H., *The Twelfth Century Renaissance* (London)
Haskins, C.H., *Studies in the History of Medieval Science* (London)
Haskins, C.H., *Norman Institutions* (New York)
Hunnisett, R.F., *The Medieval Coroner* (Cambridge)

John, E., *Land Tenure in Early England* (Leicester)

Ker, W.P., *English Literature: Medieval* (London)
Knoop, D., and Jones, G.P., *The Medieval Mason* (London)
Knowles, D., *The Monastic Order in England 943-1216* (Cambridge)

Leach, A.F., *The Schools of Medieval England* (London)
Lennard, R., *Rural England 1086-1135* (Oxford)
Loyn, H.R., *Anglo-Saxon England and the Norman Conquest* (Oxford)

Maclagan, E., *The Bayeux Tapestry* (King Penguin)
Maitland, F.W., *Domesday Book and Beyond* (Cambridge)

Oakeshote, W., *The Sequence of English Medieval Art* (London)

Poole, A.L., *From Domesday Book to Magna Carta* (Oxford)
Poole, A.L., *Medieval England* (Oxford)
Poole, R.L., *The Exchequer in the Twelfth Century* (Oxford)
Power, E.E., *Medieval English Nunneries* (London)
Power, E.E., *Medieval People* (London)

Rickert, M., *Painting in Britain: The Middle Ages* (London)
Round, J.H., *Feudal England* (London)

Seebohm, F., *The English Village Community* (London)
Smail, R.C., *Crusading Warfare* (Cambridge)
Stenton, D.M., *English Society in the Early Middle Ages* (London)
Stenton, D.M., *English Justice 1066-1215* (Philadelphia)
Stenton, F.M., *The First Century of English Feudalism* (Oxford)
Stenton, F.M., *Norman London* (Historical Association Pamphlet)
Stone, L., *Sculpture in Britain: The Middle Ages* (Pelican)

Tait, J., *The Medieval English Borough* (Manchester)
Trow-Smith, R., *English Husbandry* (London)

Vinogradoff, P., *Villeinage in England* (Oxford)
Vinogradoff, P., *Growth of the Manor* (London)

Webb, G., *Architecture in Britain: The Middle Ages* (Pelican)

Zarnecki, G., *English Romanesque Sculpture 1066-1140* (London)

Biographies

AILRED OF RIEVAULX (1109-1166), English chronicler, born at Hexham, was steward to the King of Scotland. He became a monk at Rievaulx Abbey; wrote sermons and historical works. He died Abbot of Rievaulx, and left 'the memory of gentle devotion and of unceasing love and care for his fellow monks'.

ANSELM, ST. (1033-1109), nobly born at Aosta in N. Italy, and a pupil of Lanfranc at the abbey of Bec in Normandy. In 1078 he became Abbot of Bec, the most famous school of the eleventh century. He visited England, where William Rufus appointed him Archbishop of Canterbury in 1093. After embroilments with the king he withdrew to Rome. He returned to England as Archbishop under Henry I. Anselm, perhaps the last of the great monastic teachers, wrote many theological and philosophical works, among them the famous *Monologion, Proslogion,* and *Cur Deus Homo.*

BERNARD, ST. (1091-1153), a great French ecclesiastic, first Abbot of the monastery of Clairvaux, which he founded. He was the most famous member of the Cistercians, or white monks. They followed through their constitution and the writings of St. Bernard the precepts of St. Benedict by renouncing all feudal possessions, and by forswearing all luxuries. In the schism of 1130 between Anacletus and Innocent II, Bernard strongly supported Innocent. He preached the second Crusade; was an adversary of Abelard. Indeed he has been called 'practically dictator of Christendom'. He wrote many epistles, sermons and theological treatises, and was one of the founders of Latin hymnody.

CHRÉTIEN DE TROYES (*d.*1183), writer of courtly romances for the French feudal aristocracy in the twelfth century. He enjoyed the patronage of Countess Marie de Champagne, daughter of Louis VII. His extant works are *Erec and Enide, Cligés, Yvain and Lancelot,* great metrical Arthurian romances. *Perceval* or *Le Conte du Graal,* his last great work, was the start of the cycle of romances interweaving the Holy Grail and the legend of King Arthur. His popular works had great influence in France and England.

CRISPIN, GILBERT. A monk at Le Bec with Lanfranc, and was Abbot of Westminster from 1085 to 1117. His *Life of Herluin, Abbot of Bec,* is the most authoritative source of the Norman career of Lanfranc, and tells us a great deal of the genuis and character of this famous archbishop.

EADMER (1064-1124), a monk of Canterbury, and devoted friend of Archbishop Anselm. He wrote a Latin chronicle of the events of his own time down to 1122, *Historia Novorum in Anglia,* and a biography, *Vita Anselmi;* both works are of the highest value.

FITZNIGEL, RICHARD (1130-1198), notable Anglo-Norman, Bishop of London, and treasurer of the Exchequer from about 1160 to 1198. He wrote the *Dialogus de Scaccario,* a monumental work in the form of a dialogue between *Master* and *Disciple,* a detailed exposition of the practice of the Exchequer in the twelfth century. F.W. Maitland says, 'That such a book should be written, is one of the most wonderful things of Henry's wonderful reign'.

FITZSTEPHEN, WILLIAM. The best description of twelfth-century London is given as a preamble to his *Life of Thomas Becket,* written about 1180.

FLORENCE OF WORCESTER (*d.*1118), monk of Worcester, author of *Chronicon ex Chronicis,* which was based upon the work of Marianus Scotus, an Irish monk who lived at Fulda and later at Mainz. These annals are on the whole very accurate.

GERALD OF WALES, GIRALDUS CAMBRENSIS (1146-1220), of Pembrokeshire, and son of Nesta, a Welsh princess. He studied at Paris before 1176, and was later Archdeacon of Brecon. A prolific writer. Among his most important works are *Topographia Hibernica; Expugnatio Hibernica; Itinerarium Cambriae; Gemma Ecclesiastica; De Rebus a se gestis.* He records the history of Wales and of Ireland, and speaks frankly of Church reform.

GERVASE OF CANTERBURY (*d.*1210), monk and chronicler, entered the house of Christchurch, Canterbury. His *Chronica de tempore Regum Angliae Stephani, Henrici II et Ricarda I* gives the history of his time. His *Gesta Regum* traces the fortunes of Britain from the days of Brutus.

GUIBERT DE NOGENT, a monastic writer who bemoaned the insults of his rivals . . . 'if they cannot learn, let them at least suffer their fellows to publish what they hold to be true'.

HAYWARD, SIR JOHN (1564-1627), educated at Cambridge, was the author of various historical works, following the style of great Roman historians. Among his chief works is the *Lives of the III Normans, Kings of England.*

HENRY OF HUNTINGDON (1084-1155), was brought up by Bloet, Bishop of Lincoln, and eventually became Archdeacon of Huntingdon. His *Historia Anglorum* comes down to 1154, and contains a number of popular songs and stories of the time.

HERBERT DE LOSINGA (1054-1119), first Bishop of Norwich; a learned scholar of writings of the Fathers of the Church, but his great love was the classics. His correspondence with his pupils points to the New Learning.

HOLINSHED, RAPHAEL (*d.*1580), was of a Cheshire family, and is said by Anthony à Wood to have been 'a minister of God's word'. His *Chronicle* consists of a description of England followed by a history down to the Conquest; a description of Ireland and a chronicle; a description of Scotland and a history down to 1575; the history of the English kings to 1577. These, known by his name, include the work of other writers.

JOCELIN DE BRAKELOND (*fl.*1200), a monk of Bury St Edmunds. His *Chronicle* gives a picture of monastic life in the twelfth century. Carlyle devoted seventeen chapters of his *Past and Present* to a study of this work.

JOHN OF SALISBURY (1115-1180), English scholar and divine, born at Salisbury, studied at Paris, and was clerk of Pope Eugenius III. In 1176 became Bishop of Chartres. One of the most learned classical writers of the time, he wrote lives of Anselm and of Becket; *Polycraticus*, a church and state diplomacy; *Metalogicon*, a treatise on logic and Aristotelian philosophy; *Entheticus; Historia Pontoficalis.*

LANFRANC (1005-1089), Archbishop of Canterbury, was born at Pavia, and educated for the law. Esteemed as a teacher, he was Prior of Bec in Normandy from 1045. As Archbishop he worked in accord with William I. His chief writings are *Commentaries* on the Epistles of St Paul, a *Treatise* against Berengaria, and *Sermons.*

MAP, WALTER (*fl.*1200) a Welshman, was Archdeacon of Oxford under Henry II. He wrote *De nugis curialium,* which included *Dissuasio Valerii ad Rufinum de non decenda uxore.*

NECKAM, ALEXANDER, NECKHAM, NEQUAM (*d.*1217), was a famous teacher at Paris and Oxford, and in 1213 became Abbot of Cirencester. Dante put him in the same part of Hell as his tutor was, where the considered vices of schoolmasters were punished. In his *De naturis rerum* and *De utensilibus,* Neckam was the first in Europe to describe the use of the magnetic needle by sailors. Other works were *Novus Aesopus; Novus Avianus; Sacerdos ad Altare.*

ORDERICUS VITALIS (1075-1143), a Norman born near Shrewsbury in England, and educated in the Norman abbey of St Evroul, where he spent most of his life. He wrote *Historia Ecclesiastica,* extending from the beginning of the Christian era down to 1141; a standard authority for the Norman period.

PARIS, MATTHEW (*d.*1259), historian and Benedictine monk of the monastery of St Albans. A man of great accomplishments, expert in writing, drawing, painting, in working gold and silver. He was a poet, theologian, mathematician, diplomat, especially notable as an historian. In his *Chronica Majora,* and *Historia Minor* he stands before every other English chronicler.

PETER OF BLOIS (*d.*1212) was descended from a noble Breton family. He studied in Paris and was invited to England by Henry II. He held various clerical appointments, was Archdeacon of Bath, and became Archdeacon of London. As a satirist his letters emphasize the darker side of politics and customs of his time.

REGINALD, monk of DURHAM, wrote the Life of St Godric before the saint's death in 1170. He often took notes of St Godric's words as they were uttered, so we have what is close to an autobiography.

RICHARD OF HEXHAM, in a valuable narrative written before 1154, he gives an account not only of the Scottish invasion, but of conditions in the north of England at the time of the anarchy.

ROBERT OF GLOUCESTER (*fl.*1260-1300), is believed to have written a metrical chronicle from earliest times to 1272. Not the work of one man, though probably the whole was composed in the abbey of Gloucester.

ROGER OF SALISBURY (*d.*1139) was a priest of Caen, and became Chancellor, Bishop of Salisbury, justiciar, and regent of England. He rebuilt Salisbury Cathedral, and reorganized the royal Exchequer under Henry I, on lines which were continued by his great-nephew, Richard FitzNigel.

SCOTUS, MARIANUS. An Irish monk, who lived at Fulda and later at Mainz. He wrote a chronicle of world events, upon which Florence of Worcester grafted his historical annals of the twelfth century.

SIMEON OF DURHAM (*d.c.*1138), a monkish chronicler who wrote *Historia Ecclesiae Dunelmensis; Historia Regum Anglorum et Dacorum.*

SPEED, JOHN (1552-1629), historian and cartographer. He made several maps of English counties, and was encouraged to write his *Historie of Britaine* (1611). The maps are more valuable than the history.

TURGOT (*d.*1115), Saxon monk of Durham, where he became an archdeacon, and helped to found the new cathedral. He was Bishop of St Andrews from 1109 to 1115, and confessor to St Margaret and probably wrote her *Life.*

WACE OF JERSEY (*d.c.*1171), French poet who, embodying the Arthurian legends based on Geoffrey of Monmouth's *History of the Britons,* wrote *Roman de Brut* dedicated to Eleanor, queen of

Henry II. This was one of the sources of Layamon's *Brut*. Wace also wrote *Roman de Rou* or *Geste des Normands*, a history of the dukes of Normandy.

WALTER OF HENLEY, wrote early in the thirteenth century the standard treatise on the management of an estate, advised the sowing of two bushels of wheat per acre, which ought to yield threefold.

WILLIAM OF JUMIÈGES (*d.c.*1090), Norman Benedictine monk, whose *Gesta Normannorum Ducum* is of considerable importance as he was a contemporary authority, representing Norman sentiment and Norman opinion of the invasion of England.

WILLIAM OF MALMESBURY (*d.*1143), historian, was educated at Malmesbury Abbey, and became librarian. His works include *Gesta Regum Anglorum* (440 to 1127), and its sequel, *Historia Novella,* dealing with English history to 1142. He also wrote in the same lively style *De Antiguitate Glastoniensis Ecclesiae.*

WILLIAM OF NEWBURGH (1136-1198), educated at the Augustinian priory of Newburgh, Yorkshire. He was the author of *Historia Rerum Anglicarum* in Latin. This covered the period from 1066 to 1198, with particular attention to the reigns of Stephen and Henry II. Highly esteemed for this work, he was called 'the father of historical criticism'.

WILLIAM OF POITIERS, a Norman born near Pont-Audemer. He studied at Poitiers, and then returned to Normandy as a soldier. Later as a priest he was made chaplain to Duke William and Archdeacon of Lisieux. His *Gesta Willelmi ducis Normannorum et regis Anglorum,* written shortly after 1071, provides, together with the Bayeux Tapestry, the best contemporary description of the battle of Hastings. He wrote this of Duke William: 'He dominated the battle, checking his own men in flight, strengthening their spirit, and sharing their danger.'

INDEX

Figures in **bold type** refer to illustrations

Abingdon Abbey, **157**, 159, 160, 303
Abingdon Chronicle, 157-160, 303
Acts of King Stephen, 287-289, 309-310, 311
Adrian IV (Nicholas Breakspear) pope, 257-258
Agriculture, open field system, **44**
Ailred of Rievaulx, 170, 234-235, 325
Altfranzosische Romanzen und Pastourellen (Bartsch), 62
Ancient Laws and Institutes of England, 140-141, 213-216
Ancient Lives of Scottish Saints, 13, 189-190
Ancren Riwle, 127
Anglo-Saxons, 47-49, 51
    calendar, **102**
Anglo-Saxon Chronicle, 1, 4, 52, 64, 104-105, 107-108, 204-205, 206, 226, 229-230, 251-255, 264, 273, 277-280, 285-287, 289-292, 301-302, 304-306
Anglo-Saxon Documents (Robertson), 134
Anseys de Mes, 195, 321-322
Antiquities of the Common People (Bourne), 92
Antiquities of Warwickshire (Dugdale), 25, 131
Antiquities Repertorium, vol.ii, 92
Archery, 87-88
Architectural History of Canterbury Cathedral (Willis), 131-133
Architrenius III (Jehan de Hauteville), 73
Arnold, Ralph, 76
Arts, 74-84

Balancing, **94**
Barns, 26
Baron's costume, 63
Bath, city of, 55
Bathing a child, **50**
Battle Abbey, 3, 16
Battles
    Battle of Hastings, 296-302
    Battle of Pentraeth, 315
    Battle of Stamford Bridge, 291
    Battle of the Standard, 312-314
    Battle of Tinchebrai, 308-309
Bayeux Tapestry, 2, 262, 263, 265, 272
Bedford, siege of, 311
Beds and bedding, 52, **58**,
    Bedchamber fittings, 56-57
Bells, 91
Benedictine monks, 173-179
Berkeley, The Witch of, 259-261
Berkhamstead, **283**
Black Book of Peterborough, 39-41
Blacksmiths, **106**, **122**
Bolton Priory, **180**
Book of Beasts, The (White) 78, 80
Boor's Right, 100
Borley, Essex, 43
Braunton Great Field, Devonshire, **44**
Bridlington Dialogue, The (Robert of Bridlington), 189
Britain, description of twelfth century countryside, 53-56
Builders, **29**
Buildings in England down to 1540 (Salzman), 20, 21
Buildings, 18-45
Bury St. Edmunds, abbey of, 134, 136-137, 142, 147-148, 182-183, 190, 211-212
Byland Cartulary, 185, 187, 188

Cadbury, Devon, **38**
Calder Abbey, 174
Canterbury, 20, 55
    cathedral, **84**, 131-133
    monastic procedures, 156-157, 160, 162, 171, 173
Carlisle Castle, Cumberland, **285**
Carpenters, 127, 130
Cartularium Monasteri de Rameseia (Rolls Series, 1893), 41-42
Castles, 23-24, **32**, 279, 280, 283, **285**, 287, 289, 303, 309-310, 318-319
Castle Hedingham, Essex, **32**
Cats, 78
Cavalryman, **316**
Celtic Miscellany, A, 169-170, 170-171, 223-224, 315

Chancellor's duties, 120-121
Charroi de Nimes (Shortnose), 45
Charters, (Stubbs), 212
Cheddar, Somerset, 56
Chepstow, Monmouth, 290
Chess, 86, 93
Chester, 27-30
Chichester, 55
Chretien de Troyes, 325
Christ Church, Canterbury, 3
Christchurch Priory, Hampshire, 178
Christmas dinner, 64
Chronicle (William of Malmesbury), 8
Chronicle of Jocelin of Brakelond, concerning the Acts of Samson, Abbot of the Monastery of St. Edmund, 182-183, 190, 255-257
Chronicles (Holinshed), 52, 53, 198
Church, contents of a, 193-194
Church Historians of England, The (Stevenson), 156, 264-265, 303-304
Cistercian monks, 60, 167, 169, 183, 185, 187, 188
Claverley Church, Shropshire, 77
Cluniac monks, 145-147, 183, 185, 192-193
Co-education, 70
Coining, pubishments for, 220
Collective nouns, 58-59, 86-87
Comets, 108, 159, 263
Concerning the unjust persecution of William, Bishop of Durham, 237
Constitution (Lanfranc) 143-145
Conte del Graal (Chretien de Troyes), 129
Corn prices, 64
Cottar's Right, 99
Court Baron, The (Maitland) 67, 222
Cripple, 51
Crispin, Gilbert, 326
Crop failures, 104-105
Cross and pile, 92
Cruck building, 23
Crusades, 308
Curfew, 203

Daily Living in the Twelfth Century, based on the Observations of Alexander Neckham (Holmes), 44, 56-58, 63, 69, 70, 97, 125-129, 193-194, 197, 318-321
Dairymaids, 126
Dancing, 91
David, king of Scotland, 312
Deeds of Stephen, The, 312, 317-318
Deeds of William, Duke of the Normans and King of the English, The (William of Poitiers), 302-303
De Nugis Curialium, 197
De reliquiis S. Audoeni (Eadmer), 131-133
Descriptio Noblissimae Civitatis Londonae (FitzStephen), 43, 89-90
De Vita sua (Gilbert de Nogent), 71
Dialogue of the Exchequer, 51, 240
Dialogues de Scaccario, The Course of the Exchequer, and Constitutio Domus Regis, edited by C. Johnson, 112-115, 116, 117, 119-125
Dialogus de Scaccario, 268-269
Digging, 114
Dogs, 78
Domesday Book, 19, 27-37, 76, 206-208, 267-268, 268-269
  Survey for, 201-202, 204-205, 210-211, 266-267, 269-270
Domesday Survey of Cheshire (Tait), 27-30, 65-66
Dover, 302
Dress, 59-63, 197
Drinking, aftere-dinner, 65
Dunfermline Abbey, 168
Dunstable, 37-38
Durham 56
  cathedral, 164
Dyeing cloth, 129

Eadmer. mpnk of Canterbury, 14-15, 131-133, 182, 246-251, 326
Eadmeri Monachi Cantuariensis Historiae Novorum, 182
Eadwine, monk and scribe, 238
Earthquakes, 107
Education, 70-73
Edward the Confessor, 18
Ely, Isle of, 26-27, 56, 304-306
Embroidery, 63
Enfoeffments, 162, 163
English Historical Documents, Vol.II, 1, 2, 3, 4, 5, 12; 25, 26, 46-47, 52, 99-104, 148-150, 160, 162-163, 199-201, 209-210, 226, 229-232, 237, 240, 242-245, 247-252, 261-264, 266-268, 273-275, 277-279, 286-

287, 289-292, 304-306, 308-309, 312-314
English Historical Review, Vol. XLIV, 34-36
English Society in the Early Middle Ages (Stenton) 201, 202, 212, 221
Entheticus (John of Salisbury) 82
Epistolae (Peter of Blois), 316-317
Erec et Enide, 307
Executioner, 220
Exchequer, 119-120, 222
Exeter, city of, 55
Castle, 309-310
Exhortatio ad milites Templi (St. Bernard of Clairvaux), 165, 167

Family life, 46-69
Farming, 114
Faversham Abbey, 16
Fens, The, 26-27, 42-43, 56, 304-306
Feudalism, 303
First Century of English Feudalism (Stenton), 213
First Register of Norwich Cathedral Priory, The, 115
FitzNigel, Richard, 326
Fitzstephen, William, 43, 89-90, 326
Fleta, 126
Florence of Worcester, 1, 263, 326
Food and drink, 63-69
Forde Abbey, 176
Forest charter, 212
Forest law, 201
Fountains Abbey, 146
Funeral, 56

Games and pastimes, 85-94, 310
Geneat's Right, 99
Geoffrey de Mandeville, 240-242
Geoffrey Plantagenet, Count of Anjou, 231
Gerald of Wales, 76, 326
Gerald the Welshman, Itinerary through Wales, 183, 185
Gervase of Canterbury, 326-327
Gesta Abbatum Monasterii Sti. Albani, 75
Gesta Normannorum Ducum, 294-295
Gesta Regum Anglorum (William of Malmesbury) 5, 6, 23, 24, 47-49, 59-61, 67, 108-109, 225, 239-240, 243, 261, 270-272, 277-278, 306-307, 308
Gesta Willelmi ducis Normannorum et regis Anglorum, 292-294
Gilbert de Clare, earl of Pembroke, 242
Girl's costume, 62
Glass-making, 108-109
Gloucester candlestick, 81
Godmersham, Kent, 26
Godric the merchant, 232-234
Godwin, Earl, 227-228, 263
Gregory VII, pope, 148, 149
Grimsby, 264
Growth of English Industry and Commerce (Cunningham) 47-49
Guibert de Nogent, 71, 327

Hair styles, 59-61
Hali Meidenhad, 126
Harold, king of England, 1, 159, 236-237, 260, 261-163, 291
coronation, 262
Harvesting, 114
Harvest-time, 63
Hastings, 159
Battle of Hastings, 296-301, 301-302
Hawking, 85, 87
Hayward, Sir John, 7, 327
Heads or tails, 92
Health, 95-98
Hecham, Essex, 269-270
Henry I, king of England, 8-12, 9, 16, 22, 154-155, 278-279, 280, 308-309
coronation, 273-275
court and household, 112-117
journeys, 197
justice, 213-220
Henry of Blois, 234
Henry of Huntingdon, 12, 46-47, 53-56, 63, 327
Henry of Poitou, 252-255
Herbs, 96, 97
Hereford, 55
Hereward 'the Wake', 26, 304-306
Hermits, 195
Historiae Anglicanae Scriptores Varii, 43
Historie Anglorum (Henry of Huntingdon), 12, 46-47, 53-56, 63
Historiae Coenobii Burgensis, 43
Historia Ecclesiastica, 198-199, 242-243, 296-301
Historia Novum in Anglia (Eadmer) 15, 246-251

Historia Rerum Anglicarum (William of Newburgh), 231-232, 238-242
Historical Charters and Constitutional Documents of the City of London, 202, 281-282
Historie of Great Britaine (Speed), 320
History of Domestic Architecture, Vol.I (Turner), 22
Holinshed, Raphael, 52-53, 198, 203, 327
Horse-racing, 89-90
Housemaids, 127
Hugh the Chantor, 230
Hugo, the illuminator, **227**
Hunting, 85, **88**
Huntingdonshire, 30-34
Husbandry (Walter of Henley), 68
Hywel ab Owein, prince of North Wales, 314-315

Ille et Galeron, 97
Investiture controversy, 182
Iona, 170171
Ipomydon, 94
Ireland, 4

Johannes Sarisburiensis de Nugis Corialium, 85
John of Salisbury, 257-158, 315, 327
John of Worcester's Chronicle, **11**
Jousting, 310
Jurisdiction, separation of spiritual and lay, 140-141
Justice, 198-224

Kilpeck Church, Herefordshire, **155**
Kitchen utensils, 57-58
Knighthood, ideals and realities, 315-317
Knights Templars, 165, 167

Lacock Abbey, **184**
Lance, use of, 307-308
Lanfranc, archbishop, 5, 20, 75, 138, 143-145, 149-150, 156-157, 192, 243-245, 247, 328
La vie d'Edouard le confesseur, 127
Leprosy, 98
Liber Eliensis (Clark) 27
Life of King Edward the Confessor, The, (Barlow), 19, 196, 227-229, 236-237
Life of St. Godric (Reginald, monk of Durham), 232-234
Life of St. Margaret (Turgot) 13, 189-190
Lincoln, 56
Jew's house, **45**
Lives of the III Normans, Kings of England (Hayward), 7
Llandaff Cathedral, Glamorgan, **135**
London, 18, 19, 20-22, 43, 55
assizes, 21-22
first charter, 202
Henry I charter, 281-282
Losinga, Herbert de, bishop of Norwich, 36, 115, 327
Losinga, Robert, bishop of Hereford, 34-36, 266

Magi, Adoration of the, **79**
Magna Carta, origins of, 213
Malaterra, Geoffrey, 51
Malcolm, king of Scotland, 303-304
Malmesbury Abbey, Wiltshire, **153**
Map, Walter, 328
Marianus Scotus, 266
Marlborough, 318
Marriage, 53, 192
Masons, **118**
Matilda, queen of England, 14-15, **14**
Matins, 189
Maud, daughter of Henry I, 280
May-day, 92
Mealtimes, 63, 67
Meat, treatment of unsound, 67-68
Medieval Fenland, The (Darby), 43
Medieval Latin Lyrics (Waddell), 53
Melter's duties, 121-123
Merton Priory seal, **80**
Mery Geste of Robyn Hode, A, 87-88
Mice, 80
Milling, 68-69
Monastic Constitutions of Lanfranc, The 157, 160, 162, 171, 173
Monastic Order in England, The (Knowles), 170
Monasticon Anglicanum, A History of the Abbies and other Monasteries, Hospitals, Frieries and Cathedral and Collegiate Churches, 38, 145, 147, 185, 187, 188
Monks, orders of:
Benedictine, 173-179
Cistercian, **60**, 167, 169, 183, 185, 187-188

Cluniac, 145-147, 183, 185, 192-193
monks' clothing, 179, 181
cellarer's dues, 182-183
monastic life, 143-145, 195
Mummers, 92

Neckham, Alexander, 328
New Forest, 203-204, 306-307
Nobles, 46-47
Normans, The, 46, 47-49, 51
Norman fleet, 320

Odo, bishop, 3, 131, 148, 242-243, 302
Of Knyghthode and Batayle, 307
Opera (Langfranc), 138
Ordericus Vitalis, 211, 226, 242-243, 247-248, 296-301, 328
Organ music, 83
Origines Murensis Monasterii, 109-110
Oxford, 36, 303

Paris, Matthew, 16, 328
Patrologia Latina (Migne), 136
Peasantry, dress, 59
duties, 100-104
marriage and, 126
needs of, 128-129
rents and services, 109-111
Pembroke Castle, 287
Pentraeth, Battle of, 315
Peterborough, 43
sack of, 304-306
abbey of, 39, 221
Peterborough Chronicle, 201-202, 219
Peter of Blois, archdeacon of Bath, 316-317, 328
Pilgrims, 193
Plough, 111
Ploughing, 114
Policraticus (John of Salisbury) 315
Priests, 78
wives of, 156
Psalter of St. Albans, 77
Puppets, 90
Pytchley, Northamptonshire, 221
Quintain, 300

Ramsey Abbey, 25, 68-69
Ramsey Chartulary, The, 64, 68-69
Ranulph Flambard, 225-226
Reading Abbey, 16, 105-106
Rectitudines Singularum Personarum, 99-104
Reeve, duties of, 49-50
Reginald, monk of Durham, 329
Religion, 131-195
Religious education, 134-136, 143-145
Rents and services, 109-110, 111, 117-119
Richard of Hexham, 312-314, 329
Rievaulx Abbey, 161, 170
Robert, earl of Mellent, 67
Robert of Belleme, earl of Shrewsbury, 243
Robert of Brudlington, 189
Robert of Gloucester, 25, 329
Robert of Junieges, 228-229
Robert of Mortain, 242
Rochester, 56
castle, 289
Roger, archbishop of York, 231-232
Roger of Salisbury, 238-240, 329
Roman de Brut (Wace of Jersey) 83, 321, 322
Roman roads, 25
Rou (Wace of Jersey) 130
Royalty, 1-17
Rule of St. Benedict, The, 173-179, 181

St. Albans Abbey, 74
St. Anselm, archbishop of Canterbury, 163, 165, 182, 192, 248-251, 325
St. Bernard, 134-136, 325
St. Bernard of Clairvaux, 165, 167, 192-193
St. Columba's island, 170-171
St. Dunstan, 246
St. Edmund, pilgrimage to the shrine of, 133
St. Margaret, 12-13, 189-190
St. Mary in Furness Abbey, 172
St. Michael's Mount, 166
Salisbury, 55, 317-318
Salt, 65-66
Samson, abbot, 182-183, 190, 211-212, 255-257
Scotus, Marianus, 329
Scribes, 74-75, 82
Scrofula, remedy for, 97
Shepherds, 191
Sheriff's duties, 123-125
Ships and the sea, 320-322
Shortnose, William, 45
Simeon of Durham, 156, 264-265, 303-

304, 329
Slings, military weapons, 305, 307
Social History of England, A (Arnold), 76
Sowing, 114
Speed, John, 320, 329
Sports and Pastimes, 85-94, 310
Stephen, king of England, 15-17, 15, 16, 283-289, 309-311
Sterling, term introduced, 220
Stonehenge, 56
Street cries, 45
Studies in the History of Medieval Science (Haskins), 82
Stukeley, Huntingdonshire, 41-42
Sweyn, king of Denmark, 304
Swimming, 89
Sword-dance, 295

Thegn's Law, 99
Thorney Abbey, 154
Threshing, 114
Thurstan, 229-230
Tinchebrai, Battle of, 308-309
Tintagel, 276
Tools, 49-50
Topographia Hibernica (Gerald of Wales) 76
Tostig, earl, 159, 236-237
Tournaments, 94
Tower of London, 279
Towns, 18-45
Travel, 196-197
Treasurer's duties, 121
Trepanning, 98
Trouvere Wace, 282-283
Tunics, 61
Turgot, 329

Urban II, pope, 308

Villeinage in England (Vinogradoff) 43

Wace of Jersey, 83, 130, 321-322, 329
Waddell, Helen, 53
Wages, 99-130
Wallingford Castle, 303
Walter of Henley, 68, 330
Warfare, 291-319
Warwick Castle, 280
Wasdale, Cumberland, 35
Weaving, 125-126
Welsh law, 223-224
Wenlock Abbey, 149
Westcott Barton, 20
Westminster Abbey, 18-19
Westminster Hall, 16
Whitby Abbey, 186
White Ship, The, 277
White Monks, The (Lekai) 167, 169
William I, king of England, 1, 2, 4, 16, 19, 25-26, 46, 52, 147-148, 150, 152, 154, 159, 198-211, 260, 262-264, 292-295, 296-302, 320
William II, king of England, 5, 6, 6, 8, 16, 154, 211, 270-272
William Longespee, earl of Salisbury, 252
William of Jumieges, 261, 294-295, 330
William of Malmesbury, 5, 6, 8, 12, 17, 23-24, 47-49, 59-61, 67, 108-109, 225, 239-240, 243, 261, 270-272, 277-278, 306-308
William of Newburgh (Stevenson) 15, 47
William of Poitiers, 262-263, 292-294, 302,303, 330
William of St. Calais, bishop of Durham, 237
Winchester, 20, 55, 289-290
  cathedral, 137, 151
Winchester Psalter, The, 75
Winds, 107, 108
Windsor Castle, 303
Winnowing, 114
Winter, 106-107
Wistasce li moines (Usamah), 98
Witch of Berkeley, The, 259-261
Women's costume, 60, 62
Woodstock, 23
Worcester, 55
  cathedral, 144
Work, 99-130
Wrestling, 88, 89
Writing lesson, 72-73
Wulstan, bishop of Worcester, 138, 140

Yarmouth, 115
York, 55, 159, 317